CHILDREN'S RIGHTS

Children's Rights and the Law discusses the rights of children and considers the extent to which the law gives adequate recognition to and protection of these rights.

Historically the legal protection of rights has focused on the rights and duties of parents rather than children, and the rights of children have only recently become recognised and certain. This book takes a thematic approach to children's rights and considers:

- underlying concepts such as the welfare of the child and safeguarding;
- the right to education;
- the right to medical treatment;
- the right to freedom from abuse and/or sexual and commercial exploitation, including contemporary challenges arising from forced marriage, FGM, modern slavery and trafficking;
- the role of the State in protecting children in need of care;
- children's rights in the criminal justice system; and
- a brief introduction to children's contract and employment rights.

The book also provides an overview of key aspects of domestic and international law, including the Children Act 1989, the UN Convention on the Rights of the Child, the European Convention on Human Rights and the Human Rights Act 1998.

Children's Rights and the Law will be of particular interest to law and social science students in the areas of child development and protection, human rights law, family law, child law and child studies, as well as to parents, social workers, police officers, magistrates, probation officers and other related professions.

Hilaire Barnett is formerly Senior Lecturer in Law at Queen Mary University of London.

CHILDREN'S RIGHTS AND THE LAW

An Introduction

Hilaire Barnett

Routledge
Taylor & Francis Group

LONDON AND NEW YORK

First published 2022
by Routledge
2 Park Square, Milton Park, Abingdon, Oxon OX14 4RN

and by Routledge
605 Third Avenue, New York, NY 10158

Routledge is an imprint of the Taylor & Francis Group, an informa business

British Library Cataloguing-in-Publication Data
A catalogue record for this book is available from the British Library

Library of Congress Cataloging-in-Publication Data
A catalog record has been requested for this book

ISBN: 978-1-138-32124-3 (hbk)
ISBN: 978-1-138-32125-0 (pbk)
ISBN: 978-0-429-45271-0 (ebk)

DOI: 10.4324/9780429452710

Typeset in Bembo
by Deanta Global Publishing Services, Chennai, India

For Matthew and Essie, George, Amy and Toby

CONTENTS

Preface   *xiii*
Table of cases   *xvii*
Children legislation   *xxiii*
List of abbreviations   *xxviii*

1 Introduction and legal framework   1
   Introduction 1
   The evolution of rights 2
   Children and childhood: a very brief note 4
   The legal framework 5
      The UN Convention on the Rights of the Child (CRC) 7
      The European Convention on Human Rights (ECHR) 8
      The Hague Convention on Abduction (The Convention
         on the Civil Aspects of International Child Abduction
         1980) 12
      The Human Rights Act 1998 15
      The Children Act 1989 17
      The Equality Act 2010 20
      Wardship: the inherent jurisdiction of the High Court 21
      Judicial review of administrative action 23
   Children and legal proceedings 25
      The Official Solicitor 25
      CAFCASS: the Children and Family Court Advisory
         Support Service 25

Legal aid 25
Summary 27
Notes 27

2 **Basic principles, status, and identity** 30
Introduction 30
Parental responsibility 31
Part A: fundamental concepts 34
   The welfare of the child 34
   The right to contact 36
   The right to be heard 37
Safeguarding 40
The right to equality 41
Part B: status and identity rights 42
   Introduction 42
   Proof of parentage 43
   Assisted reproduction 44
   Surrogacy 48
   Adoption 49
   Gender identity 49
Summary 54
Notes 54

3 **Children and medical treatment** 58
Introduction 58
Standards of living and health 59
The right to life 60
Consent to medical treatment 61
   Confidentiality 64
Refusing consent to medical treatment 64
Withholding/withdrawing medical treatment 66
Immunisation 70
The rights of children with disabilities 72
Children and young people's mental health 75
   The data 75
   Child and Adolescent Mental Health Service (CAMHS) 76
Culture, religion, and medical treatment 77
   Jehovah's Witnesses 77
Circumcision 79
The relevance of financial resources 81
Summary 82
Notes 83

4 Children and education   86
   Introduction 86
   The duty to provide education 87
      Education Supervision Orders 88
   State schools 89
      School standards: OFSTED (Office for Standards in
         Education, Children's Services and Skills) 90
      School governance 90
      Class sizes 91
      Admissions 91
      School uniform 92
      Religious Education (RE) 93
      Discipline 94
      Bullying 95
   Truancy 96
   Special Educational Needs or Disabilities (SEND) 97
      Children under five 98
      Children between five and 15 99
      Young people aged 16 or over in further education 99
      Education, Health, and Care Plans 99
      Evaluating the system 101
   Exclusions from school 103
      The rules on exclusion 104
      Challenging exclusions 105
      Provision of education for excluded children 106
      Alternative Provision (AP) 106
      'Managed' moves 107
      Off-rolling and gaming practices 107
   Independent schools 108
   Taking a child out of school in term time 109
   Unregistered schools 110
   The liability of schools 111
   Education in Scotland and Wales (in outline) 113
      Scotland 113
      Wales 113
      Northern Ireland 114
   Summary 114
   Notes 114

5 Freedom from abuse   118
   Introduction 118
   Child abuse within the family 118

A remaining controversy: corporal punishment in the home 123
Forced marriage 124
    Forced Marriage Protection Orders 126
Female Genital Mutilation (FGM) 129
    UK FGM statistics 131
    The law: the Female Genital Mutilation Act 2003 131
    Protecting the identity of victims 132
    The duty to protect girls from the risk of FGM 132
    The duty of professionals to report to the police 132
    Female Genital Mutilation Protection Orders (FGMPO) 132
    The application process 133
Circumcision 135
Exploiting children 136
    County Lines 136
    Modern slavery and trafficking: see also the protection of
        refugee children discussed in Chapter 6 137
        The National Referral Mechanism (NRM) 139
        The Anti-Slavery Commissioner 140
    Child Sexual Exploitation (CSE) 141
        The Rotherham scandal 142
        The Independent Inquiry into Child Sexual Abuse
            2015–2022 143
    Internet abuse 144
    Extremism and radicalisation 146
Summary 151
Notes 152

6 **Protecting vulnerable children**   157
Introduction 157
The duties of local authorities 158
    Children in need 159
    Referrals 160
    The duty to provide services for children in need 160
    The duty to investigate: Children Act, section 47 160
    Care plans: Children Act, section 31A 161
    The duty to provide accommodation: the Children Act
        1989 section 20 161
Court orders 163
    Child Assessment Orders (CAOs): Children Act, section 43 163
    Emergency Protection Orders (EPOs): Children Act,
        section 44 163
    Taking a child into police protection: Children Act,
        section 46 164

Care and Supervision Orders: Children Act, section 31 165
Supervision Orders: Children Act, section 31 166
Education Supervision Orders: Children Act, section 36 –
     see Chapter 4 167
Adoption 167
Special Guardianship Orders (SGOs) 168
Adoption or special guardianship? 169
Evaluating the system 170
Missing children 171
The liability of local authorities 171
Protecting child refugees 174
     Asylum support for families 183
Conclusion 184
Notes 184

7 **Children and the criminal justice system**   188
Introduction 188
The Age of Criminal Responsibility (ACR) 190
Preventing children from offending 191
     Child Safety Orders 191
     Parenting Orders 191
Diverting children out of the criminal justice system 192
     Youth cautions 192
Civil injunctions 193
Statistics on youth crime 194
Arrest, remand, and prosecution 195
     Arrest 195
     Legal advice and legal aid 197
     Remand on bail 197
     Remand in custody 198
     Prosecution 198
Children on trial 199
Protecting children in court 200
     The arrangement of the court 200
     'Special measures' 201
     Reporting restrictions 202
The powers of the Youth Courts 202
     Sentencing 202
     Referrals to the Youth Offending Panel 203
     Youth Rehabilitation Orders 204
     Criminal Behaviour Orders 205
     The Intensive Supervision and Surveillance Programme
          (ISSP) 206

Detention and Training Orders (DTOs) 206
Ethnicity and detention 207
Young Offender Institutions (YOIs) 207
Secure Training Centres (STCs) 208
Young Offender Institution rules 209
Separation/solitary confinement of children 210
The use of physical restraints against children 211
    Evaluating YOIs and STCs 213
Secure Schools (SS) 214
Secure Children's Home (SCH) 215
Child protection and youth justice in Scotland 216
    The Children's Hearing System 216
    Guiding principles 216
    The Children's Panel 217
    The hearing 217
    Child Assessment Orders and Child Protection Orders
        (CPO) 217
    Exclusion Orders 217
    Compulsory Supervision Orders (CSO) 218
Summary 218
Notes 218

8 **Children: Contract and employment**   222
Introduction 222
Contract 222
    Introduction 222
    Categories of contract 222
    Capacity to contract 224
    Contracts for necessities and contracts of employment,
        apprenticeship, or education 224
    The Minors Contract Act 1987 227
Employment 228
    Introduction 228
    Permitted working hours 230
    Health and safety requirements 232
    Live performances: theatres, etc. 233
    Employment in the armed forces 233
Summary 234
Notes 234

Children Appendix   *237*
Index   *242*

PREFACE

Very gradually, and over the centuries, governments in the United Kingdom have recognised that adults have rights which are protected, and enforceable in law. The right to vote, for example, an early battle long resisted by governments, was finally won by the first half of the 20th century, having evolved from a right confined to the privileged 'male' property-owning few to the universal franchise. The rights of women – to the franchise, to property ownership, to equal rights over children, and to equal employment rights – have slowly been recognised and protected in law. The right to non-discrimination on grounds of race, nationality, ethnic origins, etc., was first enshrined in law in the 1960s and has since evolved. The rights of those with disabilities were slower to be recognised and protected by law but are now legally secure.

And what of children and their rights, the focus of this book? What rights do they have? How, and to what extent, does the law protect the right to life, to health and medical care, to education, to participate in decision-making affecting their lives? And how, and to what extent, does the law protect vulnerable children from abuse and exploitation? And where families need the support of the State, what institutions and procedures are in place to provide for children in need? Where children come into conflict with the law, how does the criminal justice system provide for the special needs of children? *Children's Rights and the Law* addresses these issues: it is an inquiry into the rights of children which have been recognised and protected by the law. It is also an inquiry into the extent to which the law has reacted, and continues to react, to changes in society which present new challenges if the rights of children are to be given adequate protection. In recent years, globalisation, immigration, and multiculturalism have introduced new challenges to the protection of children from harm: Female Genital Mutilation (FGM) and forced marriage being two contemporary and culturally sensitive issues affecting children's rights. The rapid development and expansion of technology, bringing the internet and its infinite resources within the reach of both adults and children also creates further challenges to children's rights.

With many intersecting and overlapping concepts and issues, the organisation of the book has been challenging but the material has fallen reasonably coherently into eight chapters. The devolution of law-making powers to the Scottish and Welsh parliaments and the Northern Ireland Assembly complicates the discussion, but for the most part the law provides equivalent rights throughout the UK and where there are significant differences these are explained. Throughout the book I have used examples from real cases in order to illustrate the extent to which law protects rights and also the complexities involved in many aspects of decision-making relating to the lives of children. The book is written for the general reader and no knowledge of the law is presumed.

Chapter 1 outlines the main aspects of the international and domestic legal framework underlying and supporting the rights of children. I have deliberately separated out the legal framework from the main text on the basis that many readers will be very familiar with the law, while others may have little interest in the legal rules: it is here to be referred to as and when needed. Under international law, the UN Convention on the Rights of the Child, the European Convention on Human Rights, and the Hague Convention on Abduction are of particular importance in the protection of children's rights. Under domestic law, the English Children Act 1989, the Human Rights Act 1998 which enables European Convention rights to be enforced before the local courts, and the Equality Act 2010 are central to the protection of rights. The ancient and inherent jurisdiction of the English High Court (wardship) over children is discussed. There is also a brief introduction to Judicial Review of Administrative Action – the legal mechanism through which the law keeps the exercise of power by public bodies/agencies within their correct legal boundaries in order to avoid the abuse of power.

Chapter 2 considers the basic concepts which infuse the law relating to children. In the first part the welfare of the child, safeguarding, and the meaning and scope of parental responsibility is explained. The rights of children within the family – the right to contact with caring and absent parents and the right to be heard – are also considered. Also discussed is the right to equality and non-discrimination. The second part considers questions of identity. On status, the importance of answering the question 'who, in law, is my parent?' and how, if doubts exist, this is proven, is addressed. Identity also includes the complex issue of gender identity and the law's response to gender dysphoria (anxiety). Central to this is the question of whether a child has the legal capacity – i.e. sufficient understanding and maturity – to consent to procedures potentially leading to gender reassignment with its lifelong ramifications.

Chapter 3 discusses children's right to medical treatment, including when a child may consent to or refuse that treatment. The right to life is considered here as are the complexities entailed in decision-making over questions of life and death with which the medical profession and the courts are occasionally faced. When children have physical or mental disabilities the law has developed to reduce, as far as possible, the inequalities which result from disabilities. Families, the courts, and the medical profession also face particular challenges when a child's need for medical treatment conflicts with cultural or religious beliefs about treatment. In times of financial stringency the availability of financial resources for medical treatment becomes a key issue. How the law faces these various challenges is considered here.

Children's right to education is the subject considered in Chapter 4. The focus here is primarily on the State system in England. The duty to provide education, the governance of schools, and school standards are discussed. The rights of children with Special Educational Needs or Disabilities, and the extent to which these are protected, are considered here. The 'right' of schools to exclude children from school and the rights of excluded children are also discussed. The liability of schools is also considered.

Chapter 5 introduces a number of issues where the criminal activities of adults violate the rights of children. Included here is a discussion of abuse within the family. In recent years two culturally and politically sensitive issues – forced marriage and Female Genital Mutilation – have been recognised: how the law has reacted to protect the rights of children against these practices is discussed here. The exploitation of children and the violation of their rights through criminal activities such as organised sexual abuse and involvement in County Lines operations is discussed. Over recent years the law has also had to react to the problem of children who become radicalised and led into extremist ideology, and this issue is also discussed in this chapter.

The focus of Chapter 6 is the role of the State when parental care fails and the range of local authority powers designed to protect children from harm. The State recognises that the family is the basic building block of society and the family is legally protected from unjustified interference by State institutions: the law lays down specific grounds for intervening in family life and the European Convention on Human Rights (ECHR) protects the privacy of the family from State intrusion. But the State also has a duty of protection towards children: the State is *parens patriae* – the protective parental figure – with the power and duty to intervene where families fail their children and abuse their rights. Whether the balance between family autonomy and child protection has been correctly achieved is a key question for children's rights. Increasingly, law and society have had to adapt to the needs of both adults and children who arrive in the UK having fled their homelands in search of safety and security. The law relating to the protection of child refugees is discussed in this chapter.

Children and the criminal justice system are the focus of Chapter 7. The (controversial) age of criminal responsibility at which a child becomes answerable for his or her criminal actions is considered. Procedures for diverting children away from the adult criminal justice system are discussed. The powers of the police, the right to representation, the right to fair trial, and powers of the youth courts are all considered. As will be seen, there are significant differences in the manner in which the law treats children in trouble with the law in England and Scotland. The conditions in institutions for children sentenced to detention by the court, many of which breach the rights of children, are also considered here.

Chapter 8 looks briefly at children's rights to enter into contracts and employment. Children's contractual rights are regulated by statute, but vagueness surrounds their enforceability. Depending upon their age, children may enter employment and special rules apply to reflect their age and maturity. A child's right to financial support when families break down is also introduced as is the right to financial support and the State benefits designed to lessen the inequalities caused by the financial hardship faced by families.

Finally, Appendix A briefly explains the differing ages at which children can lawfully undertake disparate tasks – some of these are of considerable importance such as getting married without parental consent, voting in elections, joining and serving in the armed forces. Other, less fundamental but nevertheless important issues such as bank accounts, being left alone, driving, the ownership of weapons, and gambling are also covered.

Sincere thanks go to Yvonne Lincoln M.Ed for her help with the chapter on Education and to Brenda Offredi JP (Ret'd) for her advice on youth court procedure. Any and all errors are mine alone. Many thanks also to Russell George and Chloe James and the team at Routledge for all their help in the production of this book.

Hilaire Barnett
September 2021

TABLE OF CASES

A

A (FGMPO Application) [2020] EWHC 323 (Fam)
A and Others (Human Fertilisation and Embryology Act 2008) [2015] EWHC 2602 (Fam)
A v A (Habitual residence) [2014] AC 1
A Local Authority v A Mother [2018] EWHC 2056 (Fam)
A Local Authority v HB [2017] EWHC 1437 (Fam)
A London Borough v X [2019] EWHC 816 (Fam)
A v Liverpool City Council [1982] AC 363
A v The United Kingdom [1998] ECHR 85
A, B, C and D (Immunisation) [2011] EWHC 4033 (fam)
Agar-Ellis, Re (1878) 10 Ch D 49, CA
A City Council v A Mother and A Father (Care Proceedings: Radicalisation) [2019] EWHC 3076 (Fam)
A Hospital Trust v Child B [2014] EWHC 3486 (Fam)
Aintree University Hospital NHS Foundation Trust v James [2013] UKSC 67
An NHS Foundation Trust Hospital v P [2014] EWHC 1650 (Fam)
An NHS Trust v Child B [2014] 3486 EWHC Fam
Aintree University Hospital NHS Foundation Trust v James [2013] UKSC 67; [2013] 3 WLR 1299
A Hospital NHS Trust v LP [2019] EWHC 2989 (Fam)
An NHS Foundation Trust Hospital v P [2014] EWHC 1650 (Fam)
Armes v Nottinghamshire County Council [2017] UKSC 60
AT (Article 8 ECHR) [2016] UKUT 227 (IAC)
Attorney-General's Reference No 3 of 1994 [1994] 3 WLR 421
Aylesbury Peerage Case (1885) 11 App Cas 1

B

B (A Child; Post Adoption Contact) [2019] EWCA Civ 29
B (A minor), Re, [1990] 3 All ER 206
Barrett v Enfield LBC [1999] 3 WLR 79
Bell v Tavistock and Portman NHS Foundation Trust [2021] EWCA Civ 1363
Bellinger v Bellinger [2003] 2 All ER 593
Bracking v Secretary of State for Work and Pensions [2013] EEWCA Civ 1345
Butt v Secretary of State for the Home Department [2019] EWCA Civ 256

C

Cameron Mathieson v Secretary of state for Work and Pensions [2015] UKSC 47
Campbell and Cozens v United Kingdom (1982) 4 EHRR 293
Chaplin v Leslie Frewin (Publishers) Ltd [1996] Ch 71

D

De Francesco v Barnum (1889) 45 Ch D 430
Doyle v White City Stadium [1935] 1 KB 110

E

E v the United Kingdom [2002] ECHR 763

F

F v F (MMR Vaccine) [2014] 1 FLR 1328
Fornah v Secretary of state for the Home Department [2006] UKHL 46

G

G and D (Risk for forced marriage: FMPO) [2010] NI Fam 6
Gaskin v United Kingdom (1989) 12 EHRR 36
Gillick v Norfolk and Wisbech AHA [1986] AC 112

H

Haase v Germany [2004] ECHR 342
Hernehult v Norway [2020] ECHR 214

I

In the matter of an application by the Northern Ireland Human rights Commission for Judicial review [2018] UKSC 27
In the matter of E (Children) [2011] UKSC 84
Ireland v United Kingdom

J

J v C [1970] AC 668

K

Kenlin v Gardner [1967] 2 QB 510

L

L and B (Children: Specific Issues) [2016] EWHC 849 (Fam)
Langley v Liverpool City Council [2005] EWCA Civ 1173

M

M v Children's Hospital NHS Foundation Trust v Mrs and Mrs Y [2014] EWHC 2651 (Fam)
Mahmood v Mahmood [1993] SLT 589
Mahmud v Mahmud [1994] SLT 599
Mikulic v Croatia [2002] 1 FCR 720
Murray v Express Newspapers [2007] EWHC 1098; [2008] 1 FLR 704

N

O

Oxfordshire County Council v AD and Others [2019] EWHC 866

P

P (A child) [2014] EWCA Civ 1174.
Patel v Mirza [2016] UKSC 42
Pedersen v Norway [2020] ECHR 213
Phelps v Hillingdon LBC [2000] 4 All ER 504
Proform Sports Management Ltd v Proactive Sports Management Ltd [2006] EWHC 2903 (Ch)

Q

R

R (AA) v Secretary of State for the Home Department [2016] EWHC 1453 (Admin)
R (AB) v Secretary of State for Justice [2019] EWCA Civ 9
R (Axon)v Secretary of State for Health [2006] EWHC 37 (Admin)
R (B) v Brent Youth Court [2010] EWHC 1893 (Admin)
R (B) v Brent Youth Court [2010] EWHC 1893 (Admin)
R (Begum) v Head Teacher and Governors of Denbigh High School [2015] UKHL 15
R (Bourgass) v Secretary of State for Justice [2015] UKSC 54
R (FD) v X MBC [2019] EWHC 3348 (Admin) check
R (HC) (a child) v Secretary of State for the Home Department [2013] EWHC 982 (admin)
R (London Oratory School) v The School Adjudicator [2015] EWHC 1012 (Admin)
R (London Oratory School) v The School Adjudicator [2015] EWHC 2012 (Admin)
R (London Oratory) v The School Adjudicator [2015] EWHC 1012 ewca (Admin)
R (McConnell) v Registrar General for England and Wales [2020]
R (McConnell) v Registrar General for England and Wales [2020] EWCA Civ 559
R (Quincy Bell) and A v Tavistock and Portman HNS Trust [2020] EWHC 3274 (Admin)
R (VC) v Newcastle City Council [2011] EWHC 2673
R (Williamson) v Secretary of State for Education and Employment [2005] UKHL 15
R v Arthur [1981] 12 BMLR 1
R v Cambridge Health Authority ex parte b [1995] 1 WLR 898
R (Williamson) v Secretary of State for Education and Employment [2005] UKHL 15
Re A (A Child: Female Genital Mutilation: Asylum) [2019] EWHC 2475 (lFam)
Re A, B, C, D, E, F and G (minors) [2012] EWHC 435 (Fam)
Re A, B, C and D (Immunisation) [2011] EWHC 4033 (Fam)
Re A (Children) (Conjoined twins) [2000] EWCA Civ 254
Re Agar-Ellis (1993) 24 Ch D 317
Re B (A Child) [2013] UKSC 33
Re B (a minor) (Wardship: Medical Treatment) [1990] 3 All ER 206
Re B and G (Children) (No 2) [2015] EWFC 3; [2015] 1 FLR 905
Re A (Children) (Conjoined Twins) [2000] EWCA Civ 254
Re Agar-Ellis (1883) 24 Ch D 317
Re B and G (Children) (No 2) [2015] EWFC 3
Re C (Abduction) [1999] 1 FLR 1145
Re C, D and E [2016] EWHC 3088 (Fam)
Re D (A Child) [2019] UKSC 42
Re D (Sterisisation) [1976] Fam 185
Re Dunhill (1967) 111 SJ 113
Re F (paternity: jurisdiction) [2007] EWCA Civ 873

Re G (Education: Religious Upbringing) [2012] ewca cIV 1233
Re HK (Serious Medical treatment) (No 3) [2017] EWHC 2992 (Fam)
Re J (A Child) [1999] EWCA Civ 3022
Re J (a minor) (Wardship: Medical Treatment) [1990] 3 All ER 930
Re Jake (Withholding Medical treatment) [2015] EWHC 2442 (Fam)
Re K (Children with Disabilities: Wardship) [2012] 2 FLR 745
Re K (Forced Marriage: Passport Order [2020] EWCA Civ 190
Re M (Children) (Children) [2007] UKHL 55
Re M (Children) (Habitual Residence) [2020] EWCA Civ 1105
Re M (secure Accommodation Order) (1995) 1 FLR 418
Re NY (A Child) [2019] UKSC 49
Re P [2008] EWCA Civ 535
Re R (a minor) (Wardship: Consent to Medical treatment) [1992] Fam 11
Re S (A Child) [2007] EWCA Civ 54.
Re S (Parental aliennation: cult) [2020] EWCA Civ 568
Re SL [2017] EWHC 125 (Fam)
Re T and S (Wardship) [2011] EWHC 1008 (Fam)
Re W (a minor) (Wardship: Consent to treatment) [1992] Fam 11
Re W [1971] 2 All ER 49
Re X (A Child) (No 4) [2017] EWHC 2084 Fam
Re X (FGMPO No 2) [2019] EWHC 1990 (Fam)
Re Y (Children) (Radicalisation) [2016] EWHC 3827 (Fam)civ 559
Re Z (a minor) (Freedom of Publication) [1996] 1 FLR 191
Re W (a minor) (Medical Treatment) [1993] Fam 64
Re X (A Child) (No 4) [2017] EWHC 2084 (Fam)
Re X (FGMPO No 2) [2019] EWHC 1990 (Fam)
Roe v Wade 410 US 113 (1973)
Rose v Secretary of State for Health [2002] EWHC 1593 (Admin)
Royal Borough of Kingston Upon Thames v Wendy Price, Marie Emma Prince [1998] EWCA Civ 1891

S

SC v United Kingdom (2005) 40 EHRR 10
Scott v Sebright (1886) 12 PD 21
Secretary of State for the Home Department v K [2006] UKHL 46.
St George's Healthcare Trust v S, R v Collins ex p S [1998] 3 All ER ...
Sunday Times v UK [1979] 2 EHRR 245

T

TP and KM v United Kingdom [2001] 2 FLR 549.
T & V v United Kingdom (1999) 30 EHRR 121
The Aylesbury Peerage Case (1885) 11 App Cas 1

The Catholic Welfare Society v Various Claimants [2012] UKSC 56
Tyrer v The United Kingdom [1978] 2 EHRR 1

U

V

Vo v France [2004] ECHR 326

W

W, Re, [1971] 2 AC 682; [1971] 2 All ER 49.
W v Essex County Council [2000] WLR 601
Willliams v LB of Hackney [2018] UKSC 37

X

X (A Child) No 2 (Private Surrogacy Arrangement) [2016] EWFC 55
X v B [2004] EWHC 2015 (Fam)
X, Re (Female Genital Mutilation Protection Order No 2) [2019] EWHC 1990 (Fam)
X (Minors) v Bedfordshire County Council [1995] 2 AC 633

Y

Yousef v The Netherlands [2002] ECHR 716

Z

Z v United Kingdom [2001] 2 FLR 612.

CHILDREN LEGISLATION

A

Abortion Act 1967
Abortion (Northern Ireland) Regulations 2020
Adoption and Children Act 2002
Affiliation Proceedings Act 1957
Age of Criminal Responsibility (Scotland) Act 2018
Age of Legal Capacity (Scotland) Act 1991
Age of Majority (Northern Ireland) Act 1969
Anti-social Behaviour, Crime and Policing Act 2014.

B

Bail Act 1976
Bastardy Laws Amendment Act 1871
Borders, Citizenship and Immigration Act 2009

C

Children Act (Amendment) (Female Genital Mutilation) Act 2019.
Children Act 1989
Children Act 2004
Children and Families Act 2014
Children and Young Persons Act 1933
Children and Young Persons Act 1963
Children and Young Persons Act 1969
Chimney Sweeps Act 1834

Chimney Sweeps Act 1840
Children's Hearing (Scotland) Act 2011
Civil Partnerships Act 2004
Civil Partnership (Opposite-sex Couples) Regulations 2019
Children (Abolition of Defence of Reasonable Punishment) (Wales) Act 2020
Children Act 1989
Children Act 2004
Children and Families Act 2014
Child Care Act 1980
Children (Equal Protection from Assault) (Scotland) Act 2019
Children's Hearing (Scotland) Act 2011
Coal Mines Regulation Act 1860
Coroners and Justice Act 1009
Counter-terrorism and Security Act 2015
Counter-terrorism and Border Security Act 2015
Crime and Disorder Act 1998
Children and Families Act 2014
Children (Northern Ireland) Order 1995
Children (Scotland) Act 1995
Criminal Justice Act 1948
Criminal Justice Act 1991
Criminal Justice Act 2003
Criminal Justice Act 2009
Criminal Justice and Court Services Act 2000
Criminal Procedure (Scotland) Act 1995

D

Day Care and Child Minding (National Standards) (England) Regulations 2003, SI 2003/1996
Disability Discrimination Act 1995
Domestic Proceedings and Magistrates Courts Act 1978
Domestic Violence, Crime, and Victims Act 2004

E

Education Act 1880
Education (No 2) Act 1986
Education Act 1993
Education Act 1996
Education Act 2002
Education and Inspections Act 2006
Education and Skills Act 2008
Education (Pupil Registration) (England) Regulations 2006–2016

Education (Schools) Act 1992
Elementary Education (School Attendance) Act 1893
Equality Act 2010

F

Factory Act 1831
Factory Act 1833
Factory Act 1844
Factory Act 1891
Factories and Workshop Act 1878
Family Law Act 1996
Family Law Reform Act 1969
Family Law Reform Act 1987
Family Law (Scotland) Act 2006
Female Circumcision Act 1985
Female Genital Mutilation Act 2003
Forced Marriage (Civil Protection) Act 2007
Forced Marriage (Civil Protection) Act Northern Ireland 2007
Forced Marriage etc (Protection and Jurisdiction) (Scotland) Act 2011

G

Gender Recognition Act 2004
Guardianship of Infants Act 1925
Guardianship Act 1971
Guardianship Act 1973

H

Human Fertilisation and Embryology Act 1990
Human Fertilisation and Embryology Act (Disclosure of Identity) Regulations 2004 SI 2004/1511
Human Rights Act 1998

I

Immigration Act 2009
Immigration and Asylum Act 1991
Immigration, Nationality and Asylum (EU Exit) Regulations 2019
Immigration Act 2016
Immigration Rules
Infant Life (Preservation) Act 1929
Inquiries Act 2005

J

K

L

Law of Property Act 1925
Legal Aid, Sentencing and Punishment of Offenders Act 2012
Local Government Act 1999

M

Marriage Act 1949
Marriage (Same Sex Couples) Act 2013
Matrimonial Causes Act 1973
Malicious Communications Act 1988
Mental Health Act 1983
Minors Contract Act 1987
Modern Slavery Act 2015

N

National Health Service Act 2006
Nationality, Immigration and Asylum Act 2002
Northern Ireland (Executive Formation) Act 2019

O

P

Parish Apprentices Act 1802
Police Act 1964
Police and Criminal Evidence Act 1984
Powers of the Criminal Courts (Sentencing) Act 2000
Prohibition of Female Circumcision Act 1985
Prohibition of Female Genital Mutilation (Scotland) Act 2005
Protection of Children Act 1989
Protection of Children (Scotland) Act 1995

Q

R

Registration of Births Marriages and Deaths Act 1953
Rehabilitation of Offenders Act 1974.
Religious Education (Meetings of Local Conferences and Councils) Regulations 1994, SI 1994/1304

S

Safeguarding Vulnerable Groups (Northern Ireland) Order 2007
School Governance (Constitution) (England) Regulations 2012
School Standards and Framework Act 1998
Senior Courts Act 1981
Serious Crime Act 2015
Slave Trade Act 1807
Surrogacy Arrangements Act 1985
Settled Land Act 1925

T

Terrorism Act 2000

U

V

W

X

Y
Youth Justice and Criminal Evidence Act 1999.

Z

ABBREVIATIONS

ACR	Age of Criminal Responsibility
AHC	After Housing Costs
AID	Artificial Insemination by Donor
AP	Alternative Provision
ASBO	Anti-Social Behaviour Order
ASC	Agreed Syllabus Conference
B&B	Bed and Breakfast
BAME	Black, Asian, and Minority Ethnic
BHC	Before Housing Costs
CAB	Citizens Advice Bureau
CAFCAS	Children and Family Court Advisory and Support Service
CAMHS	Child and Adolescent Mental Health Service
CAO	Child Assessment Order
CBO	Criminal Behaviour Order
CMS	Child Maintenance Service
CPC	Child Protection Committee
CPO	Child Protection Order
CPP	Child Protection Plan
CPS	Crown Prosecution Service
CQC	Care Quality Commission
CRAE	Children's Rights Alliance England
CRC	Convention on the Rights of the Child
CSE	Child Sexual Exploitation
CSH	Cross-Sex Hormones
CSJ	Centre for Social Justice
CSO	Compulsory Supervision Order
CSO	Child Safety Order
CYP	Children and Young People
DCMS	Department for Culture, Media and Sport

DfE	Department for Education
DLA	Disability Living Allowance
DTO	Detention and Training Order
DWP	Department for Work and Pensions
ECHR	European Convention on Human Rights and Fundamental Freedoms
EHCP	Education, Health and Care Plan
EPO	Emergency Protection Order
ESO	Education Supervision Order
EYFS	Early Years Foundation Stage
FGM	Female Genital Mutilation
FGMPO	Female Genital Mutilation Protection Order
FMPO	Forced Marriage Protection Order
GIDS	Gender Identity Development Service
IICSA	Independent Inquiry into Child Sexual Abuse
ISI	Independent School Inspectorate
ISSP	Intensive Supervision and Surveillance Programme
IWF	Internet Watch Foundation
LGBT	Lesbian, Gay, Bisexual, and Transgender
MHF	Mental Health Foundation
MMR	Measles, Mumps, and Rubella
NCA	National Crime Agency
NCLCC	National County Lines Coordination Centre
NHS	National Health Service
NRM	National Referral Mechanism
NSPCC	National Society for the Protection of Children from Cruelty
OFSTED	Office for Standards in Education, Children's Services and Skills
OSPT	Official Solicitor and Public Trustee
PBs	Puberty Blockers
PIP	Personal Independence Payment
POs	Parenting Orders
PSHE	Personal, Social, and Health Education
RCGP	Royal College of General Practitioners
RCPCH	Royal College of Paediatrics and Child Health
RCPsych	Royal College of Psychiatrists
RE	Religious Education
RO	Referral Order
SACRE	Statutory Advisory Commission on Religious Education
SCH	Secure Children's Home
SEN	Special Educational Needs
SENCO	Special Educational Needs Coordinator
SEND	Special Educational Needs or Disabilities
SGO	Special Guardianship Order
SO	Supervision Order
SS	Secure Schools
STC	Secure Training Centre
UNCR	United Nations Convention on the Rights of the Child
UNCRPD	United Nations Convention on the Rights of Persons with Disabilities

UNHCR	United Nations High Commission for Refugees
UNICEF	United Nations International Children's Emergency Fund
YOI	Young Offender Institution
YOP	Youth Offending Panel
YOT	Youth Offending Team
YRO	Youth Rehabilitation Order

1

INTRODUCTION AND LEGAL FRAMEWORK

Introduction

Do children have rights? To what extent, and how, does the law recognise and protect these rights?

Children's Rights and the Law: An Introduction aims to identify the rights of children and discuss the extent to which (primarily) English law gives adequate recognition to and protection of these rights. Children's rights enshrined in law range from the right to life, the right to care and protection, the right to education, and the right to medical treatment. Children also have the right to be treated equally and where inequalities exist, for example because of disabilities, the State has a duty to make arrangements in order to lessen that inequality. As a child grows towards maturity, it is increasingly recognised that he or she is entitled to be heard and involved when issues involving his or her well-being are decided. Children also have – depending on age and maturity – the right to enter into enforceable contracts and to the protection of employment law. Children's rights also include rights when, for whatever reason, they come into contact with the criminal justice system, whether in the form of the police or the courts and/or the prison service. However, identifying the rights of children does not by any means, as will be seen, guarantee that these rights will be adequately protected by the law.

In recent years, globalisation, immigration, and multiculturalism have introduced new challenges to the protection of children from harm. Female Genital Mutilation (FGM), forced marriage, and radicalisation and extremism are particularly difficult and culturally sensitive issues affecting children's rights. Rather differently, but equally significant is the rapid development and expansion of technology, bringing the internet and its infinite resources within the reach of both adults and children and creating further challenges to the protection of their rights to safety and security.

DOI: 10.4324/9780429452710-1

The evolution of rights

The idea of individual rights which could withstand the power of government can be traced to John Locke (1632–1704)[1] and Thomas Paine (1737–1791)[2] who laid the foundations for enforceable human rights and the limits of government power.[3] Over time the majority of countries around the world adopted a written constitution which guarantees individual rights that cannot lawfully be restricted by the country's law-making body. However, in the UK, the constitution remains largely unwritten (or uncodified) and is founded on the concept of the supremacy of Parliament. In the UK, therefore, the sovereign Parliament can create and limit individual rights as the political climate demands. However, existing alongside the idea of Parliament's supreme law-making power under the UK constitution has traditionally been the prioritisation of individual freedom over a code of enforceable individual rights. This approach translates into the maxim that the individual is free to do whatever the law does not prohibit – a freedom which lacks the powerful political resonance of legally enforceable rights.

While this constitutional arrangement suggests that rights are fragile in the face of government power, movements – both domestic and international – for the legal protection of rights have resulted in a system which, albeit gradually, has reacted to the pressure for reform and the better protection of rights.[4] At the forefront of the reform agenda throughout the 20th century was the demand for equality: discrimination on grounds of sex, race, colour, language, religion, political or other opinions, national or social origins, or disability is prohibited by law. On the rights of children, however, the law was silent. Throughout infancy and childhood the child was considered to be under the authority, care, and protection of his or her parents and largely invisible to law (unless the criminal law intervened on the basis of a crime against a child). As Heywood notes 'Before the nineteenth century, the idea that the State should intervene in relationships between parents and their children was almost unthinkable'.[5]

The recognition and legal protection of children's rights, therefore, is relatively recent. Historically the idea of, and protection of rights has focused on *parental rights* rather than the rights of the child. Moreover, the parental rights of custody and control over the person of the child and his or her property vested in the father – to the exclusion of the mother.[6] The law would uphold the rights of the *paterfamilias*, not interfering with his authority unless it had been abused. The father had a 'sacred right ... over his own children'.[7] In the 18th century, Sir William Blackstone in his *Commentaries on the Laws of England* (1765–1769), wrote that a parent owes three duties to a child: those of maintenance, protection, and education. The themes of protection and maintenance remained central to the law relating to children, conferring rights and duties on parents rather than focusing on the rights of the child.

The first Act of Parliament enabling the courts to limit parental rights and exert control over parental behaviour, the Prevention of Cruelty to, and Protection of,

Children Act 1889, made it an offence to neglect, ill-treat, abandon, or expose a child. Echoing this, section 1 of the Children and Young Persons Act 1933 made it a criminal offence for a person with responsibility for a child to 'wilfully assault, ill-treat, neglect, abandon, expose (or cause "him" to suffer any of these at the hands of another) in a manner likely to cause him unnecessary suffering or injury to health'.

The welfare of the child, however, remained largely subordinated to the authority of the parent, particularly the father. As Stephen Cretney explains, in the 1920s – notwithstanding the campaigns for equal rights for women – there was a great deal of opposition to the idea that parents should have equal rights. The official view was that there needed to be one authoritative figure within the family who could take whatever decisions were necessary in relation to the child or children: and that figure was the father.[8] Furthermore, giving mothers equal rights could lead to legal disputes which could be damaging to family unity and to the well-being of the child.[9] The Guardianship of Infants Act 1925 was passed against this background and stated that where questions were raised about a child's custody and upbringing, the court was to regard the child's welfare as 'the first and paramount consideration'. Mothers were not given equal rights with fathers until 1973.[10]

The 1933 Children and Young Persons Act recognised the importance of the welfare of the child within the context of court proceedings, stating that:

> … every court in dealing with a child who is brought before it, either as an offender or otherwise, shall have regard to the welfare of the child or young person.
>
> *Children and Young Persons Act 1933, section 44*

However, other than where a child came before a court, the focus on parental rights and duties rather than on the child, meant that the *welfare of the child* was not overtly recognised. It was to be in 1971 that the House of Lords (then the highest court in the UK, now the Supreme Court) articulated the importance of a child's welfare, insisting that this principle was the determining factor in all disputes over the upbringing of a child.[11] The Children Act 1989 later adopted this principle as the guiding factor in child law, section 1 providing that in any case regarding the upbringing of a child or the administration of a child's property, 'the child's welfare shall be the court's paramount consideration'.

At the international level, in 1924 the League of Nations, (the forerunner to the United Nations) adopted the *Geneva Declaration of the Rights of the Child*, declaring the right of a child to the means of a normal development, the right to be fed, to receive medical treatment, to shelter, and to freedom from exploitation. In 1948 the United Nations General Assembly adopted the *Universal Declaration of Human Rights*, Article 25(2) recognising the need for the special protection of motherhood and childhood and the rights of children to 'social protection'. Under the auspices of the Council of Europe, established in 1949, the European Convention on Human Rights (ECHR) came into force in 1953. The

Convention relates to human rights in general and is not child-focused, although children enjoy the same protection as adults under the Convention.

In 1998, the Human Rights Act 1998, the majority of rights and freedoms protected under the ECHR were incorporated into UK law, making them enforceable before the domestic courts. Although not child-centred, the Human Rights Act has undoubtedly contributed to a developing culture of children's rights in the UK. In 1989 the seminal *United Nations Convention on the Rights of the Child* (CRC) was published. The CRC has been ratified by all member states of the United Nations (with the exception of the United States of America and Somalia). The CRC came into force in 1990. Although the rights are not enforceable before the domestic courts, the CRC is now recognised by all State agencies – from schools to hospitals to police – as setting out the guiding principles in decisions relating to children's upbringing. The ECHR and the CRC are discussed in more detail below.

Within the UK there is still no comprehensive domestic code of children's rights and children's rights remain difficult to identify and define, being submerged under assorted domestic Acts of Parliament, common law (judicial decisions), the ECHR and CRC. In the United Kingdom, some rights are 'universal' in that they apply to all children: the right to education is one example. Others are discretionary, for example the right to certain welfare benefits. Many rights, for their enjoyment, are dependent upon the financial resources of the State. In relation to the right to medical treatment, for example, the right is qualified by the right of providers to take into account available financial resources and to an extent adapt or limit treatment accordingly.[12] It is also the case that children's rights do not exist in a vacuum but must be set within the context of the family unit (whatever form that takes) and other institutions to which a child belongs: schools, for example. This raises the issue of competing sets of rights: the right of the individual child may be compromised by the rights of others which press for recognition.

Children and childhood: a very brief note

How children and childhood are defined varies over time: it is a social construct created by adults. As Colin Heywood notes in *A History of Childhood* this means 'that "child" and "childhood" will be understood in different ways in different societies'.[13]

> A child means 'every human being below the age of eighteen years unless, under the law applicable to the child, majority is attained earlier'; 'child' means a person under the age of 18.
>
> *UN Convention on the Rights of the Child 1989,*
> *Article 1; Children Act 1989, section 105.*

In law, therefore and for the most part, a child is a person under the age of 18.[14] However, the law recognises that children have rights, capacities, or liabilities at different ages for different purposes.[15] For example, a 16-year-old has the legal right to consent to medical treatment;[16] but a 'mature minor' (as defined by the courts) may have the capacity to consent at an earlier age.[17] In this way the law recognises that the time between birth and adulthood is a developmental process with the child acquiring differing capacities and rights at differing ages.

Childhood has been explained as having four principal stages: neonatal, infancy, adolescence, and young personhood. As childhood progresses, so physical and intellectual capabilities develop enabling the maturing 'child' increasingly to participate in the adult world of choice and decision-making. It would be meaningless to speak of a neonate having the right to vote but by the time a child reaches 15 or 16 years of age, it is far from clear that he or she lacks the capacity for the rational decision-making entailed in voting (that many adults also lack this rationality does not detract from the argument about childhood and maturity). There is, of course, an arbitrariness in fixing a specific age at which a right will be recognised: denying a young person aged 17 and 11 months the right to vote is undeniably arbitrary. Nevertheless, in general, for the sake of clarity there needs to be a fixed age for the acquisition of rights that are legally enforceable.

The legal framework

Throughout this book reference will be made to the many and various laws – both domestic and international – which form the framework for the identification and protection of children's rights. The domestic law relating to children is greatly influenced by international law, and most particularly by the UN Convention on the Rights of the Child (CRC) 1989, the European Convention on Human Rights and Fundamental Freedoms (ECHR), and the Hague Convention on Abduction 1980.

Complicating an explanation of children's rights is the fact that within the United Kingdom, there is more than one legal system. England and Wales share one system, Scotland has its own system, and Northern Ireland also has a distinctive system. Under the devolution of law-making powers introduced under the 1997 Labour Government, the ultimate law-making power remains with the United Kingdom Parliament (Westminster), but large areas of law-making are devolved to the national legislatures.[18] The majority of domestic law relating to children and their care is devolved and although there are variations in some aspects of the law, for the most part, there is an equivalence in terms of children's rights.[19]

The brief overview of the legal framework which follows begins by considering the contribution of international law to the protection of rights. The first major source of law is the United Nations Convention on the Rights of the Child (CRC), dating from 1989. The CRC follows the accepted classification of rights, adopted by the United Nations and regional conventions that rights are either Civil and Political or Social and Economic.[20] Civil and Political Rights emphasise the rights of citizens (rights of free speech, assembly and association, right to vote, etc.). For the most part (and generalising), such rights require governments to create a political system capable of respecting such rights and to abstain from interfering with them. Social and Economic Rights on the other hand – and again as a generalisation – the right to decent standards of living and to health, etc., require governments to make and maintain substantial investment in providing for and upholding rights. As a result, some social and economic rights are best described as aspirational: goals to be worked towards.

As noted above, rights under the CRC are not enforceable in the local courts. Notwithstanding its unenforceability, the CRC has proved highly influential in setting standards for the protection of children's rights and all official bodies in the UK are guided by the CRC in formulating policies and practices. The second major source is the European Convention on Human Rights (ECHR). The ECHR is not child-specific, but the rights under the ECHR apply equally to children and adults. As discussed below, since 2000 when the Human Rights Act 1998 came into force, ECHR rights have been enforceable in the domestic courts, from the lowest court to the highest in the legal system. Moreover, domestic law must, where it is found to be in conflict with ECHR rights, be reformed so as to bring it in line with ECHR requirements.

A further important source of rights is the Hague Convention on Abduction. The Hague Convention, as its name suggests, is highly specific – designed to protect children from the wrongful removal from their country of residence and where that has occurred, to return them (usually) to their home country. Other important aspects of international law, for example the Refugee Convention, are relevant to children's rights and will be discussed in the text. The CRC, the ECHR, and the Hague Convention, discussed below, are arguably the most wide-ranging in their scope and application.

After introducing aspects of international law, attention then turns to the domestic law, of which the English Children Act 1989 is a major source, as is the Equality Act 2010. The 'inherent jurisdiction' of the High Court also provides an important mechanism for protecting children's rights. The origins of this jurisdiction lie in the prerogative powers of the Crown which has the duty to protect children and others who do not have full legal capacity to make decisions over their lives and can be resorted to where there are serious concerns over the welfare of a child and a decision of a court of law is considered necessary. A key mechanism for challenging the legality of decision-making by public authorities – judicial review – is also introduced. As children cannot bring legal proceedings to protect their rights, the role of the Official Solicitor is briefly discussed, as is that of the Children and Family Court Advisory and Support Service (CAFCASS), the service dedicated to supporting children who come into contact with the legal system.

The UN Convention on the Rights of the Child (CRC)

In 1989, after a decade of preparation, the Convention on the Rights of the Child (CRC) was adopted by the General Assembly of the United Nations. It came into force in 1990 and was ratified (formally approved) by the UK in 1991. Although the UK has ratified the CRC it has not been incorporated into domestic law and as noted above, unlike rights under the ECHR, does not create legally enforceable rights before the domestic courts.[21] However, in 2020 the Scottish Government announced that it intends to incorporate the CRC within its legal system: the UNCRC Incorporation (Scotland) Bill 2021 gives effect to this intention. It will be the first country to make the CRC legally enforceable in its domestic courts. The CRC is now the most ratified convention in the world. Some States, however, although signatories, have registered reservations in relation to aspects of the Convention. The right of a child to freedom of thought, conscience, and religion under Article 14, for example, has proved unacceptable to many Islamic States.

Unlike the ECHR which is confined to protecting civil and political rights, the CRC protects both civil and political and social and economic rights. In relation to social and economic rights, the CRC is in large measure aspirational: it sets standards to be worked towards by all signatory States. Article 27, for example, provides that 'State Parties recognise the right of every child to a standard of living adequate for the child's physical, mental, spiritual, moral, and social development'. Article 31 requires that 'State Parties recognise the right of the child to rest and leisure, to engage in play and recreational activities appropriate to the age of the child and to participate freely in cultural life and the arts'. For these goals to be more than utopian, a State must have an economy sufficiently developed to enable the enjoyment of the rights to become a reality.

Four CRC Articles are regarded as general principles designed to guide State Parties in their duties towards children:

- Article 2 requires that States must 'respect and ensure' CRC rights without discrimination of any form;
- Article 3 requires that in all their work in relation to children all public bodies (the legislature, courts, social welfare agencies) the interests of the child 'shall be a primary consideration', a requirement lower than that adopted under the Children Act 1989 where the welfare of the child is the paramount consideration;
- Article 6 recognises the inherent right to life of every child;
- Article 12 provides that State Parties must ensure that in all matters affecting the child (whether judicial or administrative), he or she has the right to express his or her view, the views being given 'due weight' according to his or her age and maturity.

The CRC, unlike the ECHR, does not have any formal enforcement mechanisms for alleged violations of rights. There is no court to which an aggrieved person may apply, and no political body (such as the Committee of Ministers under the ECHR) to pressurise reluctant States to comply with court rulings. There is an 18-member Committee on the Rights of the Child, based in Geneva, which has the task of monitoring and reporting on the extent to which States are achieving the obligations assumed under the Convention. States are required to report on progress, initially two years after ratification, thereafter every five years, and the Committee will assess compliance and make recommendations for improvement if necessary. The UN Convention has proved immensely influential within the UK. Public bodies across all areas use the CRC as a guiding force in their work.

However, according to the Committee on the Rights of the Child, there are many areas where the UK government has fallen short in promoting and protecting children's rights. According to the CRC, the 'welfare principle' – the paramount consideration of courts when making decisions relating to a child's care and upbringing – is narrow in its scope, and does not extend or apply uniformly across all decisions relating to children. There are also inconsistencies in the extent to which the views of children are taken into account and respected, as required by Article 12 of the UN Convention. These are apparent in divorce proceedings, adoption, education, and child protection measures and the Committee called upon governments to do more to ensure the meaningful and full participation of children in decision-making.[22]

Reporting in 2018, the Children's Rights Alliance England (CRAE) which also monitors compliance with the UNCRC, states that there has been little progress in ensuring that children participate fully in decision-making and that the best interests of the child continue to apply inconsistently. Over the past ten years local authorities have suffered huge funding cuts and this has had a significant impact on provision for children in need. The number of children being cared for by local authorities, for example, increased for the tenth consecutive year; the number of child protection inquiries increased by 122 per cent since 2010 and there was an increase of nearly 17 per cent in sexual offences against children from 2015 to 2016.[23] There are further problematic areas identified by the Committee on the Rights of the Child and the CRAE which will be discussed in the relevant chapter of this book.[24] It is clear from the evidence that there remain great challenges in the protection of children's rights.

The European Convention on Human Rights (ECHR)

The European Convention (ECHR) was drafted under the auspices of the Council of Europe and came into force in 1953. The Council of Europe was founded in 1949, and now has 47 Member States, 26 of which also belong to the European Union. The aim of the Council was to provide Europe-wide protection for the civil and political rights and freedoms which had been so violated during the course of the Second World War of 1939 to 1945. The Council is based in Strasbourg and has a parliamentary assembly which oversees and debates human rights issues, a Court (the European Court of Human Rights) and a political wing, the Committee of Ministers. The latter is made up of foreign ministers of the Member States and monitors the implementation and enforcement of Convention rights and, where a Member State has violated a right, works towards rectifying the offending law or practice.

The ECHR largely reflects those rights covered by the United Nation's Convention on Civil and Political Rights of 1946. The Convention rights – many of which will feature in this book – are:

- Article 1: the right of everyone within a State to enjoy Convention rights;
- Article 2: the right to life;
- Article 3: freedom from torture, inhuman or degrading treatment or punishment;
- Article 4: freedom from slavery, servitude, or forced labour;
- Article 5: the right to liberty and security;
- Article 6: the right to fair trial;
- Article 7: the prohibition on retrospective law;
- Article 8: the right to respect for private and family life;
- Article 9: freedom of thought, conscience and religion;
- Article 10: the right to freedom of expression;
- Article 11: the right to freedom of association;
- Article 12: the right to marry and found a family;
- Article 13: the right to an effective remedy;
- Article 14: the right to enjoy all Convention rights without discrimination.

From the perspective of the protection of children's rights, the most relevant Convention rights are Article 2, the right to life; Article 3, freedom from torture, inhuman, and degrading treatment; Article 5, the right to liberty; Article 6, the right to fair trial; and Article 8, the right to respect for private and family life. Illustrations of the Convention's contribution to the protection of children's rights will be discussed further throughout this book.

Some Convention rights are absolute: the right to freedom from torture, inhuman and degrading treatment (Article 3), and freedom from slavery (Article 4) are absolute and cannot be limited. Other rights are 'qualified': in other words, limitations may apply. The right to respect for private and family life (Article 8) may be restricted, for example where it is necessary in a democratic society to do so, or in the interests of national security, public safety, or the economic well-being of the country, for the prevention of disorder or crime, for the protection of health or morals, or for the protection of the rights and freedoms of others.

When a case comes to court, the first question for the court is whether a Convention right has been infringed. The second question is whether there are any restrictions imposed on the right and whether there is a justification for the restriction. In reaching this decision, the court will use the concept of 'proportionality', i.e. is the restriction proportionate to the aims to be achieved? Where a court finds that a restriction is justified, it must then decide whether the restriction is no more than necessary to achieve the legitimate aim. In other words, has the authority 'used a sledgehammer to crack a nut'? If it has, then that is not proportionate and will be unlawful.

CASE FOCUS: *A AND D*[25]

A, aged 14 and D aged 12 were half-siblings. TMI, the partner of the mother of A and D, with the full consent of their mother, had applied to adopt them. Neither A nor D had had a relationship with their natural father. Before the High Court, the judge had refused to dispense with the consent of A's father on the basis that it was not in A's best interests to do so and would be a disproportionate measure in that it would deprive A's father of his parental responsibility.

Before the Court of Appeal, however, this decision was criticised for its flawed reasoning. The judge had failed to consider the 'quality, substance and importance' (both in terms of welfare and in ECHR Article 8 terms) of A's father's role in the child's life. That had been minimal. TMI on the other hand had 'in almost every way become A and D's father' and he and the children's mother had a stable family unit. The judge had failed to engage in the benefits that an adoption would bring. By granting the Adoption Order in favour of TMI, the de facto family status would become a legal family status and A and D would become full siblings in the eyes of the law, something that A firmly wished for. The loss of the legal relationship with A's father, on the facts of the case, was not in any manner out of proportion. The Adoption Order was granted.

The United Kingdom signed the Convention in 1953. The Convention provides for two types of applications alleging violations of rights. The first is the 'inter-state' application: one State alleging that another State has violated individual rights. The second type of application is the right of 'individual petition', allowing individual citizens to make a claim that their rights have been violated by a public body within their State, and seek a remedy. Within the UK, however, political concerns over 'interference' from a foreign court initially led the government to refuse to allow individual citizens access to the Convention institutions. The government did accept that allegations could be made by other States, using inter-state applications. It was not until 1965 that the government accepted that citizens had the right to make applications for alleged violations to be examined. From 1965 until 2000 that remained the position: if a right was violated the individual (or organisation) had to make an application to Strasbourg for a ruling. Convention rights were not enforceable before the domestic courts. The contribution of the ECHR prior to the Human Rights Act 1998 is illustrated in the following two cases.

CASE FOCUS: *TP AND KM V UNITED KINGDOM; Z V UK*[26]

In the earlier *Bedfordshire case* (1995)[27] the local authority had been aware that children were suffering abuse at the hands of their parents. Nevertheless the authority had failed, for five years, to take any action to protect the children. The House of Lords (now the Supreme Court) ruled that local authorities did not owe a duty of care to children in their care, and as a result the children could not sue the local authority in negligence. The cases of *TP and KM* and *Z* decided by the European Court of Human Rights dealt the *Bedfordshire case* a fatal blow. The Official Solicitor (on whose role see below) applied under the ECHR on behalf of the children affected by the *Bedfordshire case*.

The ECtHR ruled that local authorities, as agents of the State, have a positive duty to protect children in their care from neglect and abuse that amounts to a violation of their Convention rights (principally Articles 2 and 3). Where rights are violated, the State must provide an 'effective remedy' (Article 13). Here, because domestic law prevented victims from suing State agencies in negligence (as a result of the *Bedfordshire case*) the children were denied an effective remedy and the State had violated Article 13.

CASE FOCUS: *THE SUNDAY TIMES* CASE[28]

Evidence had emerged that Thalidomide, a drug prescribed in pregnancy to treat morning sickness, was causing serious physical defects in newborn babies. The parents of deformed babies born as a result of taking Thalidomide intended to sue the manufacturers, Distillers, and there were protracted negotiations between parents and Distillers for some form of settlement. *The Sunday Times* raised public awareness of the problems allegedly caused by Thalidomide. Distillers sought an injunction to restrain any further publicity, arguing that further publication on the issue would prejudice negotiations. The injunction was granted but was subsequently discharged by the Court of Appeal. In 1974 the matter went to the House of Lords, which restored the injunction. The injunction prohibited the newspaper from publishing any information. Breach of the injunction would have put the newspaper in contempt of court.

The effect of the injunction was to suppress, over a long period of time, any information on the subject. *The Sunday Times* took action against the United Kingdom alleging that the injunction violated ECHR Article 10: the right to freedom of expression. The Court of Human Rights ruled that Article 10 had been violated. The case led to a major reform of the law of contempt of court.

As seen above, there is also an inter-state application. This is where one State considers that another State has violated Convention rights and seeks a ruling from the European Court of Human Rights (ECtHR). The case below is one example.

CASE FOCUS: *IRELAND V UNITED KINGDOM*

In *Ireland v United Kingdom* (1979–1980), the Republic of Ireland alleged that the British armed forces in Northern Ireland had violated Article 3 of the Convention, (the prohibition against torture, inhuman and degrading treatment and punishment). The background to these allegations was the period of civil unrest and terrorism which deteriorated from around 1970. The British Government introduced internment without trial, detaining suspected terrorists. Evidence had emerged that in seeking evidence about terrorism the British forces had used wall-standing, hooding, constant noise, sleep deprivation, and deprivation of food and drink against the suspects. The ECtHR found that these techniques caused intense physical and mental suffering leading to acute psychiatric disturbances. The treatment was inhuman and degrading, but not of sufficient severity to amount to torture. There had been a violation of Article 3 by the United Kingdom.

Since 2000, the ECHR has made a significant contribution to the protection of children's rights, as will be seen throughout this book.

The Hague Convention on Abduction (The Convention on the Civil Aspects of International Child Abduction 1980)[29]

The Hague Convention 1980 was drafted under the authority of the Hague Conference on Private International Law. The Convention came into effect in 1983, and by 2019 there were 101 State Parties to the Convention.

The primary purpose of the Convention is to protect children from their wrongful removal from the country in which they are 'habitually resident' and, where a child is abducted, to establish procedures for his or her prompt return to his or her home country. A large majority of cases involve abduction by the parent who does not have the day-to-day care of the child. The Hague Convention is supported under domestic law by the Child Abduction Act 1984 which makes it a criminal offence to send a child under the age of 16 out of the UK without the consent of his or her parents, guardians, or carer.

The policy behind the Convention is that disputes about children should be decided in the courts of the country of their 'habitual residence'. When at the start of proceedings, less than a year has elapsed since the wrongful removal of the child, the Convention places a duty on the courts to return a child to his or her country of habitual residence 'forthwith'. However, even where a longer time has passed, the courts must still return the child unless 'the child is now settled in its new environment'.

The key concept here is 'habitual residence'. To be 'habitually resident' requires more than the mere fact of being in one place for a period of time: it requires that a child has settled and has a degree of attachment to the place where he or she is now living. Where a child has been moved from one country to another, he or she may retain strong ties to the country he or she has left and may not have settled in the new country to the extent that a court would hold that he or she is habitually resident there and order the child to be returned. Conversely, where strong attachments have been formed with the child's new home country and the child has been well integrated into his or her new environment, a court may refuse to disrupt that new home by ordering the child to be returned to his or her original home country.

The focus of the question is less on whether a former habitual residence has been 'lost' and more on whether – and to what extent – a habitual residence has been established in the country where the child currently lives.

CASE FOCUS: *M*[30]

Two children, aged 6 and 8, were born in Germany. In 2017 their parents separated and in 2018 the mother brought the children to England, with the father's consent, intending to remain for '12 months or so' living with the mother and her boyfriend. The children went to school in England and settled quickly. In 2019, the mother – now remarried – found that she was pregnant and decided not to return to Germany. The father sought the return of the children and a return order was granted by the court, on the basis that the children had not lost their 'habitual residence' in Germany. The mother appealed. The Court of Appeal ruled that the correct test was not whether a habitual residence had been lost, but rather where the children were habitually resident at the date of the 'wrongful retention or abduction' (in this case 2019, when the mother informed the father that she intended to remain with the children in England).[31] Here the children had established their home in England, settled, and had 'become integrated to a very substantial degree in a social and family environment in England'. The mother's appeal succeeded and the children remained in England.

The general duty to return a child to the country of his or her habitual residence may be overridden in two situations:

- firstly, where a child is of sufficient maturity and understanding to reach a decision and does not want to return;
- secondly, where there is a grave risk that his or her return would expose the child to physical or psychological harm or otherwise place the child in an intolerable situation

Hague Convention, Article 13.

Where it is alleged that there is risk of harm to the child if returned home, the courts require:

> ... clear and compelling evidence of the grave risk of harm or other intolerability which must be measured as substantial, not trivial and of a severity which is much more than is inherent in the inevitable disruption, uncertainty and anxiety which follows an unwelcome return to the jurisdiction of the court of habitual residence.[32]

CASE FOCUS: *M*[33]

In interpreting the exceptions to the duty to return, the courts had developed the principle that it was only in exceptional circumstances that the child's objections to being returned would prevail over the objectives of the Convention. In *Re M* Baroness Hale corrected that view. The weight to be given to the policy of the Convention – the speedy return of abducted children – would vary according to the circumstances of the case. Where children objected to being returned, the courts had to decide firstly whether the child objected and secondly whether had she reached the age and maturity at which her views should be given great weight. In light of Article 12 of the CRC, courts increasingly took account of the child's views. In this case, there had been a time lapse of over two years and the children had settled in the UK. The court therefore had a discretion over whether or not to return the child. On the Convention's objective of deterring abduction, Baroness Hale commented that 'these children should not be made to suffer for the sake of general deterrence of the evil of child abduction worldwide'.[34] The father's appeal was dismissed.

A very different result is seen in the case below where emphasis was placed on the courts of the child's original residence being the best place to decide on the welfare of the child.

CASE FOCUS: E[35]

Two girls, aged seven and four, had lived all their lives in Norway until their mother brought them to England with a view to staying permanently. She did not seek the father's consent. The father applied to the Norwegian authority for the return of the children.

The mother claimed that she had suffered serious psychological abuse at the hands of the father and that she and the children were afraid of him. He denied the allegations but admitted to killing the family cat and a pet rabbit. However, he made undertakings that he would leave the family home, stay away from it, not remove the children, and would support the family financially.

The Supreme Court dismissed the mother's appeal against an order to return the children to Norway. The aim of the Convention was to ensure the best interests of the child. That was served by returning them to their home country for their futures to be decided by the Norwegian courts. The trial judge was satisfied that there were legal remedies to protect the children in Norway should they be needed.

The Human Rights Act 1998

With the election of the Labour Government in 1997 came a raft of constitutional changes. Among these was the commitment to 'bring rights home', by making Convention rights enforceable before the local courts under the Human Rights Act 1998.[36] No longer would individuals have to face the inconvenience, expense, and length of time involved in applying to the European Court of Human Rights. If an individual considers that his or her rights have been infringed, he or she may challenge the acts of a public body in the local courts. All courts, from the lowest to highest, may hear allegations about rights violations, and grant remedies to the applicant where a breach has been found.

Under the Human Rights Act (HRA), it is now unlawful for any public body to act in a way which is incompatible with Convention rights. Only a *victim* of Convention violations may apply under the HRA and the rights of children will be protected by action taken by adults on their behalf (on this see further below). Applications must be made within one year of the alleged violation of a right unless a court or tribunal allows an extension of time.[37] All courts and tribunals may hear allegations of violations of rights and, where a violation is found, can grant whatever appropriate remedy falls within their usual powers.[38] Where a public body's act or a decision violates an individual's ECHR rights, but does so because there is an Act of Parliament which requires the body to act in that way, the act or decision will be lawful. However, in this situation, the higher courts (High Court and above) may grant a Declaration of Incompatibility (DoI) which puts Parliament and the government on notice that there is a defect in the law. In this way, the law will be brought in line with the requirements of ECHR rights and further violations avoided (on Declarations of Incompatibility see further below).

A public body is defined by its functions: a body which fulfils governmental functions will be a public body.[39] For example, a privately owned care home for elderly people that accommodates residents paid for in whole or part by a local authority will be a public body. All courts and tribunals are also public bodies. The effect of this is that where a privately owned body, such as a newspaper, violates an individual's right to privacy (Article 8 ECHR), the court hearing the application is under a duty to protect the claimant's right to privacy, because not to do so would cause the court itself to violate the claimant's Article 8 right. In this way, the protection of the Convention extends beyond State/public bodies to private enterprises.

CASE FOCUS: *M*[40]

A newspaper photographer took photos of the child of a well-known writer while the family was out on a private shopping trip. The child's parents claimed that the newspaper had violated their child's right to privacy. The Court of Appeal ruled that, while a child has no guarantee of privacy, he or she nevertheless has a reasonable expectation that his or her privacy would be respected. The newspaper – a privately owned entity – had violated the Article 8 right.

There is one major constitutional limitation on the powers of the courts to protect individual rights: no court may declare an Act of Parliament invalid. This restriction is explained by the doctrine of parliamentary sovereignty or supremacy. Dating back to the Bill of Rights 1689, parliamentary sovereignty sits at the pinnacle of law-making power in the UK. Theoretically, Parliament may make any law it wishes and no one can challenge that right. In reality, this unlimited power is hedged in by the requirements of democracy, economic necessities, and international obligations. However, sovereignty means that no judicial decision can undermine Parliament's power, let alone declare an exercise of that power to be invalid. Accordingly, the Human Rights Act 1998, rather than allowing judges to invalidate an Act of Parliament, gives to the higher courts (High Court and above) the power to make a Declaration of Incompatibility. This declares that a provision in an Act violates a Convention right, and that the law needs amending. However, it leaves the offending provision in force. Parliament is not obliged to respond to the DoI by amending the law: its sovereignty means that, if it were politically acceptable to do so, it could simply ignore it. However, this will rarely happen. The Human Rights Act 1998 represents a constitutional partnership between Parliament and the courts: Parliament remains supreme but judges can declare that its provisions infringe Convention rights with the normal outcome that the law will be reformed. For example:

CASE FOCUS: *BELLINGER*[41]

The law relating to marriage required that for a marriage to be valid, the parties had to be respectively male and female. Under English law, biological sex was fixed at birth and could not be altered. The European Convention, Article 12, provides that men and women have the right to marry according to the laws of their country. In the *Bellinger* case one of the parties had undergone gender realignment surgery and therefore could not lawfully marry. When the 'marriage' broke down the other party sought a declaration that the marriage was invalid. The court held that the marriage was void (i.e. invalid; of no effect), but issued a Declaration of Incompatibility in relation to English law. In response, Parliament passed the Gender Recognition Act 2004, which enabled transsexuals to obtain a new birth certificate reflecting their new gender and with it, the right to marry.

The Children Act 1989

The principal Act of Parliament relating to children and their rights in England and Wales is the Children Act 1989 (CA) and in Scotland the Children (Scotland) Act 1995.[42] The Children Act was described by the then Lord Chancellor, Lord Mackay, as the 'most comprehensive and far reaching' piece of reforming legislation 'in living memory'.[43] The Act was the outcome of a number of inquiries into the deaths of children while under the care and supervision of social services.[44] As discussed below, these inquiries exposed the deficiencies of social work practice and led to a 1985 Review of Child Care Law.[45] The Law Commission – the body which reviews the law and makes recommendations for reform – described the law relating to the care of children as 'complicated, confusing and unclear' and called for a rationalised system of law relating to child care.[46] Although the Children Act does not regulate either adoption law[47] or the law relating to juvenile justice, it is comprehensive in its coverage of the orders a court may make in relation to children when parents separate or divorce and in its coverage of local authority duties and powers in relation to the safety and well-being of children in their area.

The Children Act firstly makes clear that the welfare of the child is a court's paramount consideration when reaching decisions about the upbringing of a child. The Act then defines parental responsibility, who has it, and how it may be acquired by those who do not automatically qualify for it. The Act defines the range of orders that a court may make when there are disputes over living arrangements or contact with a child. For example:

CASE FOCUS: S[48]

A Child Arrangements Order provided that Lara, aged 9, should share her time equally between her two parents' homes. This arrangement did not work and Lara became alienated from her father. Her father applied to have the Order varied and for Lara to live with him. His application was refused and he appealed. Lara's mother applied for a variation of the Order to restrict the time Lara spent with her father. The father's case was that Lara's mother had become involved in a cult, Universal Medicine, the effect of which was increasingly harmful to Lara's welfare. The Court of Appeal considered the law relating to freedom of belief as protected by Article 9 of the ECHR, stressing that religious belief was not the business of government or the secular courts, and that the courts would respect an individual's or family's religious principles.

However, where a parent's belief was contrary to the welfare of the child, the court would intervene to protect the child. In this case it was clear that adherence to Universal Medicine was the cause of Lara's alienation from her father. Furthermore, it was 'a pervasive source of ongoing harm to Lara, emotionally and psychologically, and may make her vulnerable to eating disorders'. The Court of Appeal ruled that Lara must be 'distanced entirely' from the cult. This could only happen if her mother made 'an immediate and definitive break' with the organisation. If her mother did not do this, the court would order that Lara should live with her father. The Court of Appeal remitted the case to the President of the Family Division for a final decision, thereby allowing the mother a brief period in which to leave Universal Medicine, undertake intensive therapy, and reverse the process of Lara's alienation from her father. Unless that happened it would be necessary to transfer Lara's care to her father where she would gain 'from growing up in the care of a good parent while attending the same school, and her childhood will not continue to be overshadowed by the baleful influences that have led to the present situation'.[49]

The Act provides for accommodation arrangements for children where, for whatever reason, they are unable to live with their natural parents. It also sets out the duties of local authorities to provide services for children in their area, and the orders that a local authority may seek from a court of law. These include Emergency Protection Orders, Supervision Orders and Care Orders, each of which is discussed in Chapter 6.

In using the powers conferred by the Children Act (and any other Act of Parliament), courts and other public bodies must comply with ECHR rights which are protected under the Human Rights Act 1998: there is thus an interaction between the Children Act and the Human Rights Act. For example, when a court is deciding whether to make an Emergency Protection Order (EPO) in favour of a local authority,[50] the court must not only apply the welfare test (or best interests test) but must also consider the child's and his or her parents' ECHR rights. An Emergency Protection Order entitles the local authority to remove a child from his or her home and family, at short notice, for his or her protection. In extreme cases, the Order may be applied for without giving notice to the parents of the child. Article 8 of the ECHR protects the right to family life. This right is not absolute and restrictions may legitimately be imposed on its exercise. An EPO adversely affects the right to family life, and must therefore be justified in order to be lawful. Not only must the statutory grounds for making the order be satisfied, but also the court must consider whether making the EPO is a *proportionate* response to the factual situation. As the courts have repeatedly made clear, this consideration entails weighing up whether the objective to be achieved – the safety of a child – requires the making of an EPO or whether some less intrusive order could achieve the same result. In other words, is the EPO necessary in all the circumstances? Is it proportionate? This was the question posed in *X v B*, discussed below.

CASE FOCUS: *X*[51]

Fearing for the safety of three children the local authority sought – without notifying the parents – and was granted EPOs, each lasting eight days. The children were removed from their home and placed with foster parents. The matter came before the High Court and the then President of the Family Division, Sir James Munby, considered the human rights aspects of EPOs. Munby J noted that EPOs were 'draconian' and 'extremely harsh' and required 'exceptional justification' and 'extraordinary compelling reasons', and acknowledged the view of the European Court of Human Rights that 'intervention must be proportionate to the legitimate aim of protecting the welfare and interests of the child'.

In this case the actions of the local authority were seriously criticised as being based on the 'inadequacy of its decision-making processes' leading to the conclusion that 'it was far from clear that there was any justification for the removal of the children into foster care'.[52]

The Equality Act 2010

The Equality Act 2010 was a major reform of discrimination law, bringing together in one statute a number of earlier Acts of Parliament. The Act protects people with 'protected characteristics' from discrimination. Those characteristics are:

- age;
- disability;
- gender reassignment;
- civil and marriage partnership;
- race;
- religion or belief;
- sex;
- sexual orientation.

The Act prohibits direct and indirect discrimination. Direct discrimination occurs if a person discriminates against another person, where, because of a protected characteristic, he or she treats the other person less favourably than he or she would treat another (without the protected characteristic). Indirect discrimination occurs where a person applies a practice to another person which, because of his or her protected characteristic, would place him or her at a disadvantage when compared with those who do not share that characteristic.

In relation to disability, the Act requires that a person or organisation must make reasonable adjustments so as to avoid discrimination, which would occur if the adjustments were not made. Adjustments might include removing an obstacle, or altering some physical features which would cause discrimination, including making adjustments to building, to exits, or access, etc., and these adjustments also include, where necessary, the provision of an auxiliary aid. On disability rights see further Chapter 3.

The Act imposes a Public Sector Equality Duty (PSED) on all public authorities,[53] and those private bodies exercising public functions. The PSED applies to Ministers and Government Departments, local authorities, education bodies, health service bodies, the police, courts, and tribunals. The PSED requires that when a body is making strategic decisions about how to exercise its functions it *must* 'have due regard to the desirability of exercising them in a way that is designed to reduce the inequalities of outcome which result from socio-economic disadvantage'.[54] This requires the authority to 'have due regard to the need to':

- eliminate discrimination, harassment, victimisation, and any other conduct that is prohibited by or under this Act;
- advance equality of opportunity between persons who share a relevant protected characteristic and persons who do not share it;

- foster good relations between persons who share a relevant protected characteristic and persons who do not share it. Fostering good relations requires having 'due regard' to the need to tackle prejudice and promote understanding.[55]

The 2010 Act imposes 'a heavy burden' upon public authorities in discharging the PSED: the PSED is now at the heart of decision-making[56] and an alleged failure by a public authority to exercise its PSED may lead to a legal challenge. For example:

CASE FOCUS: *BRACKING*[57]

In 2012 the Minister for Disabled People decided to close the Independent Living Fund (ILF) with effect from 2015. The ILF was a Non-Departmental Government Body operating a discretionary trust funded by the Minister's Department. The Fund operated in partnership with local authorities to provide care packages and services to disabled persons to assist them to lead independent lives in the community and away from residential care. The system ran alongside the mainstream social care system. It was the Minister's view that the objectives of the ILF could be met within the social care system administered by local authorities rather than the ILF.

A challenge to that decision claimed, among other things, that in making the decision the Minister had failed to discharge her PSED. The Court of Appeal ruled that to satisfy the requirements of the PSED a decision-maker had to take a 'conscious approach' to the duty and the duty had to be exercised with 'rigour and an open mind'. In this case there was insufficient evidence that the Minister had enough information regarding the effects of closing the ILF – namely, that independent living might be put seriously in peril for a large number of people'.[58] Furthermore, there was nothing to show that the Minister had focused on the precise provisions of the Act. As a result, the Minister had failed to discharge her PSED and her decision was unlawful and would be quashed by the Court.

Wardship: the inherent jurisdiction of the High Court

The wardship jurisdiction of the High Court is a legacy from the days of royal power but remains a valuable procedure for protecting children's rights. The relationship between a King or Queen and his or her 'subjects' is reciprocal. The individual owes allegiance to the Crown and the Crown in turn owes a duty of protection to the people. In relation to children, the Crown is *parens patriae*: a figure having protective parental authority over children and others lacking the capacity to care for themselves.[59] By the 19th century, the wardship jurisdiction had been delegated to the Lord Chancellor and the Court of Chancery. At that time the principal use of the jurisdiction was to protect the property of a wealthy child who was made a ward of court. The effect of being made a ward of court was and remains that the court can make all arrangements over the life of the ward. The court could stipulate with whom the child was to live and make orders binding on the child herself.

Wardship could be invoked by anyone with an interest in the child: the making of an application to the court is sufficient to make the child a ward of court. It throws an immediate cloak of protection around the child and prevents anyone other than the court from making decisions over his or her life. Increasingly the jurisdiction was used by parents, doctors, and local authorities, and occasionally by those with ulterior motives. Whereas in the 19th century the jurisdiction was used to protect a relatively small number of children, by the middle of the 20th century, the process was increasingly being used to resolve all kinds of disputes over children.[60]

CASE FOCUS: *D*[61]

A social worker made D, an 11-year-old girl with serious mental and physical disabilities, a ward of court. She had become aware that the mother of the girl had sought advice from a paediatrician and gynaecologist over the sterilisation of her daughter because she feared that D would become pregnant and her child would inherit the same disabilities as D.

The court ruled that it was not in D's best interests to be sterilised and deprived of the basic right to reproduce.

CASE FOCUS: *Z*[62]

The local authority warded Z, then aged 17. Z had a range of complex health needs and his parents were failing to follow medical advice or to take him to medical appointments. The authority considered that he was suffering or likely to suffer significant harm. The mother lacked the mental capacity for legal action and was represented through the Official Solicitor as her litigation friend (on which see below).

The local authority had been unable to issue care proceedings because of Z's age. The court ruled that Z should continue to live with his parents and that wardship should continue until his 18th birthday, thereby ensuring that the court supervised Z's treatment.

CASE FOCUS: *K*[63]

Three seriously disabled children were warded where there had been protracted conflict between the parents and the local authority over the care of
the children. The judge explained that wardship:

> ... reminds all that they remain accountable to the court for the making of
> the necessary arrangements for the care, education, and nurturing of these
> three young children and it confirms the court's powers over the control
> and delegation of parental responsibility.[64]

By the 1990s the majority of wardship applications were from local authorities
seeking to avoid the stringent conditions imposed by other proceedings such as
care proceedings. In *Re L* (1982) a mother warded her child, who was subject to
a Care Order, in an attempt to stop a local authority from reducing her contact
with the child.[65] However, when the matter reached the House of Lords (now
the Supreme Court), the court decided that wardship should not be used as a way
of challenging a local authority decision. The effect of *Re L* meant that there
was now a disparity between the rights of parents to challenge local authorities
through wardship, and the rights of local authorities to use the jurisdiction. A
brake was put on its use by local authorities under the Children Act 1989.[66]

The Children Act makes it clear that the wardship jurisdiction should not
be used to place a child in the care, or under the supervision of a local authority, or in local authority accommodation. Local authorities may now only apply
for wardship with the permission of the court and permission will be granted
only if the court is satisfied that the result the local authority is trying to achieve
cannot be achieved by the making of any other type of order. The effect of this
restriction was that whereas there were nearly 5,000 applications for wardship by
local authorities in the year before the Children Act came into force, by 1992 the
number was reduced to 492 applications.[67]

Because of its flexibility and the ease with which it can be invoked, wardship
remains an important jurisdiction in relation to children. It is most particularly
useful in relation to medical decisions concerning children, where an urgent
decision needs to be made. On these cases see Chapter 3.

Judicial review of administrative action

Judicial review is a procedure by which individuals and other eligible bodies
such as representative groups and/or pressure groups may challenge the legality
of decisions made by public bodies. It plays a major role in ensuring that governmental bodies comply with the law. The law is complex, but an awareness of the

main aspects of judicial review is a useful aid to understanding the mechanics of challenging the decision-making of public authorities.

The essence of judicial review is that it provides a process through which the courts will ensure that decision-makers are kept within the scope of powers given to them by Parliament and that they comply with the rules of natural justice developed by the judges to ensure the fairness of the decision-making process. However, while State agencies must comply with the law, they also need to be protected from challenges which have no merit and are designed simply to frustrate the legitimate exercise of government power. Accordingly, there is no absolute right to initiate judicial review proceedings: it is a discretionary process for which permission to bring legal proceedings must be granted by a court of law.

The basic rules relating to judicial review are, in outline, that:

- applications to initiate judicial review are made to the Administrative Division of the High Court;
- in order to be granted permission to proceed with judicial review, and to rule out 'unmeritorious' challenges, the applicant must have 'sufficient interest' in the matter challenged;
- the decision-making body being challenged must be a 'public body', as defined by the courts. The key determinant is whether a body – public or private – is exercising a public function, i.e. a governmental function;
- the decision being questioned must involve a matter of public – not private – law, as defined by the courts. Judicial review is concerned with the legality of *governmental functions*. If a dispute involves rights acquired under a contract or a trust, that is a matter of private law and not the concern of the High Court in judicial review;
- a challenge to a decision must be made within a strict time frame: unless extended by a court, the challenge must be made within three months of knowing that there is a potential ground for challenging the decision;
- when exercising its judicial review function, the High Court is not ruling on the merits of a particular decision (i.e. whether in the court's opinion it is right or wrong). The court is ruling on whether the public authority has acted within the confines of its legal powers given by Parliament and/or complied with the requirements of natural justice and fairness;
- the outcome of judicial review is totally different from a decision made by an appeal court. An appeal court may uphold or overturn a decision of a lower court. If the lower court has made a legally incorrect decision, the appeal court will substitute its own decision for that of the lower court. In judicial review, the court is ruling on the legality (or otherwise) of an administrative decision. If the decision-making body has made an unlawful decision, the High Court will require that body to re-make the decision according to law: it will not substitute its decision for that of the decision-making body.

Children and legal proceedings

A child cannot take legal proceedings without the assistance of an adult. A parent or guardian, a family member or friend, a solicitor or other advocate, or a person with a lasting power of attorney may all be 'litigation friends'. An individual may apply to act as a child's litigation friend, or one may be appointed by the court. A litigation friend must be someone with no conflict of interest in the case and be sufficiently competent to make decisions. In addition, the court needs to be satisfied that the applicant is a 'suitable person'. This decision will be based on the completion of a certificate of suitability. If there is no suitable person capable or willing to act as a litigation friend, the Official Solicitor may fulfil the role.

The Official Solicitor

The Official Solicitor and Public Trustee (OSPT) are two separate, independent office holders. Together they have around 135 civil service staff.[68] The role of the Official Solicitor is to help those under the age of 18 (other than those who are subject to welfare proceedings) and those who lack the mental capacity to act for themselves. In relation to legal proceedings, where there is no suitable litigation friend, the Official Solicitor will help with deciding whether to start a case, or whether to defend a case if action is threatened against a child. The Official Solicitor will usually appoint a solicitor to advise and represent the child in court. Whether or not this assistance will be free or not will depend on eligibility for legal aid.

CAFCASS: the Children and Family Court Advisory Support Service

CAFCASS was created in 2001, bringing together the services formerly provided by the Family Court Welfare Service, the Guardian ad Litem Services and the Children's Division of the Official Solicitor's Office.[69] CAFCASS's Family Court Advisers work within the family courts under the direction of the court. Their work covers both private law proceedings such as divorce or separation cases where parents are unable to agree on the arrangements to be made for the children and adoption cases, and public law proceedings where local authorities apply for Care or Supervision Orders. The primary duty of CAFCASS is to safeguard and promote the welfare of children; to represent the wishes, feelings, and best interests of the child; and to ensure that children's voices are heard within the family court setting.

Legal aid

Legal aid is the money the Government will pay to help with the costs incurred in legal proceedings. There are two forms of legal aid: criminal and civil. The administration of legal aid is different in England and Wales, Scotland, and Northern Ireland. In all cases, where legal action is contemplated, it is essential to get advice on the legal aid position.

In England and Wales legal aid is administered by the Legal Aid Board. In relation to legal aid for criminal matters, children are automatically entitled to free legal advice prior to any hearing before a Youth Court and for representation before the Court if under the age of 16, or under the age of 18 and in full-time education. In relation to legal aid for non-criminal matters, eligibility for legal aid will depend on the financial circumstances of the family/carers. Depending on finances, a financial contribution may have to be made towards the costs of a case. In Scotland, legal aid is administered by the Scottish Legal Aid Board. In relation to criminal proceedings, legal aid for advice and representation will usually be free. In civil cases, however, legal aid may be unavailable if income is above the stipulated level. If capital and income are below the level set, a contribution to costs may be required. If money or property is gained as a result of a case, there is a 'clawback': the requirement to contribute to the costs of the case. And as in England and Wales, if a civil case is lost, the court may order the loser to pay the costs of the successful party.

The structure of the legal system(s) in the UK

Court structure in England, Wales, and Northern Ireland

Supreme Court
Civil and criminal appeals from all UK Courts

Court of Appeal, Criminal Division Court of Appeal, Civil Division

Appeals from Crown Courts

Appeals from High Court and County Courts

High Court

Queen's Bench Division **Family Division** **Chancery Division**

Administrative, Contract and Tort, Commercial, Admiralty

Appeals from County Courts and Magistrates' Courts

Partnerships, Bankruptcy, Patents, Land

Crown Court **County Courts**

Trial by jury

Most civil jurisdiction, Family, Small Claims

Magistrates' Courts **Coroners' Courts**
Tribunals
Courts Martial

Court structure Scotland

Supreme Court

High Court of Justiciary (Criminal)   **Court of Session (Civil)**

                                        Outer House   **Inner House**
                                        First instance   Appeals

Sheriff Courts

Criminal   **Civil**
Summary: judge only   First instance
Solemn: judge and jury   Sheriff: principal appeals

Justices of the Peace Courts   **Coroners' Courts**
                                        Tribunals
                                        Courts Martial

Summary: criminal

Summary

In Western democracies, the demand for the better protection of individual rights against the power of the State has been insistent, fuelled by the imperatives of equality and the elimination of discrimination. The 20th century saw a gradual but persistent movement away from the focus on the rights of parents over children towards the better recognition and protection of the rights of children. The concepts of the welfare of the child, and more recently safeguarding (on which see Chapter 2), provide the foundations for the law relating to children and its implementation by State bodies and, where disputes arise, by the courts of law. The law relating to children is now a complex web of international and domestic law with children's rights being increasingly recognised as a separate and distinctive body of rights. Whether this increased awareness of the rights of children is reflected in different aspects of children's lives – in education, medical decisions, in protection from abuse, and in the criminal justice system will be discussed in the following chapters.

Notes

1 *Two Treatises on Government* 1689.
2 *Rights of Man* 1791.
3 Thomas Hobbes 1588–1679, author of *Leviathan*, 1651, one of the founders of English political philosophy, advanced a very limited conception of individual rights against the power of the State, confining it to the right to physical protection.
4 See, for example, the European Convention on Human Rights and Fundamental Freedoms 1953.

5 *A History of Childhood, op cit*, page 121.
6 Equal parental rights over children were not formally recognised in law until 1973: the Guardianship of Minors Act.
7 *re Agar-Ellis* (1878) 10 Ch D 49, CA.
8 Cretney, S., *Family Law in the Twentieth Century: A History*, Oxford: OUP, 2003, page 569.
9 ibid.
10 Guardianship Act 1973.
11 *re W* [1971] 2 AC 682.
12 See *Re B (a minor) (Wardship: medical treatment)* [1990] 3 All ER 206.
13 *A History of Childhood*, 2nd edn 2018, Cambridge: Polity Press, page 4.
14 Family Law Act 1969, section 1.
15 See Appendix 1.
16 Family Law Reform Act 1969, section 8.
17 Complexities arise when a mature minor refuses medical treatment which doctors and the courts consider to be in his or her best interests. See Chapter 3.
18 Some Acts of Parliament will apply to the whole of the UK, whereas some will apply only to England and others may apply mainly in England but parts of the Act may apply in Northern Ireland, Scotland, and/or Wales. The individual Act of Parliament states in which areas of the UK the Act applies. The Children Act 1989, for example, is the major source of child law in England and Wales, with Scotland and Northern Ireland each having their own distinctive laws. However, parts of the Children Act also apply in Scotland and in Northern Ireland.
19 There is one particularly notable difference between the legal systems in the UK: the Scottish system dealing with children in trouble with the law. On this see Chapter 7.
20 See the UN Declaration on Human Rights 1948; The International Covenant on Civil and Political Rights and International Covenant on Social and Economic Rights.
21 Under the UK constitution, even where a treaty/convention is signed and ratified (i.e. formally approved), it will not have the force of law within the UK unless and until an Act of Parliament is passed to give it legal effect. This happened with rights under the ECHR when the UK Parliament passed the Human Rights Act 1998.
22 CRC/C/15/Add.188.
23 Children's Rights Alliance England, *State of Children's Rights in England 2018*, 2019.
24 See also, Children's Commissioner, *UNCRC Mid-term Review*, November 2019; *Progress Report on the Implementation of the CRC*, 2020; *The State of Children's Mental Health Services, Technical Report*, January 2020.
25 *P (A Child)* [2014] EWCA Civ 1174.
26 *TP and KM v United Kingdom* [2001] 2 FLR 549; *Z v United Kingdom* [2001] 2 FLR 612.
27 *X v Bedfordshire County Council* [1995] 2 AC 633.
28 *Sunday Times v United Kingdom* (1979) 2 EHRR 245.
29 Brought into effect in the UK by the Child Abduction Act 1985.
30 *Re M (children) (Habitual Residence: 1980 Hague Convention Abduction Convention)* [2020] EWCA Civ 1105.
31 The correct test was laid down in *A v A (Habitual Residence)* [2014] AC 1.
32 Per Ward LJ in *Re C (Abduction: grave Risk of Psychological Harm)* [1999] 1 FLR 1145 at 1154.
33 *Re M (Children)* [2007] UKHL 55.
34 ibid., at paragraph 40.
35 In the matter of *E (Children)* [2011] UKSC 84.
36 With the exception of Article 13. The Human Rights Act instead provides that the courts may use their usual powers relating to remedies for breaches of Convention rights.

37 ibid., section 7.
38 ibid., section 8.
39 Human Rights Act 1998, section 6.
40 *Murray v Express Newspapers* [2009].
41 *Bellinger v Bellinger* [2003] 2 All ER 593.
42 And the Children (Scotland) Act 2020.
43 Official Report, House of Lords, vol 502, col 488.
44 *Report of the Committee of Inquiry into the care and supervision provided in relation to Maria Colwell*, 1975, London: TSO 0 11 320596; *A Child in Trust*, the *Jasmine Beckford Report*, London Borough of Brent, 1985; *A Child in Mind, the Kimberley Carlile Inquiry*, London Borough of Greenwich, 1987; *Report of the Inquiry into Child Abuse in Cleveland 1987*, Cm 412, 1988.
45 Review of Child Care Law, 1985.
46 Law Commission Review, Law Com No 172, 1988.
47 *Re S (Parental Alienation: cult)* [2020] EWCA Civ 568.
48 But see Chapter 6 on orders relating to local authorities.
49 At paragraph 104.
50 Under the *Children Act 1989, section 44.*
51 *X v B* [2004] EWHC 2015 (Fam).
52 At paragraph 86.
53 Excluding Parliament and the Security Services.
54 Equality Act 2010, section 1.
55 Equality Act 2010, section 149.
56 *per* LJ in *Bracking v Secretary of State for Work and Pensions* [2013] EWCA Civ 1345, at paragraph 60.
57 Ibid.
58 Ibid., at paragraph 63.
59 This authority also extended to those adults with mental illness who lacked mental capacity to protect themselves.
60 Law Commission, *Wards of Court*, Working Paper No, 101, 1987, para 3.2.
61 *Re D (Sterilisation)* [1976] Fam 185.
62 *A London Borough v X (Wardship: Parental Responsibility)* [2019] EWHC B16 (Fam).
63 *Re K (Children with Disabilities; Wardship)* [2012] 2 FLR 745.
64 ibid., Hedley J, at paragraph 40.
65 *A v Liverpool City Council* [1982] AC 363.
66 Children Act 1989, section 100.
67 The Children Act did not, however, make the inherent jurisdiction unavailable to the court. In *Re NY (A Child)* [2019] UKSC 49, the Supreme Court confirmed that it existed alongside orders such as Specific Issue Orders and also the Hague Convention on Abduction.
68 The Public Trustee acts as an administrator of estates where the beneficiary is a vulnerable person, or where there is no will or no named executor who can fulfil the role.
69 Established under the Criminal Justice and Court Services Act 2000, sections 11–15 and Schedule 2.

2

BASIC PRINCIPLES, STATUS, AND IDENTITY

Introduction

Having outlined the evolution of rights and the legal framework supporting their protection, attention turns in Part A of this chapter to three fundamental concepts which underpin children's rights. As the rights of children have been recognised and enshrined in law, albeit piecemeal and sporadically, the law has evolved from its former focus on the rights of parents to focusing on parental responsibilities and the needs and welfare of children. The welfare of the child emerged early in Acts of Parliament. The 'welfare principle' applies principally in situations where a court of law is considering questions relating to the upbringing of a child, but also operates more widely as a guiding principle in relation to the care of children. More recently the welfare principle has been supplemented by the broader concept of 'safeguarding' which imposes duties on all those who have responsibility for the care of children. The right to equality – or freedom from discrimination – has also emerged as a dominant theme in the rights of children and is discussed below.

The legal status of children and their identity rights are discussed in Part B. Status involves the identification of who, in law, is a parent; who has parental responsibility for a child and the circumstances in which that responsibility may be assumed by people who are not the biological parent of a child, for example in surrogacy arrangements or in adoption. The question 'who is my parent?' is essential to the identity and rights of a child. Another identity question is that of gender, and the increased awareness that biological sex and gender are distinct concepts which may cause anxiety and conflict within both adults and children. How the law has evolved to provide remedies for the problems caused by gender 'dysphoria' is discussed later in this chapter.

Before turning to the fundamental principles of welfare and safeguarding, the concept of parental responsibility and its continuing relevance is introduced.

DOI: 10.4324/9780429452710-2

While the law has moved from protecting the rights of parents towards protecting the rights of children, parental responsibility remains an important concept.

Parental responsibility

As noted previously, historically the rights recognised by the law have related to the rights of parents, rather than those of children. Allied to this, the State's former reluctance to interfere in the 'private sphere' of the family granted parents an area of autonomy and immunity which could not guarantee the welfare of children.[1] Even today, unless children who are harmed or at risk of harm within their family come to the attention of the authorities who step in to provide protection, they are vulnerable.

'Parental responsibility' represents the bundle of rights and duties which the law confers on parents and others with responsibility for the care of children. The Children Act 1989 defines parental responsibility, who has it, and who may acquire it. The definition of parental responsibility is, however, unhelpful in that it does no more than refer to the rights which parents have under the common law (i.e. judge-made law) and other Acts of Parliament: as a result it is necessary to look at specific aspects of parents' and children's rights to determine the scope of each. The Children Act 1989 section 3 states that:

> In this Act 'parental responsibility' means all the rights, duties, powers, responsibilities and authority which by law a parent of a child has in relation to the child and his property.

By contrast the Children (Scotland) Act 1995 offers greater clarity. Section 2 of the Act provides that in order to enable a person to exercise his or her parental responsibilities, he or she has the following parental responsibilities in relation to a child under the age of sixteen:

- to safeguard and promote the child's health, development, and welfare;
- to provide, in a manner appropriate to the stage of development of the child – direction guidance to the child;
- if the child is not living with the parent, to maintain personal relations and direct contact with the child on a regular basis, and to act as the child's legal representative.

To supplement this the Children (Scotland) Act defines the parental *rights* which support the exercise of parental responsibility as being:

- to have the child living with him or otherwise to regulate the child's residence;
- to control, direct, or guide, in a manner appropriate to the stage of development of the child, the child's upbringing;

- if the child is not living with him, to maintain personal relations and direct contact with the child on a regular basis; and
- to act as the child's legal representative.[2]

A principal parental right is to the custody of the child: to have the child in one's personal 'possession'. In relation to married couples, this very basic right from early times was essentially that of the father of the child – not the mother. It was not until 1973 that English law recognised that mothers have equal rights in relation to their children.[3] The power of the father – and powerlessness of the mother – is reflected in the following case.

CASE FOCUS: (from 1883)[4]

Before they married, Mr and Mrs Agar-Ellis had agreed that their children would be brought up as Roman Catholics. The couple separated and the mother continued to take the children to Catholic services. The father objected and was granted an injunction to prevent the mother from going against his wishes. He then removed the children from their mother's care. When one of his daughters was 16 she asked to be allowed to spend her school holidays with her mother. Her father refused and her mother applied to the courts. The Court refused to see and hear the children and then refused to interfere with the father's rights over his children. The courts would only intervene if the father was guilty of some wrongdoing.

The Children Act 1989, section 2, defines who has parental responsibility:

- where a *mother and father are married to each other* at the time of a child's birth, each has automatic parental responsibility for the child;[5]
- where a child is born to an *unmarried mother*, the mother has automatic parental responsibility. The father may acquire parental responsibility if he is registered as the child's father under the Births and Deaths Registration Act 1953. He may also acquire parental responsibility if he and the mother make an agreement (a parental responsibility agreement) for him to have responsibility, or if he applies to a court and is granted parental responsibility.[6] Once the father has acquired parental responsibility, this can only be removed on the order of a court;[7]

  There are considerations which apply to unmarried fathers which do not apply to married fathers. Most obviously, there is a distinction to be drawn between the relationship between father and child within a stable family setting and a situation where there is no ongoing relationship between the parents and/or the child has no established relationship with his or her natural father. For this reason the law has proceeded cautiously in extending the procedures through which an unmarried father may acquire parental responsibility. At the heart of the question lies the welfare of the child and the assessment of whether or not, in the circumstances of the individual case, the child's best interests would be served by granting parental rights to an unmarried father;

- where a child is born as a result of *fertility treatment*, the mother has parental responsibility. Her husband will have parental responsibility provided that he consented to the treatment. An unmarried male partner may acquire parental responsibility by agreement with the mother or under an order of the court. Where a child is born to a mother whose partner is another woman, that woman may acquire parental responsibility for the child by registering as a parent under the Birth and Deaths Registration Act 1953, or by entering an agreement with the mother, or on the order of a court;[8]
- where a child's parent who has parental responsibility is married to or in a civil partnership with a person who is not a parent of the child *(a step-parent)*, that step-parent may acquire parental responsibility if there is an agreement with both parents, or, on the application of the step-parent, the court makes a parental responsibility order;
- a person appointed as a *guardian or Special Guardian* of a child has parental responsibility;[9]
- where a child is being looked after by a local authority under an *Interim or final Care Order* or an *Emergency Protection Order*, the local authority has parental responsibility shared with the parent(s);[10]
- a person having a *residence order* stating that the child is to live with him or her has parental responsibility for as long as the order is in force;
- an *Adoption Order* confers parental responsibility on the adopters and extinguishes that of the natural parent(s), and *prospective adopters* once a child is placed with them have parental responsibility.[11]

Where a person applies for parental responsibility, the court will apply the welfare test. Parental responsibility may also be lost or removed. As noted above, the making of an Adoption Order, for example, terminates the parental responsibility of the natural parents.[12]

Where more than one person has parental responsibility it is shared on an equal basis and each person may exercise that responsibility without the consent of the other person. The fact that another person acquires parental responsibility does not affect the responsibility of the person having it and a person having parental responsibility may arrange for part of it to be met by another person acting on his or her behalf. Parental responsibility may not be exercised if it conflicts with an order of a court.

Part A: fundamental concepts

The welfare of the child

The welfare of the child is now the dominant principle in questions relating to children and their upbringing and will be considered further throughout this book.

> In all actions concerning children, whether undertaken by public or private social welfare institutions, courts of law, administrative authorities, or legislative bodies, *the best interests of the child shall be a primary consideration.*
> United Nations Convention on the Rights of
> the Child 1989, Article 3.

When a court determines any question with respect to:

(a) the upbringing of a child; or
(b) the administration of a child's property or the application of any income arising from it,
> the child's welfare shall be *the court's paramount consideration*
> Children Act 1989, section 1.

As explained above, over time there has been a gradual shift from the idea that parents (originally principally fathers) have absolute rights over their children towards an emphasis on the welfare of the child which can in some cases override the rights of parents. This prioritisation of the child's welfare over the rights of parents was emphasised in two cases decided in 1969 and 1970 respectively.

CASE FOCUS: J V C[13]

A ten-year-old child had been cared for by foster parents under an informal agreement with his Spanish natural parents for most of his life. His parents – accepted by the court as being 'unimpeachable' – sought his return. The House of Lords (now the Supreme Court) ruled that the welfare of the child dictated that he should remain with his foster family. For the first time, and controversially, a court had ruled that the child's welfare overrode the rights of parents who had done no wrong.[14]

CASE FOCUS: W[15]

Re W was an adoption case. The law provided that an Adoption Order could not be made without the consent of the natural parents, unless their consent was being withheld unreasonably in which case the court could set it aside. The law reflected an uneasy balance between the rights of the natural parent and the child to preserve their blood ties and the rights of prospective adopters and the child to a secure future which offered the best prospects for the child. At issue in this case was whether the mother was unreasonable in withholding her consent to the adoption of her child.

Was her refusal unreasonable? Lord Hailsham LC stated:

> ...the test is reasonableness and not anything else...It is reasonableness, and reasonableness in the context of the totality of the circumstances. But, although welfare *per se* is not the test, the fact that a reasonable parent does pay regard to the welfare of his child must enter into the question of reasonableness as a relevant factor.

The mother's refusal to consent was set aside as being unreasonable and the Adoption Order granted.

The welfare of the child throughout his or her life is now the paramount consideration in all adoption cases.[16] In the majority of other cases where decisions are to be made by courts, the welfare of the child is the paramount consideration.[17] The Children Act 1989 provides that in legal proceedings concerning the upbringing of a child, the court – in assessing what would best serve the welfare of the child – must take into account:

- the ascertainable wishes and feelings of the child concerned (considered in the light of his or her age and understanding);
- his or her physical, emotional, and educational needs;
- the likely effect on him or her of any change in his or her circumstances;
- his or her age, sex, background, and any characteristics of his or hers which the court considers relevant;
- any harm which he or she has suffered or is at risk of suffering;
- how capable each of his or her parents, and any other person in relation to whom the court considers the question to be relevant, is of meeting is or her needs;
- the range of powers available to the court under the Act in the proceedings in question.

And, as importantly, the court must not make an order unless doing so will be better for the child than making no order at all (the 'no-order principle').

The right of the child to his or her family life, and the maintenance of family ties, is of fundamental importance. When making decisions over the future of a child, this right includes the right to contact with parents, discussed below. The right of the child to make his or her wishes and feelings known – the right to be heard – is also of particular importance as a child develops.

The right to contact

Article 9.2 of the UN Convention on the Rights of the Child provides that where a child is separated from one or both parents, he or she has the right to maintain personal relations and direct contact with both parents on a regular basis, unless it is contrary to the child's best interests.

Where parents are separated or divorced, there is a presumption that contact with the absent parent is in the best interests of the child and parents are encouraged to reach agreements about contact without the involvement of a court. However, where the issue does end up in court, it is now unusual for a court to refuse contact with an absent parent and to do so requires 'compelling evidence' that contact would not be in the child's best interests.

The Children Act 1989, section 8, provides for 'Child Arrangements Orders' which regulate the living arrangements of children, including contact with the absent parent.[18] A court can also make Prohibited Steps Orders which sets out what a parent may not do without the permission of the court, and Specific Issue Orders which give directions to parents over a specific issue which has arisen (for example over medical treatment). Where Child Arrangements Orders are in force, the court can require the arrangements to be monitored by the Children and Family Court Advisory and Support Service (CAFCASS),[19] and where the arrangements are not complied with, without a reasonable excuse, the court can issue an enforcement notice and ultimately impose penalties.

Parents, guardians, any person with parental responsibility for the child are entitled to apply for any section 8 order. If a person is not entitled to make an application, the court may nevertheless grant leave to do so.[20] The requirement concerning entitlement to seek orders protects a child from interference in his or her life which a court does not consider to be in his or her best interests. As noted above in relation to contact, while a court will look favourably on an application from an absent father (usually), especially where there is an established relationship between the child and his or her father, the decision whether to grant the order will depend on the child's best interests.

CASE FOCUS: *X*[21]

X, aged 12 months, had been born following an informal surrogacy agreement, under which the birth mother was impregnated with the genetic father's sperm. The child had lived with the father and his wife for fifteen months from the age of three months. The birth mother could not accept total separation from her child, and campaigned publicly against it, resulting in a conviction for harassment. By the date of the hearing over contact, the birth mother was finally reconciled to the fact that X would live with her biological father and his wife. The court accepted that all parties loved the child, and that some continued contact with the birth mother would be in the child's best interests. The court made a detailed order providing for direct contact between the child and her birth mother, but stressed that the birth mother must refrain from campaigning and protesting, which would jeopardise the contact arrangements.

CASE FOCUS: *B*[22]

B was born in April 2017 to two parents suffering from mental disabilities. The local authority was concerned that her parents could not cope. A Care Order was made with a view, ultimately, that B would be adopted. In August 2017 the court approved B's move to foster parents, Mr and Mrs X, who had also been approved as adopters. The local authority's care plan for B concluded that direct contact between B and her birth parents was not appropriate, and their contact with B was reduced with a final visit in November 2017. The parents wanted post-adoption contact, but required the leave of the court to apply.[23] The application for contact, which was opposed by the adoptive parents, was refused. The adoptive parents were to have full parental responsibility for B and were to be trusted to meet all her emotional, psychological, and physical needs. It was in B's best interests not to have continued contact with her birth parents. The Court of Appeal said that it would be in a very unusual case that post-adoption contact would be ordered unless the adopters agreed.

The right to be heard

The right of a child to participate in decisions concerning his or her care and upbringing is recognised as a right under the UN Convention on the Rights of the Child (CRC)[24], the Children Act 1989, and Children (Scotland) Act 1995, as follows:

> State Parties shall assure to the child who is capable of forming his or her own views the right to express those views freely in all matters affecting the child, the views of the child being given due weight in accordance with the age and maturity of the child.
>
> *UN Convention on the Rights of the Child, Article*
> *12.1*

When a court is deciding an issue relating to the child's upbringing:

> ... a court shall have regard in particular to the ascertainable wishes and feeling of the child concerned (considered in the light of his age and understanding).
>
> *Children Act 1989, section 3(3)(a)*

A person shall, in reaching any major decision which involves:

(a) his fulfilling a parental responsibility; or
(b) his exercising a parental right or giving consent by virtue of that section,

> shall have regard so far as practicable to the views (if he wishes to express them) of the child concerned, taking into account the child's age and maturity ... a child twelve years of age or more shall be presumed to be of sufficient age and maturity to form a view.
>
> *Children (Scotland) Act 1995, section 6*

Under each of the CRC, the Children Act 1989 and Scottish Children Act, the right to be consulted and heard is dependent upon the child's level of maturity and understanding. It is notable that whereas the duty to 'have regard' to a child's wishes and feelings under the Children Act 1989 is confined to situations which come before a court, the Scottish duty is more wide-ranging and imposes a duty on anyone having parental responsibility to consider the views of a child in reaching *any major decision* affecting the child. The right of the child to be consulted and heard is accordingly clearer and stronger in Scotland than in England and Wales.

There is a lack of clarity over (and potentially a very real tension between) the weight to be given to the wishes and feelings of a child and the assessment of his or her welfare which will prevail. Assessing the weight to be given to a child's views depends on the assessment of his or her maturity and understanding: a decision which is necessarily made by adults. The wishes and feelings of the child may conflict with adults' perceptions of what is best for his or her welfare which may cause the significance of the child's views to be reduced in relation to adult decision-making about his or her care and upbringing. As noted previously, the welfare principle (or the best interests of the child) is the paramount principle in child care decisions, and there is a list of factors that a court must consider when reaching this assessment, of which the child's wishes and feelings is but one. This conflict is most clearly seen in relation to decisions over medical treatment where if a 'mature minor' refuses treatment which doctors and, ultimately, the courts, feel is in the child's best interests to receive, the child's wishes will be set aside (see Chapter 3).

The wishes and feelings of the child, therefore, cannot prevail against the assessment of welfare by the court. The justification for this paternalism lies in

the perception that a child – even when approaching the formal status of adulthood – may not have the experience, maturity, or objectivity to make important decisions about his or her life. As a result, the welfare principle makes the
language of 'rights' less convincing than advocates of children's rights would
wish. Having recognised this difficulty it has to be stressed – as judges repeatedly do – that each case is unique: there is often no one obvious 'right answer'
about arrangements for children and each case is judged on its own terms. The
decision of the court is recorded and public and, importantly, subject to appeal
if a judge strays too far from the accepted parameters of decision-making for
children. This transparency in decision-making is not reflected in decisions
made by parents, carers, teachers, social workers, or others concerned with the
care of a child and represents one of the greatest strengths of the legal system.

In 2016 the Committee on the Rights of the Child, the body of experts that
monitors the extent to which States are applying the CRC conducts periodic
reviews of each signatory State[25] expressed concerns over the extent to which
children's views are respected in decision-making outside legal proceedings and
called on the UK to establish structures for the 'active and meaningful participation' in designing laws, policies, programmes, and services at a national and
local level. One example of such participation is seen with the establishing of the
Scottish Youth Parliament (SYP) in 1999. The SYP is democratic, rights-based,
committed to inclusion and diversity and political neutrality, and its aim is 'to
provide a national platform for young people to discuss the issues that are important to them, and campaign for changes in the nation that they live in'.[26] Each
year the SYP votes on a topic which will become the focus of its work for the
coming year. In 2020 the SYP launched a digital resource, funded by the Scottish
Government, to help children and young people use social media in a way that is
beneficial to their mental and physical health. The resource was designed by the
SYP working with the Children's Parliament, a charity established in 1996 to
provide a platform for children's views. An earlier campaign, *Right Here, Right
Now,* was influential in persuading the Scottish Government to incorporate the
CRC into Scottish law, thereby making it enforceable before the local courts.

For all its strengths, the welfare principle is not without difficulties or critics.
By focusing on the child's welfare, for example, the child's right to privacy and
family life and the rights of others may be ignored, or subordinated to the assessment of the child's welfare by the court. The European Court of Human Rights
has ruled, for example, that if there is any clash between the privacy rights of
a child and his or her biological father, 'the interests of the child should always
prevail' (to the detriment of the father).[27]

The welfare principle is not uniformly applied across all aspects of decision-making in relation to children as confirmed by the UN Committee on
the Rights of the Child. In its 2016 review of UK compliance, the Committee
recorded that the right of the child to have his or her best interests taken as a
primary consideration does not apply consistently through the law and practice
relating to children and is also not reflected in all legislation, policy, and judicial

decisions. It does not, for example, apply uniformly in the juvenile justice system (see Chapter 7), or in immigration and asylum practices or in the armed forces.[28]

Safeguarding

In recent years, the focus in the law and practice of protecting children's rights has evolved into the constructive approach of promoting the well-being of children through the concept of 'safeguarding'. Safeguarding is defined as:

> ... the process of protecting children from abuse or neglect, preventing impairment of their health and development, and ensuring they are growing up in circumstances consistent with the provision of safe and effective care that enables children to have optimum life chances and enter adulthood successfully.[29]

The safeguarding principle is now relevant to all aspects of decision-making relating to children. The Children Act 1989, for example, provides that:

> It is the general duty of every local authority to safeguard and promote the welfare of children within their area who are in need, and as far as is consistent with that duty, to promote the upbringing of such children by their families by providing a range and level of services appropriate to those children's needs.[30]

At a national level, there is a Child Safeguarding Practice Review Panel, with membership appointed by the Secretary of State. The function of the Panel is to identify serious child safeguarding cases which raise issues that are complex or of national importance and, where appropriate, to arrange for those cases to be reviewed. The Panel must be informed by local authorities if there is a child who the authority knows or suspects to be abused or neglected, or if a child dies, or is seriously harmed.[31]

At a local level, safeguarding requires inter-agency cooperation. Every local authority must have in place arrangements to improve the well-being of all children. These arrangements include arrangements relating to:

- physical and mental health and emotional well-being;
- protection from harm and neglect;
- education, training, and recreation;
- the contribution made by them to society;
- social and economic well-being.[32]

In order to achieve safeguarding goals, every local authority must have a Local Safeguarding Children Board (LSCB) which brings together the Director of Children's Services, representatives of health, housing, police, and probation services. The principal function of the LSCB is 'to agree how the relevant organisations in each local area co-operate to safeguard and promote the welfare of children, and to ensure the effectiveness of what they do'.[33] While valuable, it must be recognised that the resources of local authorities, particularly in recent years, have been stretched to the limit, making the safeguarding of children the more difficult than it might otherwise be.

Safeguarding children also includes the duty to protect children from being drawn into extremism through radicalisation. All schools and childcare providers are expected to fulfil the Prevent duty by assessing 'the risk of children being drawn into terrorism, including support for extremist ideas that are part of terrorist ideology'.[34] On radicalisation see Chapter 5.

The right to equality

The right to equality and freedom from discrimination on any basis is a fundamental requirement of a fair society and all children have the right to equal status in society. Where there is inequality, for example through disability, the State has a duty to ensure, to the extent possible, that adjustments are made to minimise the effects of that disability.

Anti-discrimination law in the UK dates back to the 1960s with the Race Relations Act 1968, followed by the Racial Discrimination Act 1970, the Equal Pay Act 1970, the Sex Discrimination Act 1975, and the Disability Discrimination Act 1995. As discussed in Chapter 1, the Equality Act 2010 harmonises discrimination law, bringing together all the earlier law.[35] Achieving equality has been a long and hard-won process. Writing in 1983 on the movements towards equality and non-discrimination, Professor MDA Freeman remarked that 'First it was blacks, then women and now, in the last decade or so, children and youth'.[36] To that list can now be added the right to freedom from discrimination on grounds of disability. Today, a combination of international and national law sets out the formal requirements of equality.

> State Parties shall respect and ensure the rights set forth in the present Convention to each child within their jurisdiction without discrimination of any kind, irrespective of the child's or his or her parent's or legal guardian's race, colour, sex, language, religion, political or other opinion, national, ethnic or social origin, property, disability, birth or other status.
>
> *UN Convention on the Rights of the Child, Article 2.1*

> The enjoyment of the rights and freedoms set forth in this Convention shall be secured without discrimination on any ground such as sex, race, colour, language, religion, political, or other opinion, national or social origins, association with a national minority, property, birth or other status.
>
> *European Convention on Human Rights, Article 14*

As discussed in Chapter 1, the Equality 2010 Act imposes a 'public sector equality duty' (PSED) on all public authorities. This is the duty to 'have due regard to' eliminating discrimination, harassment and victimisation; to advance equality of opportunity and to foster good relations between those who share a relevant characteristic and those who do not share it.[37] Relevant characteristics include age, disability, gender reassignment, pregnancy and maternity, race, religion or belief, sex, and sexual orientation. There are, however, a number of exceptions built into this public sector duty. For example:

- in relation to employment, employers are entitled to pay different (and lower) minimum wage rates to 16- and 17-year-olds and 18–21-year-olds when compared with over those over 22 who are entitled to the full minimum wage;[38]
- the non-discrimination provisions do not apply to qualifications for employment;[39]
- in relation to education, neither single-sex schools nor faith schools act unlawfully on the basis of favouring children of one faith over another;[40]
- also in relation to education, schools and children's homes are not bound by the PSED with respect to age. For example, a school is not required to consider advancing equality of opportunity between pupils of different ages, nor to foster good relations between them. Schools still need to have regard to the need to eliminate unlawful discrimination, advance equality of opportunity, and foster good relations between pupils having other protected characteristics.[41]

Part B: status and identity rights

Introduction

Rights have historically been determined by legal status, and legal status was formerly dependent upon the marital status of a child's parents. A child born to married parents was 'legitimate' in the eyes of the law. The status of being legitimate carried with it the right to protection and support from both parents and the right to succeed to property on the death of a parent. A child born to an unmarried mother was 'illegitimate': *filius nullius* – 'the son of no-one' – and illegitimacy carried with it not only a stigma but also the absence of rights. However, as will be seen, the rights of children born outside marriage or civil partnership are now, for the most part, equal to the rights of children born within marriage or civil partnership.

The 'rationale' for the former discrimination against children born outside marriage lay in the law's preoccupation with the protection of property rights: a child born outside marriage posed a potential threat to the succession to property. Certainty in the law regarding property ownership dominated relationships and was more important than ideas of equality either between men and women[42] or between fathers and children. The illegitimate child had no rights to contact his or her father, or to be treated equally with any half-siblings in relation to financial support or inheritance. In order to have any financial support from the natural father the mother was obliged to take affiliation proceedings before the Magistrates' Court, a process with criminal overtones and the degrading need to provide clear evidence of paternity.[43]

Historically, a child born 'outside marriage' would be made legitimate by the subsequent marriage of his or her parents. It also used to be the case that if a marriage was declared void (i.e. where there is a fundamental defect in the requirements for a valid marriage and the court declares it to be invalid and of no legal effect) the children of that relationship would be declared illegitimate and denied rights to support and inheritance. That discrimination ended in 1976 with the Legitimacy Act of that year. The right of a child born outside marriage to financial support from both parents and to succeed to property was established under the Family Law Reform Act 1987. It was this Act which effectively abolished the status of illegitimacy, declaring that in relation to the Act itself and to any later legislation, 'unless the contrary intention appears' any references to the relationship between two people 'shall be interpreted without regard to whether or not the mother or father have or had been married to each other at any time'.[44] Civil partnerships were introduced for same-sex couples in 2004;[45] marriage for same-sex couples was introduced in 2013;[46] and civil partnerships for heterosexual couples in 2019.[47] Any children born into these families, or any children families have through adoption or surrogacy have the same status and rights as children of heterosexual married parents. All children are now equal.[48]

However, while the issue of a child's status has now been resolved in favour of equality, there are circumstances where it remains essential – both to children and to parents – formally to identify the legal tie between a child and his or her parents. Where doubts exist, this identification is achieved through Declarations of Parentage.

Proof of parentage

There can be few more important rights than the right to know one's origins. As the former President of the Family Division of the High Court put it:

> What after all, to any child, to any parent, never mind to future genera-
> tions and indeed to society at large, can be more important, emotionally,
> psychologically, socially and legally, than the answer to the question: Who
> is my parent? Is this my child?.[49]

In the 19th and early 20th century, disputes over parentage which ended up in the courts were invariably about financial support for children or their inheritance rights. On occasion, the law employs 'presumptions' and there is a legal presumption that the woman who gives birth to a child is that child's mother. While this presumption suited the time before reproductive technology such as in vitro fertilisation (IVF), the law has in recent years had to adapt to clarify the concept of motherhood.[50] There was also a presumption that a married woman's husband was the father of any child born or conceived during marriage, and this presumption was difficult to rebut since it carried with it – in the harsh language of former times – the 'bastardisation' of the child.[51] However, where a dispute over parentage reached the law courts, there needed to be proof that the alleged father of the child was in fact the biological father. This is the requirement of 'corroboration'. Today this is generally straightforward with proof being established through blood tests and/or DNA testing.[52]

Where there is doubt about the identity of a child's father, an application can be made to the courts for the matter to be resolved. The UN CRC recognises this right as follows:

> The child shall be registered immediately after birth and shall have the right from birth to a name, the right to acquire a nationality and, as far as possible, the right to know and be cared for by his or her parents.
>
> *UN Convention on the Rights of the Child, Article 7*

By law a child born to married parents must be formally registered within six weeks of his or her birth and will assume the name of his or her parents.[53] Where parents are unmarried, parental responsibility for the child lies solely with the mother unless the father registers his paternity under the 1953 Registration of Births Marriages and Deaths Act, or makes an agreement with the mother to share parental responsibility, or applies to a court for a parental responsibility order.[54] When a child is born as a result of fertility treatment, the child has no automatic legal link to his or her biological father or mother, but has the right, as discussed below, to receive information about his or her genetic father from the age of 18.[55]

Assisted reproduction

Assisted reproduction and surrogacy raise difficult questions about the child's right to information identifying his or her biological parents and this has proved controversial. While the focus here is on the rights of the child, it has to be recognised that in questions over the identity of a child there are other competing, adult interests and rights in play: a number of rights jostle together. There is firstly the right of a child to know the identity of his or her parents.[56] This identity right may conflict with the right of a mother to her privacy and her desire that the (probably) unknown biological father should not disrupt her family life. The right of the donor to his privacy also comes into play: donors may be reluctant to come forward to aid fertility treatments if they do not want to have their identity revealed to any child or children born as a result of that treatment.[57] However, a case decided by the European Court of Human Rights

(ECtHR) in 2002, discussed below, favoured the rights of the child over those of her father and the law is now firmly on the side of openness about biological parentage.

CASE FOCUS: *M*[58]

The applicant, M, was a five-year-old girl who had been born to an unmarried mother. She wanted to know the identity of her natural father. A court had ordered DNA testing, but there were no procedures to ensure compliance, or sanctions for non-compliance. M complained that Croatia had no measures in place to resolve the uncertainty about her personal identity and that this failure, or lack of action, violated her rights under Article 8 (the right to privacy).

Taking into account the 'basic principle' of the child's interests, the ECtHR ruled that the inefficiency of the Croatian system left M in a state of prolonged uncertainty over her personal identity. The authorities had accordingly failed to respect her private life, and there was a violation of Article 8 by the State.

The identity rights of the child also came before the domestic courts in 2002 when children born as a result of Artificial Insemination by Donor (AID) sought the identity of their father. The judge accepted the importance of identity, and the role of Article 8 ECHR. He also referred to the greater openness in society compared with 20 years previously and said that whereas secrecy formerly did not have to be justified, by 2002 justification was needed.[59] In the same year the UN CRC had expressed its concern over the lack of rights of children (whether born outside marriage, or adopted, or born as a result of assisted fertilisation) to know the identity of their biological parents and called on the government to take measures to allow all children to know the identity of their parents, 'to the extent possible'.

The right to know one's origins is advanced by the welfare principle which applies to disputes over parentage. For example, a court may order paternity tests on a child even where a mother objects, if it is in the child's best interests to do so.[60] Once parentage is established, it will then be difficult for a mother to keep the information from her child and a court would require good reasons to justify her withholding the father's identity, and if these are not forthcoming, a court can order the mother to disclose it.[61]

The Human Fertilisation and Embryology Act 1990[62] regulates the creation, storage, and implantation of human embryos. In 2018 there were over 74,000 fertility treatments in the UK. An estimated 20,000 children are born every year as a result of fertility treatment. For the husband or partner of the woman receiving fertility treatment to acquire the status of parenthood and thereby ensure a child's right to the security of having two legal parents, consent forms must be signed by both the woman and her partner before fertility treatment is commenced.

The law makes it clear that the woman who gives birth to a child as a result of fertility treatment, whether by the placing of an embryo or of sperm and eggs, is to be treated as the mother for all purposes. In relation to fatherhood, the law states that where the man and woman are married, and the creation of the embryo was the child, provided that he consented to the treatment.[63] A deceased husband is also to be treated as the father of the child where he or she has been born as a result of fertility treatment provided that the husband had consented to the treatment. Similar provisions apply to unmarried couples, and to same-sex couples, where the woman receives fertility treatment using the donation of a third party. Her partner will be treated as the parent of the child provided that he or she consented to the treatment.[64]

The complexity entailed in the identity of parentage and the right of the child is revealed in the following case.

CASE FOCUS: *MCC*[65]

McC was registered as female at birth. At the age of 22 she transitioned to live in the male gender. In 2013 he began testosterone therapy and in 2014 underwent a double mastectomy. In 2016 MC suspended testosterone treatment and commenced fertility treatment to fertilise one or more eggs in his womb. At the time he was registered with the clinic as male.

In 2017 McC applied for, and was issued with, a Gender Recognition Certificate, confirming his gender as male. The legal effect of the Certificate is that the person to whom it is issued becomes, with some exceptions, 'for all purposes the acquired gender'. McC then underwent successful fertility treatment at the clinic, became pregnant, and in January 2018 gave birth to a son, YY.

When registering his son's birth, McC was informed that he would have to register as YY's mother, although he could register in his current male name. He sought judicial review of that decision and made an application for a Declaration of Incompatibility under the Human Rights Act 1998 (on which see Chapter 1) and YY applied for a declaration of parentage.

There are exceptions to the right to be treated 'for all purposes' as the acquired gender. These include, firstly that this right 'does not affect things done...before the certificate is issued'[66] and secondly that acquiring a different gender 'does not affect the status of the person as the father or mother of a child'.[67]

The Court of Appeal considered various authorities, including the legal position of parents under both surrogacy and adoption, the European Convention on Human Rights and the UN Convention on the Rights of the Child. Emphasising that Parliament intended that every child should have a mother because that is in the child's best interests, the Court of Appeal ruled that McC would remain, in law, YY's mother.

When first enacted, the Human Fertilisation and Embryology Act 1990 provided that children born as a result of fertility treatment had no right to know the identity of the donor.[68] However, when a child reached the age of 18, he or she could ask the Human Fertilisation and Embryology Authority for information about the donor, other than information disclosing his identity.[69] The information to be disclosed includes:

- the sex, height, weight, ethnic group, eye colour, hair colour, skin colour, year of birth, country of birth, and marital status of the donor;
- whether the donor was adopted;
- the ethnic group or groups of the donor's parents;
- the screening tests carried out on the donor and information on his personal and family medical history;
- where the donor has a child, the sex of that child and where the donor has children, the number of those children, and the sex of each of them;
- the donor's religion, occupation, interests and skills and why the donor provided sperm, eggs, or embryos;
- matters contained in any description of himself as a person which the donor has provided;
- any additional matter which the donor has provided with the intention that it be made available to an applicant.

The pressure for greater openness about a child's biological origins prompted reform, although its implementation was delayed. From 2023 it will be possible for a person over the age of 18 to request and receive all information about donors, including identifying information, held by the Human Fertilisation and Embryology Authority and treatment clinics. From the age of 16 (down from 18), children will be able to receive non-identifying information.[70]

The right of the child to know his or her origins is dependent not just upon the law but also on the workings of fertility clinics, as the case focus below shows.

CASE FOCUS: *A*[71]

In 2013 an audit of 109 fertility clinics had been ordered following the disclosure that one clinic had failed to comply with the conditions of its licence. The audit revealed that there had been administrative errors in no fewer than 51 clinics, throwing into doubt the parentage of the children born as a result of fertility treatment. In *A & Others* (2015) there had been a failure on the part of the clinic to ensure that the required consents had been given. The essential elements of this scheme were forms giving the woman's consent to her partner being the legal parent of the child and forms giving the man's consent to be the legal parent. The situation was described by Sir James Munby, then President of the Family Division, as 'alarming and shocking' and as revealing 'widespread incompetence across the sector'. The court had no hesitation in granting the Declarations of Parenthood sought by the eight applicants.

Surrogacy[72]

Surrogacy involves the creation of an embryo in a surrogate mother, with a view to providing a child for another mother and/or father. Commercial surrogacy is illegal in the UK, but not-for-profit organisations exist to facilitate surrogacy. Surrogacy takes two forms. 'Straight' or traditional surrogacy is when the surrogate mother provides her own eggs to achieve pregnancy, with the intended father providing the sperm. Conception will be achieved through sexual intercourse, self-insemination, or through insemination at a fertility clinic. 'Host' surrogacy on the other hand involves either the eggs of the intended mother fertilised with sperm of the intended father or the eggs of a donor fertilised with sperm of the intended father being created in vitro and then transferred into the uterus of the surrogate mother.

A Surrogacy Agreement is usually drawn up between the parties, but such agreements are unenforceable in the courts.[73] In all surrogacy cases, the welfare of the child is the paramount consideration. To ensure legal certainty for children born through surrogacy, their rights are protected by the rule that the birth mother is the legal mother of the child (and if married or in a civil partnership her spouse of civil partner provided that he consented will be her spouse or civil partner) unless and until a formal Parental Order is granted by a court. In order for the commissioning mother and/or father to become the legal parents of the child, a Parental Order must be sought from the courts. Applications will normally go to the Magistrates' Court, but if a child is born overseas or there are doubts over whether the requirements for an order have been met, to the Family Division of the High Court.

An application must be submitted to the court within six months of the birth. The court will request a report from the Children and Family Court Advisory Support Service (CAFCASS, see Chapter 1) to investigate the case and submit a report to the court. If the court grants the Parental Order a copy will be sent to the General Register Office, following which the commissioning parents will be able to order new birth certificates for the child. In Scotland Parental Orders are sought through the Court of Session or Sheriff Court, and in Northern Ireland through the Courts and Tribunals Service.[74]

Once a Parental Order is granted, the child becomes the legal child of the commissioning parents who assume full parental responsibility for the child.

Adoption

In relation to adoption it used to be thought that the welfare of an adopted child would be served best by being integrated into his or her new family without the knowledge of the identity of his or her biological parents. This has changed and research has shown that children benefit from being told of their biological origins at an early age, and that revealing their identity later in life causes confusion and distress.[75]

The Adoption and Children Act 2002 makes clear that it is the child's welfare 'throughout his life' that is the paramount consideration of a court or adoption agency. The right to information about adoption arises at the age of 18.[76] The adopted person has the right to information held by an adoption agency to enable him or her to obtain a copy of his or her birth record. If there are 'exceptional circumstances' the High Court may allow the agency to withhold the information.

The Human Rights Act 1998, making European Convention Rights enforceable before the domestic courts, has played a key role in developing the right to identity. As noted above, Article 8 ECHR protects the right to respect for private and family life and this has been interpreted broadly by the European Court of Human Rights, for example so as to allow decisions on the relationship between a child born outside marriage and her natural father.[77][78]

Gender identity

The right to an identity includes gender identity and the issue of gender is currently one being addressed both by governments and by the courts. The gender issue raises important questions about equality and the extent to which the law protects those who, for whatever reason, experience doubts about their own gender. Gender identity and the recognition that gender is socially constructed and may change has, in recent years, become increasingly understood and the law has been developing to reflect the needs of those with doubts about their gender and those who seek help in changing their gender identity. NHS England explains that:

> Gender identity refers to an individual's subjective sense of being male, female, both, neither or something else.
> Gender Dysphoria (GD) describes the distress that is caused by a discrepancy between a person's gender identity and that person's sex classified at birth.[79]

Gender change or reassignment is thought to be irreversible, and whereas adults may be free to make decisions of such magnitude, there are real doubts over the capacity of a child to have the maturity and understanding to make such a decision. In 2020, the Minister for Women and Equalities, said that while it is for adults to make their own decisions, children should be protected from making irreversible decisions about their bodies.[80] In addition to questions over a child's capacity to consent to treatment (on which see further Chapter 3), the gender debate also involves the right of parents to make or participate in decisions for children, the role of medical practitioners, and of schools in dealing with such a sensitive issue. The Gender Recognition Act 2004 allows those over the age of 18 who have undergone gender-changing treatment to apply for a new birth certificate reflecting their chosen gender. Children, however, have no such right: the 2004 Act does not assist those under the age of 18, and it is with children that most controversy over gender change is centred.

The Act lays down strict criteria for gender change: there must be certification by two doctors and the person must have lived in their 'new' gender for a period of two years. In 2017, the then Conservative Prime Minister, Theresa May, proposed relaxing the rules to allow people to 'self-identify' and have their birth certificates changed without a medical diagnosis. This proposal led to a clash of rights, for both adults and children, pitching the right to identity against the right to privacy of others, and was dropped by the government in 2020. A consultation into the working of the Gender Recognition Act was undertaken in 2018. In its response to the consultation, the government reported that the legal requirements for gender change would remain the same, but that the process would be modernised and the cost of a Certificate reduced.

Currently, children with gender dysphoria may be referred by a General Practitioner for specialist help. After a telephone assessment a child should have three to six therapy sessions before being referred for treatment. If physical treatment is recommended, an adolescent can be given hormone blockers to suppress puberty (but see below on the recent legal challenge to this treatment). Blocking puberty could be followed up with Cross-Sex Hormones (sex steroids of the preferred gender) and ultimately gender affirming surgery. In 2018–2019 there were 2,590 children referred to the Tavistock Clinic's Gender Identity Development Service (GIDS), more than triple the 2014–2015 total. NHS England states that some children wish to make the social transition to their preferred gender long before puberty, but recognise that the issue is controversial and something about which health professionals have divergent views. Research has shown that the average age for referral is 14.6 years, but the range is from 12.2 years to 15.3.

Transgender children face a number of related practical and psychological difficulties. The GIDS has identified the three most common problems associated with gender dysphoria. These are bullying (47 per cent), low mood/depression (42 per cent), and self-harming behaviours (39 per cent).[81] The Equality and Human Rights Commission records that research suggested that 91 per cent of transgender boys and 66 per cent of transgender girls experienced harassment or bullying at school.[82]

One of the difficulties in schools is the lack of awareness and knowledge about gender dysphoria and how to deal with the issue leading to a lack of support for trans children.[83] The Government states that transgender issues are included in the Personal, Social and Health Education (PSHE) Programme of Study and that this includes teaching pupils about diversity. However, it is clear that there is concern at the government level over the question of advising on gender. In 2019, the Department for Education and Skills issued guidelines for schools which stated that 'Gender identity should be explored at a timely point and in a clear, sensitive and respectful manner'. As the number of children seeking gender reassignment increases, the Government has altered its tone. The Department for Education Guidance issued in September 2020 which applies to schools in England, states that:

> You should not reinforce harmful stereotypes, for instance by suggesting that children might be a different gender based on their personality and interests or the clothes they prefer to wear … materials which suggest that non-conformity to gender stereotypes should be seen as synonymous with having a different gender identity should not be used and you should not work with external agencies or organisations that produce such material. While teachers should not suggest to a child that their non-compliance with gender stereotypes means that either their personality or their body is wrong and in need of changing, teachers should always seek to treat individual students with sympathy and support.[84]

The practical consequences of gender reassignment include entitlement to compete in athletics and other sports and the right to use gender-neutral facilities such as toilets and changing rooms. Respecting trans rights in schools, for example, potentially conflicts with the right to privacy of female pupils: a matter which will fall to be decided by the courts. In April 2020 the Crown Prosecution Service had to withdraw its guidance to schools on transphobic bullying in schools after claims that the guidance gave the impression that girls objecting to biological boys accessing their toilets were breaking the law. Oxfordshire County Council's guidance that boys transitioning to girls can use female toilets, changing rooms, and dormitories on school trips, was withdrawn after a 13-year-old girl applied for judicial review of the policy, on the basis that the guidance was unlawful and undermined both safeguarding and the Equality Act 2010.[85] Other concerns expressed by transgender children include the recording of birth gender on official documents, including passports and birth certificates. However, the government has taken the view that there cannot be changes in official recording of birth gender before a wider review of gender recognition law has been undertaken.[86] In September 2020 the NHS announced that it would launch an independent review into gender identity services for children and young people. The Review will be led by Dr Hilary Cass, former president of the Royal College of Paediatrics and Child Health.

Two recent cases from British Columbia and a recent case from the English High Court reveal the difficulties entailed in children seeking gender reassignment. Note that the British Columbia Infants Act 1996, section 17, provides that an 'infant' may consent to medical treatment provided that the health care provider is satisfied that the child understands the 'nature and consequences and the reasonably foreseeable benefits and risks of the health care' and has 'made reasonable efforts to determine and has concluded that the health care is in the infant's best interests'.

CASE FOCUS: *SB*, 2020[87]

SB, a 17-year-old girl, had consented to and was receiving hormone therapy, without her parent's consent, and was scheduled to have a double mastectomy. The day before the operation was due to take place, her mother, AM, sought, and was granted, a temporary injunction preventing the operation and prohibiting doctors from counselling or advising the girl in preparation for the operation.

AM blamed British Columbia's education ministry for distributing material designed to foster inclusivity and argued that the material pushed 'depressed and anxiety-ridden girls to gender-change clinics when what they need is psychiatric care'.

CASE FOCUS: *a teenager*, 2019

An unidentified (by order of the court) 14-year-old started publicly identifying as a boy at the age of 11. Supported by her/his mother the teenager requested hormone treatment to assist the transition from female to male. The child's name and birth certificate had been changed to reflect the fact that he identified as male. The father took legal action to stop the treatment: he did not oppose the child's transitioning, but argued that the decision was too complex to be made by a child. The Lower Court, and the Appeal Court, upheld the right of the child to receive the treatment and ruled that the teenager's consent to the treatment was valid.

The issue of children and gender change came to a head in 2020 when the High Court considered the competence of children to consent to treatment leading to gender change.

CASE FOCUS: *BELL AND A*[88]

Keira Bell, aged 23 in 2020, was born a female. She had been treated for gender dysphoria and given puberty-blocking drugs from the age of 15 and later transitioned to a male. Mrs A feared that her 15-year-old autistic daughter would be prescribed puberty-blocking drugs (PBs). Together they sought judicial review of the lawfulness of the Tavistock Clinic's Gender Identity Development Service (GIDS) treatment of children.[89] Central to the lawfulness of giving children Puberty Blockers was the question whether – and at what age – a child could give valid consent to such treatment. The Court re-examined the *Gillick principle* (discussed in more detail in Chapter 3). To recap briefly, the case of *Gillick* concerned a challenge to the legality of guidance issued by the Health Minister to the effect that girls under the age of 16 could be given contraceptive treatment.[90] The Court there decided that the key to the matter lay in the degree of maturity and understanding which a girl had in relation to the treatment and to its consequences.

In Bell and A's case the Court considered the increased numbers of children seeking gender treatment, noting that in 2009 97 children and young people were referred to the GIDS but that by 2018 that number had increased to 2,519. In terms of gender split, in 2011 it was 'roughly 50/50' between natal girls and boys: by 2019 76 per cent of referrals were female. In the year 2019/2020, 26 of the 161 children referred were aged 13 or younger, and 95 were under the age of 16. Furthermore, there was a disproportionate number of children referred with Autistic Spectrum Disorder. The Court also noted that 'the vast majority of cases of children who take PBs move on to take cross-sex hormones' and that once they had embarked on that clinical pathway, it was 'extremely rare for a child to get off it'.

The High Court ruled that the treatment of children with Puberty Blockers by the GIDS, without the approval of a court, was unlawful. However much information he/she was given, he/she would not be able to weigh up the implications of the treatment to a sufficient degree. In order to be competent to give valid consent, a child would have to 'understand, retain and weigh up':

(i) the immediate consequences of the treatment in physical and psychological terms;
(ii) the fact that the vast majority of patients taking PBs go on to take cross-sex hormones (CSH) and therefore that s/he is on a pathway to much greater medical interventions;
(iii) the relationship between taking CSH and subsequent surgery, with the implications of such surgery;
(iv) the fact that CSH may well lead to a loss of fertility;
(v) the impact of CSH on sexual function;

(vi) the impact that taking this step on this treatment pathway may have on future and lifelong relationships;
(vii) the unknown physical consequences of taking PBs; and
(viii) the fact that the evidence base for this treatment is as yet highly uncertain.

The court held that is was 'highly unlikely' that a child aged 13 or under would be competent to give valid consent and that it was doubtful that 14- and 15-year-olds could understand and weigh up the long-term consequences of taking PBs. Furthermore, although there was a statutory presumption that the consent of 16-year-olds was valid, given the long-term consequences of the treatment and the fact that it is 'as yet innovative and experimental', doctors would be well-advised to seek the authorisation of a court before commencing treatment.

The Court of Appeal overturned the decision of the High Court. An appeal to the Supreme Court is expected.[91]

Summary

The focus of the law relating to parents and children has, over decades, moved away from its emphasis on the rights of parents towards recognising the rights of the child and the priority of his or her welfare. The safeguarding principle complements the welfare principle, imposing duties on all public bodies to protect the well-being of all children.

Status and identity rights are inextricably linked to the status, rights, and duties of parents: who is my parent? who is my child? are two of the fundamental questions in both law and society. The emerging right of a child to change his or her gender identity has become one of the most controversial issues in recent years, with many questions remaining unresolved by society, Parliament, and the courts.

Notes

1 This 'hands-off' approach also explains why domestic violence was not officially 'discovered' until the 1970s.
2 Children (Scotland) Act 1995, section 2.
3 Guardianship Act 1973.
4 *Re Agar-Ellis* (1883) 24 Ch D 317.
5 ibid., section 2.
6 ibid., section 4.
7 ibid., section 4(2A).
8 ibid., section 4ZA.
9 ibid., sections 5 and 14C.
10 ibid., section 33(3).

11 Adoption and Children Act 2002 section 67; Adoption and Children Act 2002 section 25.
12 Adoption and Children Act 2002, section 46.
13 *J v C* [1970] AC 668.
14 Overturning a 1931 decision that notwithstanding the 1925 Act, the wishes of the child's parents could not be disregarded unless there had been some wrongdoing: *Re Carroll* [1931] 1 KB 317.
15 *Re W* [1971] 2 All ER 49, at 55.
16 Adoption and Children Act 2002, section 1(2).
17 Children Act 1989, section 1.
18 Children Act 1989, sections 8–11.
19 Established under the Criminal Justice and Court Services Act 1990.
20 Children Act 1989, section 10.
21 *X (A child) No 2 (Private Surrogacy Arrangement: Contact with Birth Family)* [2016] EWFC 55.
22 *B (A Child: Post-Adoption Contact)* [2019] EWCA Civ 29.
23 Adoption and Children Act 2002, section 51A(4)(c).
24 UN CRC Article 12.
25 *Concluding observations on the fifth periodic report on the United Kingdom of Great Britain and Northern Ireland*, CRC/C/GBR/CO/5, 2016. The next review is scheduled for 2022.
26 https://syp.org.uk/about-syp/
27 *Yousef v The Netherlands* [2002] ECHR 716; (2002) 36 EHRR 20.
28 The UN Committee on the Rights of the Child has criticised the lack of uniformity in the application of the welfare principle. See CRC/C/15/Add.188, 2002.
29 Ofsted: *Safeguarding Children*, 2005; www.safeguardingchildren.org.uk/Safeguarding-Children/2005-report.
30 Children Act 1989, section 17.
31 Children Act 2004, sections 16A–C.
32 Children Act 2004, section 10.
33 UK Government response to Freedom of Information Request, *Local safeguarding children's boards*, March 2011.
34 Department for Education: *The Prevent duty: advice for schools and childcare providers*, 2015.
35 The Disability Discrimination Act 1995 remains in force in relation to Northern Ireland.
36 MDA Freeman, *The Rights and Wrongs of Children*, London: Frances Pinter, 1083, Prologue.
37 Equality Act 2010, section 149.
38 ibid., Schedule 9.
39 ibid.
40 ibid., section 85(1) and Schedule 11.
41 Equality Act, Schedule 18.
42 The right to own property in her own right was not achieved by women until the Married Women's Property Act 1882; the right to equal parental rights in 1973.
43 Affiliation Proceedings Act 1957, repealed by the Family Law Reform Act 1987. The origins of the law lie in the Bastardy Laws Amendment Act 1972.
44 Family Law Reform Act 1987, section 1.
45 Civil Partnerships Act 2004.
46 Marriage (Same Sex Couples) Act 2013.
47 Civil Partnership (Opposite-sex Couples) Regulations 2019, amending eligibility criteria under Civil Partnerships Act 2004.
48 A minor exception relates to the inheritance of titles.
49 ibid., at paragraph 2.

50 See the Surrogacy Arrangements Act 1985 and Human Fertilisation and Embryology Acts 2008, 2008 and 2008.
51 Bastardy Laws Amendment Act 1871, section 4.
52 The Family Law Reform Act 1969 made blood testing available as proof of paternity.
53 Registration of Births Marriages and Deaths Act 1953.
54 Children Act 1989, section 4.
55 Human Fertilisation and Embryology Act 1990 as amended by HFEA 2008.
56 Which is an accepted part of the ECHR Article 8 right to privacy.
57 Donors under the Human Fertilisation and Embryology Act are not 'parents' and do not incur any liability to maintain a child born as a result of their donation.
58 *Mikulić v Croatia* [2002] ECHR 27.
59 *Rose v Secretary of State for Health* [2002] EWHC 1593 (Admin).
60 Family Law Reform Act 1969, section 21(3)(b).
61 *Re F (paternity: jurisdiction)* [2007] EWCA Civ 873; [2008] 1 FLR 225.
62 As amended by the 2008 Act.
63 Human Fertilisation and Embryology Act 1990, sections 27 and 28.
64 Human Fertilisation and Embryology Act 2008, sections 33 to 50.
65 *R (McConnell) v The Registrar General for England and Wales* [2020] EWCA Civ 559.
66 Gender Recognition Act 2004, section 9(2).
67 ibid., section 12.
68 HFEA (Disclosure of Identity) Regulations 2004 SI 2004/1511, reg. 2(2).
69 Human Fertilisation and Embryology Act 1990, section 31(4).
70 ibid., sections 31ZA–31ZB.
71 *A & Others (Human Fertilisation and Embryology Act 2008)* [2015] EWHC 2602 (Fam)
72 See the Surrogacy Arrangements Act 1985, as amended by the HF&FE Acts 1990 and 2008.
73 ibid., section 1A.
74 See Department for Health and Social Care, *The Surrogacy Pathway*, November 2019.
75 Triseliotis, J, 1973, page 20.
76 Adoption and Children Act 2002, section 60.
77 See also Article 8 of the UN Convention on the Rights of the Child.
78 *Mikulić v Croatia* [2002] 1 FCR 720.
79 NHS England, *Gender Identity Development Service for Children and Adolescents*, Schedule 2, 2016.
80 See the Government response and analysis of responses to the consultation: www.gov.uk/government/speeches/response-to-gender-recognitiion-act-2004-consultation and Government Equalities Office, Gender Recognition Act Analysis of consultation responses, CP 294, September 2020.
81 NHS England, 2015, op cit., page 6.
82 Equality and Human rights Commission; Women and Equalities Select Committee, *Transgender Equality Inquiry Response to call for written submissions*.
83 Children's Rights Alliance England, *See it, Say it, Change it: Children speak out on transgender issues*, p 3.
84 www.gov.uk/guidance/plan-your-relationships-sex-and-health-curriculum 24 September 2020.
85 The case was withdrawn after the Council withdrew its guidance. See the *Oxford Mail* 7 May 2020. The challenge was to be funded through crowdfunding backed by the Safe Schools Alliance.
86 Government Equalities Office, *Government Response to Women and Equalities Committee Report on Transgender Equality*, 2016, Cm 9301.
87 Reported in *The Times*, 12 November 2020.
88 *R (Quincy Bell) and A v Tavistock and Portman NHS Trust* [2020] EWHC 3274 (Admin).
89 The Tavistock Gender Identity Development Service (GIDS) in London, with clinics in Exeter and Leeds, is the only specialist gender treatment clinic. Waiting months

for appointments, appointments far away and fixed for impossible times of day are reported to lead to depression and self-harm and, allegedly, many attempted suicides.

90 Note that there is a legal presumption that a child aged 16 is capable of giving valid consent: Family Law Reform Act 1969, section 8. However, if a court considers that the treatment consented to is not in the child's best interests, the child's consent may be overridden.

91 [2021] EWCA Civ 1363.

3

CHILDREN AND MEDICAL TREATMENT

Introduction

In this chapter we look at the laws and practices surrounding children and medical treatment. The language of rights is particularly difficult in relation to health and medical treatment. Standards of health and access to medical treatment are inextricably linked to a range of other factors which may undermine the standard of health which is achievable for a child. Accordingly, as the UN Convention states, States recognise the right of the child to the 'highest attainable' standard of health:

> State Parties recognize the right of the child to the enjoyment of the highest attainable standard of health and to facilities for the treatment of illness and rehabilitation of health. State Parties shall strive to ensure that no child is deprived of his or her right of access to such health care services.
>
> *UN Convention on the Rights of the Child,*
> *Article 24.1*

The right to health, employment, a decent home and standard of living are social and economic rights which come at a high cost to the State and require significant investment if standards are even to be maintained, let alone improved.[1] The Secretary of State for Health is under a duty to provide a comprehensive health service designed to secure the improvement of physical and mental health and the prevention, diagnosis, and treatment of physical and mental illness.[2] However, with the financial crisis of 2008, the UK entered into an extended period of fiscal austerity: all government departments were required to reduce their annual estimates for expenditure. The official belt-tightening inevitably led to cuts in service provision, whether education, health, or social services.[3] The King's Fund records that NHS spending on medicines, for example, in England

DOI: 10.4324/9780429452710-3

grows at an average five per cent per year, while the NHS budget grows by an average of only one per cent.[4] Such financial restraints have a severe impact on the rights of families and children to the care and support needed to ensure and maintain satisfactory levels of health.[5]

Standards of living and health

The links between poverty and health, both physical and mental, are well established. Housing problems also feature significantly in children's quality of health.

A British Medical Association report in 2017, *Health at a price: reducing the impact of poverty*, stated that:

> Poverty can have a significant impact on child health, from the point before a child is even born ... Babies born in the poorest areas in the UK weigh on average 200 grams less than those born in the richest areas, which may impact on subsequent cognitive development. Babies living in poverty are also more likely to die within their first year of life. After birth, poverty is associated with postnatal depression in the mother and lower rates of breastfeeding ... Children born into poverty are more likely to suffer from chronic diseases, such as asthma, as well as diet-related problems such as tooth decay, malnutrition obesity and diabetes...As well as poverty affecting their physical health, children living in low-income households are over three times more likely to suffer from mental health problems compared to their more affluent peers.

Research conducted by the Royal College of Paediatrics and Child Health (RCPCH) in 2017 records the responses of some doctors in relation to health and housing as follows:[6]

> It is not unusual to hear about extended families of five to seven people, maybe more, living in one bedroom apartments, or single mothers with two or three children living in bedsits with a shared kitchen and bathroom. According to parent reports a lot of the housing seems to be damp as well. This exacerbates both acute and chronic lung infections and conditions such as asthma.
>
> The burden on social housing and social services for emergency and planned housing leads to placements in houses that are unsafe, have mould, [are] damp, overcrowded. This has a direct effect on deterioration of child health, both physical and emotional well-being.
>
> I recently saw a child who was living in a mouse-infested house – the mum and baby plus four other kids were living upstairs as the mice had totally destroyed their living room. Mum was worried that their poor living conditions had made her baby ill.

The Mental Health Foundation (MHF) reports that the link between poverty and mental health has long been recognised, and that the relationship between the two operates in two directions. 'Being poor can bring about mental health problems (most commonly anxiety and depression), but mental health problems can also lead people into poverty due to discrimination in employment and the reduced ability to work'.[7] The MHF states that there is a 'social gradient' with people on the lowest income having worse health problems than those in the highest levels, and that this is evident in childhood with children as young as three and five showing a link between poverty and behavioural difficulties. Other factors affecting mental health include being part of a disadvantaged group (BAME; LGBT); experiencing discrimination, abuse or neglect, and homelessness can all affect mental health.

The right to life

Under English law, from the time when a child is capable of being born alive and maintaining an existence independent of his or her mother, he or she is entitled to the full protection of the law. Prior to that point in time, the embryo or foetus is not recognised as a 'legal person' entitled to the same level of legal protection as a child which is capable of being born alive. However, as discussed below, this does not mean that the unborn child is devoid of legal protection.[8]

> State parties recognise that every child has the inherent right to life. State parties shall ensure to the maximum extent possible the survival and development of the child.
>
> *UN Convention on the Rights of the Child, Article 6*

The beginning of life debate – and the protection of that right – are both highly contested on moral and religious grounds. The debate is also inextricably linked to the right of a woman to exercise control over her body and her choice (controlled by the law) whether or not to have a child. In the United States of America, for example, the right to terminate a pregnancy has, since 1973, been regarded as a woman's constitutional right to privacy and is thus controlled by the Supreme Court and its interpretation of the law.[9] In the UK, by contrast, the right to terminate a pregnancy is regulated under an ordinary Act of Parliament, currently the Abortion Act 1967 as amended.[10] Note that the Act 1967 Act does not apply in Northern Ireland. In Northern Ireland abortion was unlawful until 2020. After a sustained campaign for reform and the judgment of a majority of the Supreme Court in 2019 that the prohibition of abortion violated the right to privacy under the ECHR Article 8, the government finally acted to reform the law.[11]

The first Act of Parliament to deal specifically with the right of the unborn child was the **Infant Life (Preservation) Act 1929**[12] which created the offence of child destruction. Section 1 provides that it is an offence (punishable to penal servitude for life, later interpreted as a life sentence or less[13]) if

> ... any person who, with intent destroy the life of a child capable of being born alive, by any wilful act causes a child to die before it has an existence independent of its mother, shall be guilty of a felony.

While the Act does not state at precisely which point 'a child' comes into being for the purposes of legal protection it is clear that this is determined on the factual basis of when the child is 'capable of being born alive' and can sustain 'an existence independent of its mother'. It is a defence to prove that the act causing the death of the child was done for the purpose 'only of preserving the life of the mother'.[14] At first sight, the offence of child destruction comes into conflict with a woman's right to terminate a pregnancy, first officially recognised under the Abortion Act 1967[15] which makes the termination of a pregnancy lawful when conducted in accordance with the Act. However, the Abortion Act makes it clear that where a pregnancy is lawfully terminated, no offence is committed under the 1929 Act.

Article 2 of the European Convention on Human Rights (ECHR) guarantees the right to life. This right, however, is not absolute and does not protect the unborn foetus – accordingly the Article 2 right to life cannot be used in opposition to abortion. In *Vo v France* (2004)[16] a medical mistake led to a woman being forced to have a therapeutic abortion. The Court of Human Rights (by a majority) acknowledged that the 'embryo/foetus belongs to the human race', and that its potential to become a human being justified States giving it some protection under the law. However, that could be so 'without making it a "person" with the "right to life" for the purposes of Article 2'.[17] Furthermore, the Court stated that 'it is neither desirable, nor even possible as matters stand, to answer in the abstract the question whether the unborn child is a person for the purposes of Article 2 of the Convention'.[18]

Consent to medical treatment

In order for medical treatment to be lawful, there must be a valid consent given by the patient or his or her parent or guardian. If there is no valid consent a doctor giving treatment would be committing a trespass upon the person of the patient. While a mentally competent adult has the right to consent to medical treatment, the question of whether a girl under the age of 16 has the same right raises the question of competence. The Family Law Reform Act 1969, section 8, creates a rebuttable presumption that the consent of a 16-year-old is valid and does not rule out the validity of consent of a child under the age of 16 (on this see further below).

> The consent of a minor who has attained the age of sixteen years to any surgical, medical or dental treatment...shall be as effective as it would be if he or she were of full age.
>
> *Family Law Reform Act 1969, section 8(1)*

On whether a child under the age of 16 can give valid consent, the issue will turn on whether or not he or she is regarded as having sufficient intelligence and maturity to understand what is involved and the consequence of any treatment. The 1969 Act provides that where a child who has reached the age of 16 has the capacity to consent to surgical, medical, and dental treatment and where such consent is given it is unnecessary to obtain consent from a parent or guardian.

The 1969 Act also states (rather awkwardly) that 'nothing in this section shall be construed as making ineffective any consent which would have been effective if this section had not been enacted'. In other words, a child under the age of 16 may be capable of giving consent (i.e. has the capacity to consent), depending upon his or her level of understanding and maturity. As will be seen from the case below, as a child grows towards the age of majority he or she will acquire greater rights to make decisions about his or her care and upbringing, including decisions concerning medical treatment.

Where there is an emergency situation threatening the life of a child, the question of valid consent becomes less relevant.[19] Consent should be sought but if it is not possible to obtain consent, doctors should provide treatment that is in the best interests of the patient, and necessary to save life or prevent a deterioration of the patient's condition.

For consent to treatment to be valid, patients must:

- have the capacity to make the decision;
- have been offered sufficient information to make an informed decision;
- be acting voluntarily and free from undue pressure;
- be aware that they can refuse.[20]

In *Gillick v West Norfolk and Wisbech AHA,* (1986)[21] the capacity of a child to make independent decisions was examined. Victoria Gillick, a Roman Catholic, had five daughters under the age of 16. In 1980, the Department of Health and Social Security (DHSS) issued Guidelines to the effect that doctors could, in exceptional circumstances, give contraceptive advice or treatment to a girl under the age of 16 without parental consent. Mrs Gillick objected. When her request to the local Health Authority that her daughters would not receive such advice or treatment was refused, she sought a declaration from the court that the guidance was unlawful. Although successful before the Court of Appeal Mrs Gillick lost by a majority of three to two in the House of Lords (now the Supreme Court). The *Gillick* case has implications far beyond the narrow issue of contraceptive advice and treatment and represents a comprehensive judicial analysis on the respective rights of parents and children in relation to decision-making as a child matures.

The key concept in *Gillick* is that of the 'mature minor' and the point at which he or she has the right to make independent decisions even if these conflict with the wishes of parents or others with parental responsibility. The essential principle established in this case is that a child under the age of 16 has the right to make decisions when:

> … he reaches a sufficient understanding and intelligence to be capable of making up his own mind on the matter requiring decision *per* Lord Scarman at paragraph 186.
>
> Lord Scarman, paragraph 186

Just what amounts to a 'sufficient understanding and intelligence' is the key question. Lord Scarman required a high level of understanding of the issues involved, including her relationship with her parents, the problems associated with the emotional impact of pregnancy and its termination and the risks to health of sexual intercourse at an early age which are not wholly eliminated by contraception. As discussed below, the courts continue to insist on a high level of understanding and intelligence, particularly when it comes to refusing medical treatment.

A number of questions arise from this case. What happens to the parental right to make decisions for the child? Is the consent of a 'mature minor' valid if her decision conflicts with her welfare as perceived her parents or a court of law? Does the capacity to consent to medical treatment include the right to refuse medical treatment?

Lord Scarman in *Gillick* stated that 'the parental right yields to the child's right to make his own decisions', suggesting that the parents' rights are extinguished when the child is considered to have sufficient maturity to reach a decision. Lord Fraser in *Gillick* adopted a more cautious approach, stating that there were five conditions which had to be met before a doctor could be satisfied that he or she could lawfully proceed without parental consent. The 'Fraser guidelines' are:

(1) that the girl will understand his advice;
(2) that he cannot persuade her to inform her parents or allow him to do so;
(3) that she is very likely to begin or continue having sexual intercourse with or without contraceptive treatment;
(4) that unless she receives advice or treatment her physical or mental health or both are likely to suffer;
(5) that her best interests require him to act without consent.[22]

In addition to valid consent to medical treatment, there is the fundamental principle that medical treatment must be in the child's best interests and that the paramount principle of the welfare of the child will be served by a particular treatment.

Gillick was decided before the Human Rights Act 1998 (HRA) came into force. In force from 2000 the HRA enables European Convention (ECHR) rights to be enforced before the domestic courts. Article 8 protects a person's right to respect for private and family life and this encompasses the question of consent to medical treatment. The UN Convention on the Rights of the Child 1989 (CRC) is also relevant. As discussed in Chapter 1, although not enforceable in the national courts, the CRC has a persuasive effect and guides State agencies over all areas of decision-making related to children and young people. These two international Conventions bolster the claim of children to rights. In 2006, for example, a judge recognised that there was 'a change in the landscape of family matters, in which the rights of children are becoming increasingly important'.[23] However, in the context of consent to medical treatment, the claim to the right of the child to make binding decisions is qualified by the *Gillick* requirement of competence (i.e. the mature minor test) and by the welfare principle.

CASE FOCUS: *AXON* (2006)[24]

Government Guidance on the provision of advice and treatment on sexual matters to young people without their parents first being notified was challenged by a mother who wished to protect her young daughters from making decisions which they might later regret. The Court recognised that this raised a tension between the rights of a child to consent to medical treatment and a parent's responsibility for her child's welfare.

The Guidance stated that such treatment would be lawful provided that the Fraser Guidelines in *Gillick* were followed. In *Axon* following the Guidance was held to be mandatory. The Court ruled that in order for the advice and treatment to be lawful, the Fraser Guidelines had to be 'strictly observed' and warned that medical professionals could expect to be disciplined by his or her professional body if they were not adhered to.

Confidentiality[25]

Running through considerations of a child's right to consent to medical treatment is the issue of medical confidentiality: patient confidentiality applies to children as well as adults. The NHS Code of Confidentiality requires that the disclosure of medical information should be anonymised unless it is essential for the purposes of the disclosure. The patient should be informed about the use of information and the patient's consent should be sought before any disclosure is made. The disclosure of information without consent should only be made when there is 'an overriding public interest in the disclosure' or the disclosure is in the best interests of a child who is not *Gillick*-competent, or where the information is required by law, or on the order of a court.[26]

Refusing consent to medical treatment

As the *Gillick* case made clear, the mature minor can consent to medical treatment. Can the mature minor also refuse medical treatment? The answer to that question is, it depends. If the child patient, his or her parents, and the doctors concerned are all in agreement over a proposed course of action there is no problem. Where, however, a child refuses to consent to treatment, the position is more complex. In Scotland, if a competent child refuses to consent to treatment, a parent cannot override that decision.[27] In England, Wales, and Northern Ireland, however, where a child refuses medical treatment which parents and/ or doctors regard as serving his or her welfare the matter may end up before a court for a decision.

Under the *Gillick* principle, where a child is competent to make a decision over medical treatment, that decision must be respected. However, the difficulty in respecting a mature minor's *refusal* to consent to medical treatment is that his or her decision may be contrary to his or her welfare. In relation to refusal to consent, therefore, the right of the child will depend on whether or not that decision will be in his or her best interests and promote his or her welfare.

CASE FOCUS: *R*[28]

A fifteen-year-old girl suffered from episodes of mental illness and suicidal behaviour. She refused drug therapy and the matter went to court. The Court of Appeal ruled that R was not '*Gillick*-competent': she lacked the intelligence and understanding to be capable of making up her own mind. The Court of Appeal overrode R's decision.

CASE FOCUS: *W*[29]

W, aged 16, suffered from anorexia nervosa. She refused to be moved from a residential unit to a hospital specialising in eating disorders. The Court of Appeal overrode her decision.

The Court acknowledged that it had to give great weight to the wishes of a mature minor. However, where respecting her decision would lead to her death or permanent injury, her decision could not stand. Furthermore, the Family Law Act 1969 did not apply to decisions refusing medical treatment.

CASE FOCUS: *P*[30]

P, aged 17 and a half, took an overdose of paracetamol. When admitted to hospital she refused to consent to treatment. Treatment was needed urgently (within eight hours) in order to avoid liver failure and death. The Trust sought a Declaration that it was lawful to treat her, notwithstanding her refusal to consent, and that if it proved necessary to sedate or restrain P when administering the treatment, doing so would not be unlawful.

The judge had taken into account P's wishes and feelings but had not been able to talk to her. Her wishes were important and formed part of her ECHR Article 8 right. However, the balance came down firmly in favour of overriding her wishes. Her rights were not absolute and in this case were outweighed by her right to life protected under Article 2. The court granted the order sought.

Withholding/withdrawing medical treatment

As noted above, from the moment that a child is capable of being born alive and sustaining life independently from his or her mother he or she is entitled to the full protection of the law. However, difficult questions arise where the child is incapable of sustaining his or her life without medical assistance.

For the doctors and nurses treating very sick patients, there is also the question of liability should a patient die as a result of their care, or lack of it. The criminal law of murder and manslaughter exists to call to account those whose wrongful actions cause death. Accordingly, when there are difficult decisions to be made about continuing treatment, or withholding treatment, doctors may turn to the courts for authorisation for their proposed actions.

CASE FOCUS: *JOHN*[31]

In 1980 a baby boy was born with a severe and irreversible handicap. He was rejected by his parents and Dr Leonard Arthur, a respected senior consultant paediatrician at Derby City Hospital, made a note 'Nursing care only'. The baby, John, was given sedation and kept comfortable. He died within three days of his birth.

The police were called and in February 1981 Dr Arthur was charged with murder. He pleaded not guilty. The medical evidence relied on by the prosecution turned out to be inaccurate. The judge ordered the charge of murder to be dropped and replaced with a charge of attempted murder. Dr Arthur did not give evidence. Evidence by a number of doctors and specialists testified on his behalf: what was revealed was that Dr Arthur had acted in accordance with the accepted standards of medical practice. The jury unanimously acquitted Dr Arthur.

The case of *Re J* (1990) remains influential in decision-making on continued medical treatment and the words of Lord Donaldson MR are frequently cited before the courts.[32] J was four and a half months old, and suffered severe brain damage and predicted paralysis, deafness, limited intellectual ability, and no speech. The question before the court was whether doctors, having resuscitated J twice, were obliged to do so again. It was an invasive process which caused J distress. The judge ruled, on the recommendation of the consultant neonatologist that, in the event of further convulsions requiring resuscitation, J should not be revived by means of mechanical ventilation unless to do so seemed appropriate to those involved in his care in that situation. The Official Solicitor appealed. In the House of Lords (now the Supreme Court), Lord Donaldson stated that:

> ... a very strong presumption must be attached to the prolongation of life because the individual human instinct and desire to survive is so strong and must be presumed to be strong in the patient. But it is not absolute, nor necessarily decisive; and may be outweighed if the pleasures and the quality of life are sufficiently small and the pain and suffering or other burdens of living are sufficiently great.[33]

The court dismissed the appeal. If it was in the best interests of the child, it was not unlawful to choose a course of action which did not prevent death. The court stressed that there was no question of a court approving a course of treatment aimed at terminating life or accelerating death which would be unlawful.

In *Re Jake* (2015) Sir James Munby, then President of the Family Division of the High Court, set out the law relating to withholding or limiting treatment in the differing circumstances in which these difficult decisions arise in relation to children. The language of rights becomes especially difficult in relation to medical treatment when the best interests of the child – the guiding principle in decision-making for children – dictate that withholding or withdrawing treatment may be in the child's best interests. On the law Munby J stated that:

> It is clear, as a matter of law, that if the primary purpose is to relieve distress, the fact that, as a side effect, medication may have the effect of shortening life does not in any way prevent that treatment being lawful.[34]

Munby J set out two principal categories of cases. The first is where there is a limited quality of life. In this case 'if treatment is unable or unlikely to prolong life significantly, it may not be in the child's best interests to provide it'. Within this first category, there are three possible scenarios:

- brain death: 'when death is diagnosed following formal confirmation of brain stem death by agreed medical criteria, intensive technological support is no long appropriate and should be withdrawn'.
- imminent death: where 'despite treatment, the child is physiologically deteriorating. Here it is no longer appropriate to provide lifesaving treatment because it is futile and burdensome to do so'.

- inevitable demise: where death is inevitable, but not imminent, and it is possible to prolong life but this may 'provide little or no overall benefit for the child' then a shift in focus of care from life prolongation per se to palliation is appropriate.

In relation to the second category of case, where there is a limited quality of life and there is no overall qualitative benefit from treatment, Munby J recognised that decisions may be more difficult as a result of differences of opinion between the healthcare team and children and families as to what constitutes quality of life. There are three main determinative considerations:

- the burden of treatments: some treatments cause pain and distress. 'If a child's life can only be sustained at the cost of significant pain and distress it may not be in their best interests to receive such treatments';
- the burdens of illness and/or underlying condition: 'some children have such severe degrees of illness associated with pain, discomfort and distress that life is judged by them (or on their behalf if they are unable to express their wishes and views) to be intolerable. All appropriate measures to treat and relieve the child's pain should be taken. If, despite these measures, it is genuinely believed that there is no overall benefit in continued life, further lifesaving treatments should not be provided';
- the lack of ability to derive benefit: in other cases 'the nature and severity of the child's underlying condition may make it difficult or impossible for them to enjoy the benefits that continued life brings. Examples include persistent vegetative state or minimally conscious state, or those with such severe cognitive impairment that they lack demonstrable or recorded awareness of themselves and their surroundings'. Here, 'continuation of lifesaving treatment may not be in their best interests because it cannot provide overall benefit to them'. Given that there may be disagreements over whether continued treatment might be of benefit, it is particularly important in this situation to take into account the parents' wishes or preferences.[35]

Establishing what action best fits with the welfare of a patient, whether adult or child, is inevitably a complex issue. In 2013, Baroness Hale JSC gave guidance:[36]

> The most that can be said, therefore, is that in considering the best interests of this particular patient at this particular time, decision-makers must look at his welfare in a wider sense, not just medical but social and psychological. They must consider the nature of the medical treatment in question, what it involves and its possibilities of success. They must consider what the outcome of that treatment for the patient is likely to be. They must try and put themselves in the place of the individual patient and ask what his attitude to the treatment is or would be likely to be and they must consult

others who are looking after him or interested in his welfare, in particular for the view of what his attitude would be.

In 2017 the *Charlie Gard case* attracted international attention and highlighted the tensions between the rights of parents and the medical profession and the principle of the best interests of the child.

CASE FOCUS: *CHARLIE GARD*[37]

Charlie Gard was born in 2016. Within two months he was admitted to intensive care at Great Ormond Street Hospital (GOSH) and diagnosed with a rare genetic disorder. He was paralysed and unable to breathe without respiratory support. By January 2017 GOSH was convinced that further treatment would be ineffective and in February applied to the High Court for permission to withdraw life support and provide palliative care only. The parents appealed, but the Court of Appeal, the Supreme Court, and the European Court of Human Rights upheld the decision of the High Court. In July 2017 the parents accepted that further treatment would not help their child, life support was withdrawn, and Charlie was allowed to die.

CASE FOCUS: *JAKE*[38]

Jake was ten months old. He suffered from severe epilepsy[39] and his condition was deteriorating. His parents both had learning difficulties, and his mother lacked the capacity to consent to medical treatment. In 2014 an Interim Care Order was made, with the effect that the local authority shared parental responsibility with the parents.[40]

An application was made to the court for a decision on Jake's further treatment. Detailed medical evidence was given to the court, together with three options for treatment if Jake's condition continued to deteriorate. Option A was for palliative/end of life care with a no resuscitation order. Option B was for continued medical treatment and full resuscitation. Option C was for continued treatment, with resuscitation for a limited time.

The court ordered that Option A should be adopted. In the event of serious deterioration in Jake's medical condition, it was lawful for treatment to be withheld. The local authority and the guardian (appointed to represent Jake's interests) agreed to the order. The parents 'did not actively oppose the order'.

The case outlined below is not one of withdrawing or terminating treatment, but rather one where a court is asked to authorise a procedure which would, inevitably, result in the death of a child.

CASE FOCUS: *JODIE AND MARY*[41]

Mary and Jodie were born in August 2000. They were conjoined twins, 'each having their own brain heart and lungs and other vital organs, and they each have arms and legs'. However, they were joined at the lower abdomen. They could be surgically separated but to do so would involve the death of either Mary or Jodie. Their parents, devout Roman Catholics, were unable to give their consent to the operation.

Mary was the weaker twin. To survive she was dependent upon a common artery which enabled her sister to circulate oxygenated blood for both of them. Had Mary been born without a twin she would have died shortly after her birth. Jodie, the stronger twin, could not continue to support Mary indefinitely and the strain of supporting Mary would lead to her death. If the children were not separated, both would die within six to 12 months. If they were separated Mary would die within minutes but there was a good chance that Jodie would survive.

Would the separation be lawful? The welfare of the child was the paramount consideration, but here the interests of Jodie and Mary were in direct conflict: both had a right to life, but neither would survive without the surgery to separate them. The Court of Appeal declared that the proposed operation would be lawful. Jodie had a good chance of surviving but continued life for Mary would hold nothing but pain and discomfort, 'if she could feel anything at all'. In was in the interests of both children that the operation be carried out.

Immunisation

The NHS publishes the schedule of immunisation for children. As a result of immunisation, smallpox, polio, and other killer diseases have been almost eradicated. However, there remain doubts and fears over vaccinations which, fuelled by inaccurate social media reporting, lead to reductions in the take-up of vaccinations for children. In 1998, controversy over the MMR (Measles, Mumps and Rubella) vaccine was ignited by a former doctor who published a research paper in *The Lancet* claiming that there was a link between the MMR vaccine and autism. The research was discredited as false and the paper retracted from the journal. The doctor was subsequently struck off for acting 'dishonestly and irresponsibly' and not in the interests of children. A research study in 2014 involving 1.2 million children revealed that there was no relationship between vaccination and autism.[42]

In 2019, the World Health Organisation removed the UK's 'measles free status' as a result of outbreaks of the disease. Public Health England warned that one in seven five-year-olds were not up to date with MMR immunisations, and that 30,000 children starting primary school in 2019 would do so with no protection against measles, mumps, and rubella.[43] Vaccination is compulsory in some

European countries including France and Italy. The Prime Minister, however, has ruled out making immunisation compulsory in the UK, despite continuing downwards trends in the take-up of all immunisations of children.[44]

While refusing to have children vaccinated is within a parent's rights and no action will be taken when this remains within the family, once the State is involved – usually in the form of a local authority – disputes may arise which lead to court.

CASE FOCUS: *A, B, C, AND D*[45]

In 2009 four children, aged between thirteen years and five years, were removed from their parents' care on the basis of chronic neglect by both parents. In 2011 final Care Orders were made in favour of the local authority which then proposed to have the children immunised. The authority wished to have booster immunisations relating to immunisations the children had while in their parents' care and the seasonal flu and MMR immunisations for A. The parents objected to the plan to give A (then aged 13) the MMR vaccine on the ground that they believed there was a connection between the side effects of the vaccine and autism, from which A suffered. The issue went to the Family Division of the High Court.[46]

The court accepted that the parents' views should be treated with respect and not 'lightly set aside'. However, where the views of the parent and the court diverge:

> … the role of the court is to exercise an independent and objective judgment … it is the duty of the court, after giving due weight to the view of the devoted and responsible parent, to give effect to its own judgment. That is what it is there for.'[47]

The court gave careful consideration to the medical evidence and concluded that there was no competent body of professional opinion that supported the link between the MMR vaccine and autism. The court made declarations authorising the vaccinations.[48]

CASE FOCUS: *SL*[49]

SL was seven months old. In the course of care proceedings, the local authority applied to the court, under its inherent jurisdiction, for a declaration that it was in SL's best interests for the local authority to arrange the Hib and PCV vaccines for SL. The mother objected (the father was unknown). The court heard expert medical evidence which made clear that the vaccinations would protect SL from serious diseases such as meningitis and pneumonia and that there were no contra-indications to offset the clear benefits.

The mother argued that vaccinating SL against her wishes and without her consent would breach her rights under the ECHR, Article 8 (the right to respect for private and family life). The court accepted that there was an interference with her right and that for the interference to be lawful the action proposed had to be justified and proportionate. The court's primary duty was to the welfare of the child. The court therefore granted the declaration authorising the vaccinations.

The rights of children with disabilities

Please note that the rights of children with Special Educational Needs and Disabilities are discussed in Chapter 4.

The Equality Act 2010 prohibits direct discrimination, indirect discrimination, harassment, and victimisation. The Equality Act defines disability as:

> A person (P) has a disability if –
> (a) P has a physical or mental impairment, and
> (b) the impairment has a substantial and long-term adverse effect on P's ability to carry out normal day-to-day activities.
>
> *Equality Act 2010, section 6.*[50]

Direct discrimination is treating someone with a 'protected characteristic', in this case disability, less favourably than others. Indirect discrimination is putting rules or arrangements in place that apply to everyone, but that put a disabled person at an unfair disadvantage. Harassment is unwanted behaviour linked to disability that violates a person's dignity or creates an offensive environment for them. Victimisation is treating someone unfairly because they have complained about discrimination or harassment.

The UN Convention on the Rights of the Child (CRC) deals specifically with the rights of disabled children:

1. State Parties recognise that a mentally or physically disabled child should enjoy a full and decent life, in conditions which ensure dignity promote self-reliance and facilitate the child's active participation in the community;
2. State Parties recognise the right of the disabled child to special care and shall encourage and ensure the extension, subject to available resources, to the eligible child and those responsible for his or her care, of assistance for which

application is made and which is appropriate to the child's condition and to the circumstances of the parents or others caring for the child;

3. recognising the special needs of a disabled child, assistance extended in accordance with paragraph 2 of the present article shall be provided free of charge, whenever possible, taking into account the financial resources of the parents or others caring for the child, and shall be designed to ensure that the disabled child has effective access to and receives education, training, health care services, rehabilitation services, preparation for employment and recreation opportunities in a manner conducive to the child's achieving the fullest possible social integration and individual development, including his or her own cultural and spiritual development.

Article 23[51]

Also in the realm of international law is the **UN Convention on the Rights of Persons with Disabilities (UNCRPD) 2006.**[52] Specific to children, the Convention states that:

1. State Parties shall take all necessary measures to ensure the full enjoyment by children with disabilities of all human rights and fundamental freedoms on an equal basis with other children;
2. in all actions concerning children with disabilities, the best interests of the child shall be a primary consideration;
3. State Parties shall ensure that children with disabilities have the right to express their views freely on all matters affecting them, their views being given due weight in accordance with their age and maturity, on an equal basis with other children, and to be provided with disability and age–appropriate assistance to realise that right.

UNCRPD, Article 7

In relation to disability, home, and family the UNCRPD states that:

State Parties shall ensure that children with disabilities have equal rights with respect to family life. With a view to realising those rights, and to prevent concealment, abandonment, neglect and segregation of children with disabilities, State Parties shall undertake to provide early and comprehensive information, services and support to children with disabilities and their families.

UNCRPD, Article 23

It is axiomatic that children with disabilities face a number of problems not encountered by children without disabilities. There are particular difficulties in relation to access to buildings and facilities, the funding of services; problems with the provision of Special Educational Needs (which overlaps with funding); experiencing abuse or alienation as a result of a disability. The Equality Act 2010 imposes a duty to make 'reasonable adjustments' to make life easier for disabled people. This duty encompasses the requirement to make adjustments so as to avoid any disadvantage which a disabled person may experience when compared with those who are not disabled. It also requires adjustments to physical features, for example to a building or room, to avoid the disabled person being disadvantaged. Thirdly the duty requires the provision of auxiliary aids to a disabled person so as to remove any disadvantage.[53] Where a child has Special Educational Needs or Disability (SEND: see further Chapter 4), local authorities have a duty to keep under review the provision of their services to ensure that they are sufficient to meet the needs of children with SEND.[54]

A child with disabilities is a 'child in need' for the purposes of the Children Act 1989.[55] Local authorities are under a duty to provide short break services such as holiday playschemes, care at home, aids and adaptations, and financial help, for example, towards travel costs for hospital visits.

For children under the age of 16 with mobility problems or who need much more care than a child who does not have a disability, there is a Disability Living Allowance (DLA). This is a tax-free benefit made up of a care component and a mobility component.[56] Eligibility is linked to habitual residence in the UK, Ireland, Isle of Man, or the Channel Islands and being free from immigration control. When a child reaches the age of 16 they are no longer eligible for the DLA but may apply for a Personal Independence Payment (PIP).

CASE FOCUS: *CM*[57]

Cameron had 'exceptional and complex care needs'. His disabilities were so severe that he qualified for the highest rates of DLA. He was admitted to hospital and remained there for 13 months during which time one of his parents was with him all the time. His parents were his primary carers, administering physiotherapy, giving him antibiotics, feeding him, and changing his stoma bag up to eight times a day. They provided the same level of care as they would have done at home, relieving hospital staff of the need to care for him. Their travel costs to and from the hospital amounted to £8,000.

Under the relevant DLA Regulations, payment would cease when a child had been in hospital as an inpatient for a period of 84 days. The Secretary of State suspended Cameron's DLA. The parents continued to receive other State benefits, but the suspension of the DLA amounted to a loss of some £7,000. There were appeals against the decision, all of which were dismissed. The matter finally went to the Supreme Court.

The Supreme Court ruled that Cameron was entitled to continued payment of the DLA and set aside the Secretary of State's decision. The right to welfare benefits fell within the right to 'property' protected under ECHR A1P1. The appeal was based on Article 14 of the ECHR: to right to enjoyment of Convention rights (i.e. A1P1 rights) without discrimination. Disability was a prohibited ground: there was no justification for suspending Cameron's DLA after 84 days and the suspension violated his rights. He had been treated less favourably than disabled children who did not require 84 days in hospital and who therefore remained entitled to receive continued DLA and there was no justification for the discrimination.

The European Convention on Human Rights (ECHR) Article 5 – the right to liberty – played a decisive role in the following case:

CASE FOCUS: D[58]

When he was a child, D was diagnosed with Attention Deficit Hyperactivity Disorder, Asperger's Syndrome, and Tourette's Syndrome and had a mild learning difficulty. When he was 14 he was admitted to hospital for assessment and treatment. He lived in the hospital grounds and attended school within the hospital. The external doors were locked and he was accompanied by staff whenever he left the site. The hospital sought a declaration that it was lawful for the hospital trust to deprive D of his liberty in this way. The court ruled that it fell within its parental responsibility and was lawful.

D was then discharged from hospital and placed in residential care, with his parents' consent, where he was under constant supervision.[59] When D turned 16 a declaration was sought that it was lawful for D to be deprived of his liberty because his parents had consented to it, D not having the mental capacity to consent. The matter ended up before the Supreme Court.

It was accepted that D's liberty had been restricted. But was that restriction lawful? By a majority of three to two the Supreme Court ruled that it was lawful on the basis that the authorisation of the court – protecting D's rights – had been sought and granted. Accordingly there was no violation of D's Article 5 rights. Parental responsibility, however, did not include the right to consent to the deprivation of liberty of a child over the age of 16.[60]

Children and young people's mental health

The data

An NHS survey of children and young people's mental health in 2017 found that 12.8 per cent of those between the ages of 5 and 19 had at least one mental disorder.[61] One in six, 16.9 per cent, of those between the ages of 17 and 19 had more than one mental disorder. Among those aged 5–10, disorders were more common in boys than girls (12.2 per cent to 6.6 per cent). Among the ages 17–19, girls had a higher prevalence than boys (23.9 per cent to 10.2 per cent).

Boys were found to be more likely to have behavioural and hyperactivity disorders than girls while girls more were more likely to have emotional disorders (anxiety and depression) than boys. Children from poorer families who were in receipt of benefits were almost twice as likely to have a mental disorder (19.2 per cent) as those who were not (9.8 per cent). Children from families where an adult was receiving disability benefits were three times more likely to have a mental disorder (31.8 per cent) than those who were not (9.8 per cent).

Public Health England (PHE) reports that ten per cent of children aged five to 16 years suffer from a clinically significant mental illness, but that only 25 per cent of children who need treatment receive it. Fifty per cent of those with lifetime mental illness (excluding dementia) will experience symptoms by the age of 14.[62]

In 2017 the Royal Colleges of GPs (RCGP), Paediatrics and Child Health RCPCH) and Psychiatrists (RCPsych) announced five shared principles that they hope will lead to action to improve and support children and young people (CYP) with mental health problems. An effective mental health system for children and young people requires:

- acknowledgment that CYP mental health is everybody's business and should be supported by a shared vision for CYP mental health across all government departments, particularly health, education, and justice;
- a preventative, multi-agency approach, focusing on mental health and early intervention in CYP;
- a system of national and local accountability for CYP mental health and well-being, delivered via integrated local area systems;
- training and education for the whole children's workforce in their role and responsibilities for CYP mental health;
- more support for professionals dealing with CYP who do not meet the referral threshold to a Child and Adolescent Mental Health Service (CAMHS).[63]

Child and Adolescent Mental Health Service (CAMHS)

The Child and Adolescent Mental Health Service (CAMHS) is a localised service, made up of child mental health professionals. These include child and adolescent psychiatrists, clinical psychologists, child psychotherapists, family therapists, social workers, and mental health practitioners. Paediatricians, educational psychologists, art therapists, and speech and language therapists may also form part of the local CAMHS. CAMHS work at community CAMHS clinics, through outpatient appointments in local hospitals, in schools and some

GP practices, in children's centres and alongside social services such as Youth Offending Services (on the latter see Chapter 7).

However, there are problems with accessing the services, with wide variations in waiting times for treatment. The Care Quality Commission (CQC) has found that 'whilst most specialist services provide good quality care, too many young people find it difficult to access services and so do not receive the care that they need when they need it'.[64] Across all providers the median waiting time for a first appointment is one month, and two months until the start of treatment. Some children may have to wait as long as ten months for treatment, but 18 months is not uncommon. The Education Policy Institute[65] in 2016 reported that 23 per cent of children and young people referred to them were turned away by specialist mental health services.[66]

In relation to eating disorders, in the second quarter of 2019–2020, 75 per cent of urgent cases received treatment within one week (the government's target was for 95 per cent). In each quarter, approximately 1,500 children and young people in England are treated for routine cases and 300 for urgent cases.[67] The Children's Commissioner reports that at the end of 2018–19, there were 7,575 children accessing treatment.[68]

Culture, religion, and medical treatment[69]

Jehovah's Witnesses

Jehovahs Witnesses was founded in Pittsburgh, Pennsylvania by Charles Taze Russell in the 1870s. Its religious basis is Christianity, from which it is distinct. Members do not celebrate Christmas or Easter or observe birthdays or national holidays: only God may be celebrated. Members do not take part in mainstream politics, salute the flag, or sing national anthems. Jehovah's Witnesses refuse to serve in the armed forces. There is a deep-rooted belief that blood transfusions violate God's law and these must be refused even in life-threatening situations. Voluntarily agreeing to a blood transfusion is an offence, which may lead to disciplinary action and even expulsion. In 2019 Jehovah's Witnesses had a membership of 8,683,117.

Article 9 of the European Convention on Human Rights (ECHR), enforceable before the domestic courts under the Human Rights Act 1998, provides that everyone has the right to freedom of thought, conscience, and religion. This right includes the right to manifest one's religion in public or private. The right is not absolute, but may be restricted (in common with several other Convention rights) only by limits laid down in law and necessary in a democratic society, in the interests of public safety, for the protection of public order, health or morals, or for the protection of the rights and freedoms of others.

In relation to medical treatment, the right to freedom of religion under Article 9 will come into conflict with the right to life protected under ECHR Article 2 when a parent – because of his or her religious beliefs – refuses to consent to a blood transfusion (or any other medical treatment) which is necessary for his or her child.

The problem for doctors when faced with a parent's refusal to consent to medical treatment which could save a child's life is whether they can lawfully give the treatment in the face of parental opposition. The Human Rights Act came into force only in 2000, and the problem of parental refusals to treatment for their children has been encountered for considerably longer than 20 years. The courts respect the belief and wishes of parents but the duty of the court is clear: the child's welfare is the paramount consideration and the religious beliefs of parents are subordinate to the child's right.

CASE FOCUS: T[70]

T, aged 13-and-a-half, was in hospital suffering with potentially catastrophic ill health from an inflammatory disease of the brain caused by a viral or bacterial infection. Urgent decisions needed to be taken about his treatment. His mother, however, was a Jehovah's Witness and unable to consent to the treatment of T on the basis of her religious beliefs. She was not, however, opposed to the court making the decision. The hospital sought the authorisation of the court for treatment to be given.

When consulted by doctors T had indicated 'thumbs up' to the treatment, although the doctors were concerned whether he had the capacity to consent because of his fluctuating levels of consciousness.

The court expressed its respect for the mother's sincere beliefs. The prospects for T's recovery without the treatment were slight. Accordingly it was in the child's best interests for authorisation to be given for the treatment to be carried out without delay.

CASE FOCUS: B[71]

B, a 'very young' child suffered severe burns requiring skin grafts. As skin grafts cause a loss of blood, the Hospital Trust wanted consent to giving B a blood transfusion should this be needed. The parents, although wanting the best medical treatment for B, refused to consent based on their religious beliefs. The Trust sought the permission of the court.

The judge stated that his decision 'must be determined by an assessment of what is in B's best interests because my paramount consideration is B's welfare'. The judge expressed his great respect for the father's views. However, these views were subordinate to B's welfare. The court granted the order authorising the treatment.

CASE FOCUS: *P*[72]

P, aged 13-and-a-half, sustained serious injuries in a road accident. There was a risk that unless a blood transfusion could be given, P's condition could suddenly and rapidly deteriorate and threaten his life. His parents refused consent to a blood transfusion on religious grounds. The court here expressed the view that the sanctity of life was a powerful factor in the case and that there is a strong presumption in favour of taking all steps to preserve life. The responsibility for assessing a child's best interests lay solely with the court, and that objective assessment necessitated subordinating the parents' religious beliefs to P's welfare. The court granted the order.

Circumcision

Circumcision is the surgical removal of the foreskin, the skin covering the tip of the penis. It may be both therapeutic and non-therapeutic. There is normally no medical need for circumcision in healthy newborn babies, although later in childhood or in adulthood it may be needed to treat several conditions. Both Judaism and Islam require circumcision. The practice in Judaism – brit milah – is usually performed as part of a religious ceremony when the baby is eight days old. It is performed by a person who has had religious and surgical training. In Islam, the procedure – the khitan – is usually performed at an early age but may also be carried out when a boy enters puberty.

It is claimed that there are medical reasons in favour of circumcision for young babies, although there are differences of opinion on the matter. However, it causes pain and may lead to complications and it has been accepted that it is capable of causing harm or the risk of harm.

Circumcision usually comes before the courts when parents are in conflict over whether it should be performed and seek a Specific Issue Order to determine whether the child should be circumcised.

CASE FOCUS: *J*[73]

J, a five-year-old boy, lived with his mother, a non-practising Christian. He had staying contact with his father, a non-practising Muslim. The father wanted the child to be circumcised, but the mother objected. The father applied for a Specific Issue Order that the boy be brought up in the Muslim religion and that he be circumcised.

The court refused the order. J would not be mixing in predominantly Muslim circles where circumcision would be the norm and the procedure was medically unnecessary. Circumcision was irreversible and should only be carried out where both parents support it or the court decides that the operation is in the best interests of the child. This was one of the few important decisions where both parents must agree, or if not agreeing then the decision of the court must be sought.

CASE FOCUS: *L AND B*[74]

The father and mother of L and B, boys aged six and four and three-quarters, had never legally married and their relationship had deteriorated. The father had dual Algerian and British citizenship and wanted to take the children to Algeria. He had threatened many times to take the children there and to remain. He also wanted the boys to be circumcised. He applied to the court for an order enabling him to take the children to Algeria.

Algeria was not a party to the Hague Convention on Abduction (on which see Chapter 1) and the Algerian courts would not respect any order of the British courts. Under Algerian law, the father had custody rights over the children giving him the right to make all decisions relating to the care and upbringing of the child: including circumcision.

The court refused the order sought. The court found that the children had many non-Muslim friends and would be in the minority if circumcised. There was no 'overriding imperative' for the children to be circumcised before puberty. The court decided to make no order, taking the view that it would be best to delay any decision until the boys were of sufficient maturity and insight to make their own decisions.

The matter could also come to the courts when a local authority seeks a Care Order over a child who it considers to be suffering or at risk of suffering significant harm, and that harm is attributable to the care being given to the child not being the care that would be expected of a reasonable parent.[75] The courts have recognised that circumcision is an important aspect of a child's identity as a member of a religion. However, as with all decisions relating to children, the determining factor will be the welfare of the child. Where a child has a potentially serious physical condition, for example, which could be alleviated by circumcision, the court may authorise it subject to conditions, such as it taking place in a hospital and under the responsibility of the specialists.[76]

At first sight there appears to be an irrationality in the law in so far as law regards all forms of Female Genital Mutilation (FGM) as a crime, but at the same time appears to be ambivalent over circumcision. Sir James Munby, then

President of the Family Division of the High Court, in the context of care proceedings, explained the approach of the law as follows:[77]

> Whereas it can never be reasonable parenting to inflict *any* form of FGM on a child, the position is quite different with male circumcision. Society and the law, including family law, are prepared to tolerate non-therapeutic male circumcision performed for religious or even for purely cultural or conventional reasons, while no longer being willing to tolerate FGM in any of its forms. There are, after all, at least two important distinctions between the two. FGM has no basis in any religion; male circumcision is often performed for religious reasons. FGM has no medical justification and confers no health benefits; male circumcision is seen by some (although opinions are divided) as providing hygienic or prophylactic benefits. Be that as it may, 'reasonable' parenting is treated as permitting male circumcision.

The relevance of financial resources

Medical procedures and/or treatments have cost implications for both the State and medical providers. When deciding whether or not a child should receive medical treatment, to what extent does the issue of cost enter into the picture? And can it defeat the rights of the child to medical treatment?

CASE FOCUS: *B*[78]

B, aged 10, suffered from leukaemia and had been treated with chemotherapy for several months. Following a relapse, the Cambridge Health Authority refused to provide funding for further treatment. This was partly on the basis that it was not in the best interests of the child, but also on the basis that the funding of further treatment, which had not been proven to be of benefit, would not be an effective use of resources.

The matter went to the Court of Appeal. Recognising that in a perfect world any treatment sought would be provided, especially if a life was potentially at stake, Sir Thomas Bingham MR ruled that that 'would be shutting one's eyes to the real world'. Health authorities faced all sorts of restrictions of resources and could not do all that they would wish. It was not for the Court to decide which allocation of resources was to be preferred. The Court would not interfere with the judgement of the Health Authority.

In a 2017 case, which came before the Family Division on four occasions, the shortages of appropriate accommodation for a disturbed and potentially suicidal teenager were revealed. Sir James Munby, expressed his concern and frustration over her situation, as the case focus below explains.

CASE FOCUS: X[79]

X had been subject to a Detention and Training Order and detained in a secure unit, ZX. While in ZX she had made a number of attempts at suicide. She was due to be released on 14 August 2017. The staff at ZX considered that any plan to send to her a community setting would be disastrous and that what was needed was a long-term adolescent mental health unit. At a hearing on 3 August there was no placement available anywhere in the country, and the only identified placement had a waiting list of six months. A further hearing was scheduled for 7 August. On 3 August the judge said this:

> If, when in eleven days' time she is released from ZX, we, the system, society, the State, are unable to provide X with the supportive and *safe* placement she so desperately needs, and if, in consequence, she is enabled to make another attempt on her life, then I can only say, with bleak emphasis: we will have blood on our hands.

Munby J directed that copies of his judgment of 3 August be sent to the Chief Executive Officer of NHS England, to the Secretary of State for the Home Department, to the Secretary of State for Health, to the Secretary of State for Education and to the Secretary of State for Justice. Finally, following an assessment of X on 4th August, institution ZZ (responding to a request by NHS England), suggested converting an adult psychiatric intensive care unit into a Low Security Unit which clinicians had deemed the most suitable for X's needs. On 10th August, X was transferred. At a hearing on 7 August the judge made an order that all NHS documentation concerning X's care and treatment plan be lodged with the court by 9th August, and commented that if necessary a further hearing would be held the following week. Munby J was determined to keep control over X's treatment and her future wellbeing.

Summary

Some aspects of the medical treatment of children raise fundamental questions over the right to life and the circumstances under which it should be protected. For any medical treatment (other than in emergency situations) to be lawful, valid consent to treatment is central. From the age of 16 children have the statutory right to give consent to medical treatment (but refusing treatment is not covered by the Act and is more complex). Younger children may acquire the right to consent if they meet the standard of the 'mature minor' laid down in the *Gillick case*.

The rights of children with disabilities are protected by equality law which requires the State to make relevant adjustments in order to lessen the impact of disabilities. Underlying consideration of the adequacy of treatment and facilities for children with mental health problems is the problem of finance and despite the vast investment in services, rising demand and need continue to challenge the resources of providers. Resources are also central to the availability of other vital medical treatments, but the allocation of resources involves value judgements by the courts and they are reluctant to interfere with the decisions of health authorities.

Notes

1 By contrast, the protection of civil and political rights – for example the right to vote, the right to free speech, and to freedom of association – require governments to abstain from interfering or restricting those rights and, for the most part, they do not require governments to invest vast sums of money in order to ensure that the rights are upheld.
2 Health and Social Care Act 2012, section 1. Health services are devolved: see NHS (Scotland) Act 1978, NHS (Wales) Act 2006, and the Health and Social Care (Reform) Act (Northern Ireland) 2009.
3 On NHS costs see the National Audit Office, *Investigation into NHS spending on generic medicines in primary care*, HC 1122, June 2018.
4 The King's Fund Press Release, April 2018.
5 Health matters are devolved to Scotland, Wales, and Northern Ireland and there are variations in approaches and standards across the UK.
6 RCPCH, *Poverty and Child Health*, May 2017.
7 Mental Health Foundation, *Tackling social inequalities to reduce mental health problems*, 2020.
8 Discussion of embryology is outside the scope of this book. For a full analysis see Warnock, M. *Report of the Committee of Inquiry into Human Fertilisation and Embryology*, Cmdn. 9314, 1988.
9 See *Roe v Wade* 410 US 113 (1973).
10 As will be seen, a child's right to life is not absolute and where a child would, because of medical problems, be incapable of sustaining life without artificial support, that child may be allowed to die.
11 *In the matter of an application by the Northern Ireland Human Rights Commission for Judicial review (Northern Ireland)* [2018] UKSC 27. The Supreme Court, by a majority, ruled that it could not issue a Declaration of Incompatibility because the Northern Ireland Commission did not have standing under the Human Rights Act 1998. Under section 9 of the Northern Ireland (Executive Formation) Act 2019, the Government repealed sections 59 and 61 of the Offences Against the Person Act 1861 and Parliament passed the Abortion (Northern Ireland) Regulations 2020 which now regulate abortion.
12 The Act does not extend to Northern Ireland or Scotland.
13 Criminal Justice Act 1948, section 1.
14 On the law relating to liability for the death of an unborn child see *St George's Healthcare Trust v S; R v Collins ex parte S* [1998] 2 WLR 936; *Attorney General's Reference No 3 of 1994* [1994] 3 WLR 421.
15 As amended by the Human Fertilisation and Embryology Act 1990, section 37.
16 *Vo v France* [2004] ECHR 326; (2005) 40 EHRR 12.
17 ibid., paragraph 84.
18 ibid.
19 The refusal to consent to medical treatment by a competent adult must be respected.
20 British Medical Association, *Consent, refusal by adults with decision-making capacity*. See also General Medical Council, *0–18 years: guidance to all doctors*: gmc-uk.org/ethical guidance.

21 (1986) AC 112.
22 ibid., at para 174.
23 *R (Axon) v Secretary of State for Health* [2006] EWHC 37 (Admin); [2006] 2 FLR 206.
24 *R (Axon) v Secretary of State for Health* [2006] EWHC 37 (Admin).
25 National Health Service Act 2006, section 251; Crime and Disorder Act 1998, section 115; Health and Social Care (Control of data Processing) Act (Northern Ireland) 2016.
26 NHS Code of Confidentiality, paragraphs 56–63.
27 General Medical Council, *Guidance for doctors, 0–18 years*, para. 31 and *Houston* [1996] 32 BMLR 93.
28 *Re R (a minor) (Wardship: Consent to Treatment)* [1992] Fam 11.
29 *Re W (a minor) (medical treatment)* [1993] Fam 64.
30 *An NHS Foundation Trust Hospital v P* [2014] EWHC 1650 (Fam).
31 *R v Arthur* (1981) 12 BMLR 1.
32 *Re J (a minor) (Wardship: medical treatment)* [1990] 3 All ER 930; [1991] (Fam) 33, at para 46.
33 See also *Re HK (Serious Medical Treatment) (No3)* [2017] EWHC 2992 (Fam).
34 Paragraph 43.
35 ibid., Annex.
36 *Aintree University Hospital NHS Foundation Trust v James* [2013] UKSC 67; [2013] 3 WLR 1299.
37 See [2017] 2 FLR 773; (2017) BMLR 59; [2017] ECHR 605; (2017) 65 EHRR SE9.
38 *Re Jake (Withholding Medical Treatment)* [2015] EWHC 2442 (Fam).
39 Epileptic encephalopathy of infancy.
40 Children Act 1989, section 33(3).
41 *Re A (children) (conjoined twins)* [2000] EWCA Civ 254.
42 Luke Taylor, Amy Swerdfeger, Guy Eslick, *Vaccines are not associated with autism: An evidence-based-meta-analysis of case-control and cohort studies: Vaccine*, vol 32.29, June 2014, p 3623.
43 See also Public Health England, *Health Protection Report*, Vol. 14.24, Second Quarterly Report for 2020/21 published 22 December 2020.
44 See Sarah Boseley, *The Guardian,* 19 August 2019.
45 *Re A, B, C, and D (Immunisation)* [2011] EWHC 4033 (Fam).
46 The application was made under the Wardship (or inherent) jurisdiction which falls under the Family Division of the High Court's jurisdiction. Wardship is discussed in Chapter X.
47 Per Sir Thomas Bingham, in *Re Z (A Minor) (Freedom of Publication)* [1996] 1 FLR 191 at 217 B - C.
48 See also *F v F (MMR Vaccine)* [2014] 1 FLR 1328.
49 *Re SL* [2017] EWHC 125 (Fam).
50 Discrimination can also arise from something which is the consequence of a person's disability: section 15.
51 Also relevant is Article 14 of the ECHR which provides that there must be no discrimination in the enjoyment of Convention rights on any ground such as sex, race, colour, language, religion, political or other opinion, national or social origin, association with a national minority, property, birth, or other status.
52 The Convention has 181 ratifications (formal State approvals). It came into force in May 2008.
53 Equality Act, sections 20–22.
54 Children and Families Act 2014, section 27.
55 Children Act 1989, section 17.
56 On the rates in 2020 see Appendix B.
57 *Cameron Mathieson v Secretary of State for work and Pensions,* [2015] UKSC 47.
58 *Re D (A Child)* [2019] UKSC 42.
59 He was accommodated under the Children Act 1989, section 20.

60 Lord Carnwath, dissenting, took the view that the European Court of Human Rights recognised that the proper exercise of parental responsibility can include consent to confinement of a child such as D (who lacked the capacity to consent).
61 NHS Digital, 2018, *Mental Health of Children and Young People in England, 2017.*
62 Mental Health England, *The Mental Health of Children and Young People in England,* 2016.
63 RCPCH, *Colleges join forces to make young people's mental health a priority,* August 2017.
64 Care Quality Commission, *Are we listening? Review of children and young people's mental health services,* March 2018.
65 An independent evidence-based research institute.
66 There are also problems with funding, with local CAMHS providers spending large amount of money on agency staff, rather than the treatment of children.
67 House of Commons, Library Briefing 6988, 23 January 2020.
68 Children's Commissioner, *The State of Children's Mental Health Service: Technical Report,* January 2020.
69 Female Genital Mutilation is discussed in Chapter 5.
70 *M Children's Hospital NHS Foundation Trust v Mr and Mrs Y* [2014] EWHC 2651 (Fam).
71 *An NHS Trust v Child B and Others* [2014] 3486 (Fam).
72 *A Hospital NHS Trust v LP* [2019] EWHC 2989 Fam.
73 *Re J (Child)* [1999] EWCA Civ 3022.
74 *L and B (Children: Specific Issues)* [2016] EWHC 849 (Fam).
75 Children Act 1989, section 31.
76 *Re T and S (Wardship)* [2011] EWHC 1008 (Fam).
77 *Re B and G (Children) (No 2)* [2015] EWFC 3; [2015] 1 FLR 905, paragraph 72.
78 *R v Cambridge Health Authority ex parte B* [1995] 1 WLR 898.
79 *Re X (A Child) (No 4)* [2017] EWHC 2084 (Fam).

4

CHILDREN AND EDUCATION

Introduction

Every child has the right to full-time education, free of charge, and provided by the State. In addition to publicly funded education there exist private fee-paying schools to which parents may choose to send their children. Education is a devolved matter and there are variations in State provision in England, Wales, Scotland, and Northern Ireland. The principal focus of this chapter is on the English education system. The main differences in other national systems are noted at the end of this chapter.

> State Parties recognise the right of the child to education.
>
> *UN Convention on the Rights of the Child*
> *1989 Article 28.1[1]*

> No person shall be denied the right to education. In the exercise of any functions which it assumes in relation to education and to teaching, the State shall respect the right of parents to ensure such education and teaching in conformity with their own religious and philosophical convictions.
>
> *European Convention on Human Rights and Fundamental*
> *Freedoms, 1953, Protocol 1, Article 2 (A1P2)*

Education as a right was not recognised in the UK until the late 19th century. The Elementary Education Act 1870 provided for education for children between the ages of 5 and 13. Its principal aim was to improve the skills of the future workforce. Elected school boards, funded by local rates, were created under the 1870 Act, to be replaced by Local Education Authorities in 1902. The 1880 Education Act made education compulsory until the age of ten, to be increased to 11 in 1893 and

DOI: 10.4324/9780429452710-4

to age 13 in 1899. The right to education for deaf and blind children was provided for under the 1893 Act.[2] Education provision today is heavily regulated by law and regulations made by the Secretary of State for Education.

Extending the right to education to all children was controversial. There were fears, for example, that educating the working class would risk destabilising the class system. However, the extension of the right to vote to working-class men under the Reform Act of 1867 made the extension of education inevitable. There were other objections to universal education. For many families dependent upon their children's contribution to the household through work, education would mean a loss of a valuable earner (on the employment of children see Chapter 8). The 1880 Education Act introduced attendance officers to ensure attendance and with the power to fine parents who kept their children out of school.

In 1918 education became compulsory until the age of 14. It was not until 1972 that the school leaving age was increased to 16. In England, however, from 2008 children were required to remain in some form of education or training until the age of 18.[3]

The law relating to education traditionally focuses on the duties of parents and local authorities to provide education for a child rather than on the rights of the child. The ECHR provides for education as follows:

> No person shall be denied the right to education. In the exercise of any functions it assumes in relation to education and to teaching, the State shall respect the right of parents to ensure such education and teaching in conformity with their own religious and philosophical convictions.[4]

The duty to provide education

Education is now compulsory for all children between the ages of 5 and 18. As noted above, in England, the school leaving age is 16, but a child must remain in some form of education or training until the age of 18. In Northern Ireland, Scotland, and Wales the leaving age is 16.

All children between the ages of five and 16 are entitled to a free place at a state school. It is the duty of parents to ensure that their children are receiving full-time education. **The Education Act 1944** states that:

> The parent of every child of compulsory school age shall cause him to receive efficient full-time education suitable:
>
> (a) to his age, ability, and aptitude, and
> (b) to any Special Educational Needs he may have,
>   either by regular attendance at school or otherwise.[5]

The duty may be fulfilled by either entering a child into a State-maintained school, an academy or an independent school, or by home schooling. Local authorities (LAs) have a duty to ensure that children are receiving suitable education.[6] In providing education, local authorities must comply with the general principle that children are to be in education in accordance with the wishes of his or her parents, *so far as that is compatible with the provision of efficient instruction and training and the avoidance of unreasonable public expenditure.*[7] In turn, parents must comply with the local authority requirements.

If a child is being educated at home and the local authority does not consider that he or she is receiving suitable education, the authority has the power to order a parent, through a School Attendance Order, to register the child with a named school.[8] It is an offence, for which a parent may be prosecuted, not to comply with a School Attendance Order.

In order to ensure that all children in their area are receiving full-time education, local authorities must identify, as far as possible, children who are not in education: 'children missing education' (CMEs).[9] On missing children, see Chapter 6. On truancy, see below.

Local authorities have a legal duty to exercise their education functions with a view to:

- promoting high standards;
- ensuring fair access to opportunity for education and training;
- promoting the fulfilment of learning potential of every person (below the age of 20, aged 20 or over where an Education, Health and Care (EHC) Plan is maintained (on these see further below).[10]

Teachers and other staff in education play a key role in safeguarding children (discussed in Chapter 2). Safeguarding is defined as the processes by which children are protected from abuse and neglect, preventing damage to their health and development, and ensuring that they grow up in safe and effective care so as to maximise their life chances.[11]

Education Supervision Orders[12]

Where a child's right to education is at risk because of non-attendance at school, parents may be prosecuted under the Education Act 1996.[13] Before prosecuting the authority has a duty whether to consider applying to the court for an Education Supervision Order (ESO).[14] An ESO will be overseen by an education supervision officer who is under a duty to advise, assist, befriend, and give directions to the child and his or her parents so as to ensure that he or she is properly educated.[15] An ESO will run for one year, but may be extended by the court. It is a criminal offence for a parent to fail to comply with any directions under the ESO.[16] However, a failure to comply will be disregarded if the parent took all reasonable steps to comply with it, or that the requirement(s) were unreasonable.[17]

State schools

Within the State sector, which receives funding from both central and local government, there are:

- local authority-maintained schools,[18] Church of England schools, or community schools which must follow the national curriculum;
- foundation schools and voluntary schools, funded by local authorities, but having more freedom in the provision of education; they follow the national curriculum but Church of England and Roman Catholic schools have additional requirements and are inspected on these;
- academies and free schools. These are run by academy trusts and are independent of the local authority being funded by central government, but can buy into LA services. Many have an external sponsor, such as a business, university, charity, or faith body. They are not bound by the national curriculum and can decide on school term dates and the length of the school day;
- grammar schools. These can be run by local authorities, a foundation body, or an academy trust. Pupils are selected on academic ability;[19]
- special schools educating children aged 11 and older and specialising in one of the four areas of special educational need (SEN):
  - communication and interaction;
  - cognition and learning;
  - social, emotional, and mental health;
  - sensory and physical needs;
- faith schools follow the national curriculum but can choose what to teach in religious studies. Anyone can apply for a place, but faith schools have their own admissions criteria;
- faith academies do not have to follow the national curriculum and have their own admissions processes;
- City Technology Colleges. These are free independent schools in urban areas, funded by central government and companies. The teaching emphasis is on science and technology;
- State boarding schools. See further below;
- pupil referral units, or Alternative Provisions either run by LAs or by private organisations and/or charities. On this see further below.

There are 38 State boarding schools in the UK. The education is free and parents pay only for the cost of boarding. Most are for pupils aged 11–18. Some State boarding schools are grammar schools with selective entry. Many of these schools are among the highest-ranking schools in GCSE and A-levels/international baccalaureate examination results. There are also State-subsidised special boarding schools.

School standards: OFSTED (Office for Standards in Education, Children's Services and Skills)

Ofsted, the Office for Standards in Education, Children's Services and Skills[20] was established in 1992.[21] The former system of school inspections was run by Her Majesty's Inspectors of Schools in collaboration with local authorities and regarded by the then government as offering a variable inspections regime. The Ofsted Board is responsible for setting strategic priorities, targets, and objectives for Ofsted while the responsibility for Ofsted's inspections work lies with the Her Majesty's Chief Inspector of Education, Children's Services and Skills.

Under the Education Inspections Framework introduced in 2019, Ofsted carries out inspections of all State-funded schools and post-16 government-funded education (but not higher education institutes or universities). It also inspects childminding services, children's daycare centres and teacher training providers, and the few private schools that are not inspected by the Independent Schools Inspectorate.

Through regular inspections Ofsted examines:

- the effectiveness of leadership and management;
- the quality of teaching, learning, and assessment;
- personal development, behaviour, and welfare;
- outcomes for children and learners.

Education providers will be assessed as outstanding, good, requires improvement, or inadequate. If a provider is judged as requiring improvement at two successive inspections, it will be subject to monitoring by Ofsted. Inadequate is subdivided into two categories: serious weaknesses and requiring special measures. Where a school requires special measures it will receive additional funding, additional help from the local authority, and frequent inspections to ensure that its standards are rising. Where a school requires special measures it must become an academy. Church of England schools are inspected independently for Religious Education teaching, usually close to the timing of Ofsted inspections.

School governance[22]

All maintained schools must have a Board of Governors, comprising at least two parent governors, the head teacher, one staff governor, one local authority governor, and a clerk to the governors. Governors are volunteers. Governors are elected (parent governors) or appointed, and the appointment runs for a fixed four-year term with eligibility for reelection and reappointment for a further term. The minutes of Board meetings are published (excepting confidential matters). The core functions of Boards of Governors are to:

- ensure clarity of vision, ethos, and strategic direction of the school;
- holding executive leaders to account for educational performance of the school and pupils and the performance management of staff;
- overseeing the financial performance of the school and making sure money is well spent.

Governors must be aged 18 and over. They may not be elected members of a local authority, or engaged in paid work for the school of over 500 hours in a 12-month period. Disqualification includes failure to attend Board meetings for six months, bankruptcy, conviction of a criminal offence carrying a three-month or greater sentence, or those barred from working with children. Appointment is subject to agreement to apply for a Disclosure and Barring Service (DBS).

Governors are involved in the work of the school, including helping a school work towards improving Ofsted requirements and assisting with buildings and procurement tasks. Governors are encouraged to visit the school, attend parent evenings, school plays, and other events.

Class sizes

Class sizes, other than infant classes (ages 4 to 7, reception and Key Stage 1), are not restricted by legislation. Infant classes are restricted to 30 pupils and local authorities must have procedures in place to ensure that limits are adhered to.[23] There are a number of limited exceptions to the 30-maximum rule, for example children with Special Educational Needs or looked-after children (i.e. cared for by the local authority) who may be admitted outside the normal admissions round.

Research evidence finds that a smaller class size has a 'positive impact on attainment and behaviour in the early years of school, but that this effect is small and diminishes after a few years'.[24]

Admissions

Maintained schools and academies must comply with the legal requirements and the Admissions Code issued by the Secretary of State for Education when drawing up their admissions arrangements. School places must be allocated in a way that is fair, clear, and objective. Schools must have 'reasonable, clear, objective, procedurally fair' oversubscription criteria. Children with Special Educational Needs (SEN), (on which see below) are given priority. If the school is not oversubscribed, all applicants must be admitted (with the exception of designated grammar schools). An alleged failure of a school to comply with the Code may be investigated by the School Adjudicator,[25] whose decision may be judicially reviewed by the High Court.[26]

There is no right to be admitted to a chosen school and parents must follow the admissions procedure, including the timing of applications, of the local authority. Every local authority will have a school admissions team to help with applications. Admissions criteria vary. They give priority to looked after children[27] and may give priority to those:

- who live within a school's allocated catchment area where parents have put the nearest school on their list;
- who have a brother or sister at the school already;
- are from a particular faith;
- who pass an entrance exam (for selective schools such as grammar schools);
- who went to a particular primary school which acts as a feeder school for a secondary school within the catchment area;
- whose parent has worked at the school for two years or more.

When applying to schools within a local authority area, up to six schools can be named in the application, including free schools and schools in other council areas. If a place at the first choice of school is not offered there is a right of appeal. The first-choice school must explain to parents why a child has not been offered a place at that school and explain the appeal process. There is a prescribed time frame for appeals and hearings. The appeal will be heard by a panel which is independent of both the school and the local authority and parents have the right to attend and make representations. The decision of the panel will be communicated to the school and the school and parents are expected to accept the ruling. If the parents do not accept the decision, there is a right to take the matter to the First-tier Tribunal.

As noted above, the European Convention on Human Rights, Article 2 of Protocol 1, (A2P1) states that 'no one shall be denied the right to education'. It also provides that the State shall respect the rights of parents to ensure such education and teaching in conformity with their own religious and philosophical beliefs. But while the Convention recognises the right to education, its focus is on the rights of parents to have their beliefs respected in the education of their children. However, if a child is wrongly denied a place or not provided with any school place, or wrongly excluded from school, A2P1 provides a means of challenging a public authority under the Human Rights Act 1998.

School uniform

The Department for Education leaves it to individual schools to decide on school uniform. Compulsory school uniform has been challenged before the European Court of Human Rights on the basis that the uniform required by the school conflicts with religious beliefs protected under the European Convention on Human Rights.[28]

CASE FOCUS: *SB*[29]

Shabina Begum attended Denbigh High School. The school had a majority of Muslim pupils and had been sensitive to their needs concerning appropriate dress, allowing pupils to wear the shalwar kameez. Shabina Begum had worn the shalwar kameez without complaint for two years, but then decided that her faith required here to wear the jilbab which concealed her body more effectively than the shalwar kameez. The school refused to allow this and Shabina withdrew from the school. She then sought judicial review of the school's uniform policy, claiming that she had been excluded from school and that the uniform policy violated her right to manifest her religion contrary to the ECHR, Article 9.2. The matter went to the House of Lords (now the Supreme Court). The House of Lords rejected her claim. Shabina had not been excluded: she remained on the school roll. Her right to practice her religion was not infringed: the school's uniform policy was compliant with Muslim requirements. Shabina also had the right to change school, but had chosen not to do so.

Religious Education (RE)

Every maintained school must provide a Religious Education syllabus for all registered pupils, except for those who have been withdrawn from RE by their parents.[30] The duty to provide RE does not apply to pupils under compulsory school age.[31] The syllabus for Religious Education in State schools must reflect the fact that 'the religious traditions in Great Britain are in the main Christian while taking account of the teaching and practices of the other principal religions represented in Great Britain.'[32] Where parents have requested that their child be withdrawn from RE, the school must respect that right. If parents want their child to receive a particular type of RE, the local authority may arrange for the pupil to attend another school, or if this is not possible, to make arrangements for RE outside school.[33]

CASE FOCUS

In a primary school, a number of parents from a local Jehovah's Witness community expressed a wish to withdraw their children from RE. The headteacher met with representatives from the community, including some of its leaders, to explain the school's approach to the subject. As a result of the meeting, the school developed a relationship of trust with the community and was able to identify those aspects of the RE programme which the parents were happy for the children to join and those from which the children would be withdrawn – mainly around the celebration of Christmas.[34]

Every local authority must appoint a Standing Advisory Council on Religious Education (SACRE), a permanent independent body representing different religious groups, the Church of England, teachers associations, and the local authority[35] and an Agreed Syllabus Conference (ASC) to review the RE syllabus. The SACRE meets in public and advises the local authority on the RE syllabus and monitors the provision and quality of RE taught, including the fostering of interfaith and community links. It may also require the authority to review the agreed syllabus.[36]

If disputes over education reach the courts, the starting point is 'respect for an individual's religious principles, coupled with an essentially neutral view of religious beliefs and a benevolent tolerance of cultural and religious diversity'.[37] Furthermore, 'The State's duty of neutrality and impartiality…is incompatible with any power on the State's part to assess the legitimacy of religious beliefs'.

Discipline[38]

Up until the 1980s the rights of children not to be subjected to physical assaults in the name of 'corporal punishment' were violated. There is now a total ban on corporal punishment in schools. The legal movement away from corporal punishment in the UK started with a case brought before the European Court of Human Rights in 1982.[39] The applicants were opposed to corporal punishment and argued that the State had failed to respect their philosophical convictions as required by the European Convention on Human Rights (ECHR).[40] The Court upheld their claim and Parliament responded by legislating to prohibit corporal punishment in state schools.[41] It was not until 1998 that corporal punishment in independent schools was prohibited.[42] In 2003 the ban was extended to protect the rights of children cared for by childminders and other children's activity/sports groups.[43] As discussed below, schools have the right to exclude pupils on defined grounds. In this section disciplinary measures short of exclusion are discussed.

It is for the governing body of a school in England and Wales to make a statement of general principles which a head teacher must take into consideration when deciding the rules on school discipline, and the statement must be published.[44] The governing body should give clear guidance to head teachers and staff, especially in relation to matters of discipline, the power to search for banned items, and the use of reasonable force in order to protect teachers from accusations that their powers have been abused. Head teachers must decide measures to 'promote' self-discipline, respect for authority, good behaviour, and the prevention of bullying and compliance with homework requirements and include rules for 'disciplinary penalties'.[45] The disciplinary penalties apply to standards of conduct and failure to obey instructions by a member of staff.

For any disciplinary penalty to be lawful it must satisfy three conditions:

- firstly, the penalty must not be in breach of any statutory requirement or prohibition and be reasonable in all the circumstances and proportionate (i.e. not excessive);
- secondly, the penalty may only be imposed by a member of staff authorised to do so;
- thirdly, the decision to impose the penalty must be taken on school premises or elsewhere when a pupil is under the control or charge of a member of staff.

In deciding whether a punishment is reasonable, the pupil's age, any Special Educational Needs or Disability he or she may have and any religious requirements affecting him or her must be considered.[46] Punishments can include detention outside normal school hours and the law lays down days on which it is permissible for the detention to take place in secondary, but not primary, schools. The confiscation, retention, and disposal of items in a pupil's possession is also lawful provided it complies with the above three conditions.[47]

A member of staff may restrain a pupil (using 'reasonable force') to prevent him or her committing an offence, causing personal injury to another person or him or herself, or damaging 'good order and discipline' at the school. 'Reasonable force' does not include corporal punishment. The Department for Education's *Use of reasonable force* advice, 2013 provides that:

> Force is usually used either to control or restrain. This can range from guiding a pupil to safety by the arm through to more extreme circumstances such as breaking up a fight or where a student needs to be restrained to prevent violence or injury.
>
> 'Reasonable in the circumstances' means no more force than is needed.
>
> Reasonable force can be used to prevent pupils from hurting themselves or others, from damaging property, or from causing disorder.
>
> Reasonable force can be used to search for prohibited items such as knives and weapons, alcohol, illegal drugs stolen items tobacco and cigarette papers, fireworks, pornographic images, any article that has been or is likely to be used to commit an offence, cause personal injury or damage to property.[48]
>
> Force cannot be used to search for items banned under the school rules.

Bullying

A child's right to physical and emotional security and freedom from abuse includes the right not to be bullied. Bullying does not have a legal definition, but is defined as behaviour that is repeated; intended to hurt someone either physically or emotionally and is often aimed at certain groups, for example because of race, religion, gender, or sexual orientation. Forms of bullying include physical assaults, teasing, making threats, name calling, and cyberbullying (abusive phone calls, emails, or text messages). Some forms of bullying are crimes. Violence, assault, theft, harassment or intimidation, or hate crimes should all be reported to the police.

State-funded schools, but not independent schools, are required to have a behaviour policy which includes measures to prevent bullying. All schools in England, Wales, and Scotland have a legal duty, under the Equality Act 2010, to prevent discrimination.[49] On the Equality Act 2010, see Chapter 1.

The statistics on bullying of children between the ages of ten and 15 in England remain fairly constant.[50] In the year ending March 2018, 17 per cent were bullied in a way that made them frightened or upset. Younger children between the ages of ten and 12 report the highest incidents of bullying. Most bullying was verbal. Of the 60 per cent who said they had been bullied, 89 per cent said that this was verbal bullying. Eighteen per cent suffered theft or damage to their property. Seven per cent of pupils reported cyberbullying.

Truancy

Truancy is the unjustified failure to attend school and is a breach of parents' duty to ensure that their children receive a full-time education.[51] Local authorities are responsible for ensuring school attendance. A majority of children who truant have Special Educational Needs or Disabilities (SEND, see below) and a high proportion will have an autism spectrum disorder. Being a victim of bullying is also a common cause of truanting. The causes of truanting are therefore complex, suggesting that what is needed to protect children's education rights is a supportive approach encouraging children to attend school while also ensuring that their special needs are met and that they are protected while in school.

Parental failure to make sure that a child is in school can result in an Education Supervision Order, a School Attendance Order, a fine, and/or ultimately prosecution.[52] A School Attendance Order requires a child to attend a named school and requires a parent to prove, within 15 days of the Order, that a child is registered with a school named in the Order or is being homeschooled. A Parenting Order may also be issued, requiring a parent to attend classes and comply with directions. The number of Parenting Orders has declined significantly, whereas the number of Parenting Contracts – a voluntary agreement between parents and schools or local authorities – had declined from 17,100 in the period 2016–2017 and had increased to 19,200 in the period 2017–2018. Under an Education Supervision Order an Education Supervisor will be appointed to advise and assist a child and his or her parents in relation to education.

Alternatively, a school, local authority, or the police may issue a penalty notice to parents for failing to ensure that their child regularly attends the State-funded school where they are registered or at the place where Alternative Provision is made for them. The penalty notice requires payment of £60 within 21 days, rising to £120. If there is a failure to pay within 28 days the local authority must either prosecute or withdraw the notice. A successful prosecution may result in a sentence of up to three months' imprisonment. In England in 2017, there were over 16,00 prosecutions of parents for failing to make sure that their children attended school.[53]

The statistics on absence from school are distorted by the number of parents taking their children out of school for holidays (on which see further below, page 109). The number of penalty notices showed a 74.7 per cent increase from 149,300 in 2016–2017 to 260,877 in 2017–2018. Of these, 85.4 per cent were issued for unauthorised family holidays, up 77.5 per cent from 2016 to 2017. Only 14.3 per cent of penalty notices were issued for other unauthorised absences. Seventy-five per cent of penalty notices issued in 2017–2018 were paid within 28 days. Ten per cent were withdrawn, seven per cent led to prosecutions, and eight per cent remained unresolved.

Special Educational Needs or Disabilities (SEND)[54]

The Children and Families Act 2014 defines special education needs as follows:

> A child or young person has special educational needs if he or she has a learning difficulty or disability which calls for special educational provision to be made for him or her.
>
> A child of compulsory school age or a young person has a learning difficulty if he or she:

> (a) has a significantly greater difficulty in learning than the majority of others of the same age, or
> (b) has a disability which prevents or hinders him or her from making use of the facilities of a kind generally provided for others of the same age in mainstream schools or mainstream post-16 institutions.[55]

In January 2019 there were over 1.3 million school-age children with SEND, representing 15 per cent of all pupils in school. Of these, just over one million were receiving SEND support and 354,000 pupils had an Education and Health Care Plan (see below), an increase of 11 per cent over 2018.[56,57] Ninety-one per cent of pupils with SEN support are educated in state-funded primary and secondary schools. EHCPs have replaced Learning Difficulty Assessments (LDAs) and Statements of Special Education Needs, subject to their being successfully transitioned from one to the other (see further below).[58]

The SEND system was reformed by the Children and Families Act 2014. The aims and objectives of the Act were:

- to introduce a coordinated assessment process to assess and child's educational, health, and care needs;

- to ensure that local education, health, and social work providers work effectively together to help young people in need;
- to make sure that Education, Health, and Care Plans for children aged 15 and above include measures to help prepare for adulthood;
- to introduce internships to help children with SEND prepare for the workplace.

Local authorities have a statutory duty to identify all children and young people in its area who have or may have SEN and/or disabilities, and NHS bodies have a duty to notify a local authority if they consider that a child or young person has, or may have, SEND.[59] In exercising its functions local authorities must take into account the view, wishes, and feelings of the child and his or her parent(s), or the young persons.

Every school must have a Special Educational Needs Coordinator (SENCO) whose role is to support pupils and teachers. Not all schools are large enough to have a full-time dedicated SENCO and many are part-time. A House of Commons Select Committee inquiry found that there was a lack of knowledge about the law and local authority procedures and that not all local authorities had invested sufficiently in training for SENCOs, leading to mistakes which let down both children and young people and their families.

Local authorities may co-operate with other local authorities to make the necessary provision for the education, health, and care provision for children with SEND. Government advice on special needs and disabilities explains the different forms of help for children of different ages.[60]

Children under five

Special education needs (SEN) support can be provided for a child from the age of two. Nurseries, playgroups, or childminders registered with Ofsted follow the government's Early Years Foundation Stage (EYFS) framework provides for children with special education needs and disabilities (SEND). SEN support for children under the age of five includes:

- a written progress check when the child is two years old;
- a child health visitor carrying out health checks for children aged under three years;
- a written assessment in the summer term of a child's first year of primary school;
- making reasonable adjustments for disabled children, such as aids like tactile signs.

If a child doesn't attend a nursery, playgroup, or childminder, a doctor or health visitor can advise on the help and support available.

Children between five and 15

Help may include:

- a special learning programme;
- extra help from a teacher or assistant;
- working in a smaller group;
- observation in class or at break;
- help taking part in class activities;
- extra encouragement in learning;
- helping with communicating with other children;
- support with physical or personal care difficulties.

Young people aged 16 or over in further education

Parents and carers should contact the college the young person is going to attend before he or she starts to enquire whether the college can provide for his or her needs.

Education, Health, and Care Plans[61]

For all children and young people up to the age of 25, if on assessment it is found that extra help is needed this can be provided through an Education, Health and Care Plan (EHCP). ECH plans are designed to identify the educational, health, and social needs of a child or young person and set out the support to meet those needs. These are administered by local authority staff who will carry out an assessment where this is considered necessary. Parents/carers can request an assessment, and young people over the age of 16 may make the request them-selves. A local authority is required to let parents/carers know whether an EHC is going to be made within 16 weeks of the original application.

Where an EHCP is to be provided, a draft of the plan will be made follow-ing which parents/carers have 15 days in which to comment. From the original assessment the local authority has 20 weeks to make the final ECH plan.[62]

The EHCP *must* specify:

- the child's or young person's Special Educational Needs;
- the outcomes sought for him or her;
- the special educational provision required by him or her;
- any health care provision reasonably required by the learning difficulties and disabilities which result in him or her having Special Educational Needs;
- in the case of a child or a young person aged under 18, any social care provi-sion which must be made for him or her by the local authority;

- any social care provision reasonably required by the learning difficulties and disabilities which result in the child or young person having Special Educational Needs, to the extent that the provision is not already specified in the plan under the paragraph above.

An ECHP *may* also specify other health care and social care provision reasonably required by the child or young person.[63] Where necessary to achieve the ECH plan, a personal budget' may be provided by the local authority, enabling schools to buy in additional help for the child.[64] Once a plan is agreed, the local authority is under a statutory duty to maintain the plan and arrange the specified educational and health needs.

The ECHP must be reviewed every 12 months and must also reassess the educational health care and social care needs of a child if requested to do so by a parent, or the young person over the age of 16, or the school which the child or young person attends. In doing so the local authority must consider whether the stated aims and objectives of the plan have been achieved and during the reassessment must consult with the parent of the child or the young person aged 16–25.[65]

Should parents/carers be dissatisfied with the local authority's decision about whether to make an EHC, or the contents of the EHC this can be raised initially with the school and then with the local authority with a view to resolving any difficulties through mediation. If mediation does not produce a satisfactory result an appeal can be made to the First-tier Special Educational Needs and Disability (SEND) Tribunal.[66] The grounds on which an appeal may be made are as follows:

- a decision by a local authority not to make an EHC needs assessment;
- following an assessment, a decision by the local authority that there is no need to make special education provision under an EHC plan;
- where an ECH plan is made, the contents of that plan;
- a decision not to re-assess the needs of the child or young person following a request to do so;
- following a review or re-assessment of the plan, a decision not to amend the plan;
- a decision of a local authority to cease to maintain a plan.[67]

The SEND Tribunal has no power to deal with:

- the way the local authority carried out an EHC assessment;
- the length of time it took to carry out the assessment;
- how the local authority or school is arranging to provide the help set out in the ECHP;
- the way the school or college is meeting the child or young person's needs under the plan;
- the outcomes sought for the child (section E of the plan);

- any disputes about the working of sections A (the views and aspirations of the child and his or her parents), J (details of how a personal budget will be spent), K (advice and information gained during needs assessment) of the plan.

Where the Tribunal cannot deal with a complaint, it can be taken to the Department for Education. There is also the Local Government Ombudsman who may be able to investigate a complaint (see further below).

The Ministry of Justice statistics for the period September 2017 to end of August 2018 reveal that appeals to the SEND Tribunal have an 89 per cent success rate. In the year 2018–2019 there were 6,374 appeals to the SEND Tribunal, an increase of 26 per cent over the previous year. Appeals to the Tribunal have been made more difficult by the 2013 cuts in legal aid which is now means-tested. If eligible for legal aid and advice, this will be given over the telephone and will not cover representation before the Tribunal.

Evaluating the system

In its 2019 Annual Report Ofsted highlighted the problems with the provision for children and young people with SEND.[68] The Report states that:

> … inspections of provision for children and young people with special educational needs and/or disabilities (SEND) has exposed a lack of coherence and coordination. Local leaders across education, health and care do not always see themselves as collectively accountable for this provision. Too often, parents encounter fractures in assessment and planning. In these cases, the system is not working well as a whole to make the best decisions and achieve the best outcomes for children and young people.

This is not the only source of criticism. In 2019 the House of Commons' Education Select Committee report, *Special Educational Needs and Disabilities*, stated that:[69]

> … the 2014 reforms have resulted in confusion and at times unlawful practice, bureaucratic nightmares, buck-passing and lack of accountability, strained resources and adversarial experiences, and ultimately dashed the hopes of many.[70]

Furthermore: 'The Department [for Education] did not need to preside serenely over chaos for five years to see that things were not quite going as planned'.

One problem identified by the Select Committee was that the focus on EHCPs and the transition from Statements to Education and Health Care Plans had caused the needs of children on SEN support to be neglected. As a result, parents were seeking EHCPs as a way of ensuring support for their children, with the result that the system is overloaded. This in turn caused local authorities to 'practices of rationing, gatekeeping and, fundamentally, children and young people's needs being unidentified and unmet'. Furthermore, 'much of this is unlawful, goes wholly against the intentions of the Act and contributes to a lack of faith in the system'.[71]

The Education Select Committee heard much evidence of 'misleading or unlawful advice' being passed from local authorities to schools and then to parents. Parents were refused a needs assessment or had been advised not to apply for an EHCP, or refused one. This wrong advice led to appeals to the Tribunal and the local authorities decisions being overturned. The Committee recorded a depressing picture of 'local authorities not meeting their statutory duties, and of schools deliberately or otherwise off-rolling [on which see below], excluding and even discouraging parents from sending pupils to their schools'.[72] The Committee has called for the Department for Education to take greater responsibility for ensuring that the system is better overseen, that local authority practice was lawful, that timescales were being adhered to, and that children's needs were being met. The Chair of the Committee, Robert Halfon MP, has called for:

> '... an end to this major social injustice, one which affects children and their families, particularly those who are not as well equipped to navigate this bureaucratic maze'.

The Local Government and Social Care Ombudsman, Michael King, added his voice to the current concerns over the SEND system. In 2018–2019 the Ombudsman's Office received 45 per cent more complaints than in the previous year (315 cases up from 217). The Office undertook 126 detailed investigations and upheld nearly nine out of ten (87 per cent) complaints. The Ombudsman concluded that his investigations 'suggest a system in crisis'. The main problems the Ombudsman identified were:

- severe delays of up to 90 weeks but regularly more than one year;
- poor planning and anticipation of needs, such as councils without the specialist provision which is available to them;
- poor communication and preparation for meetings;
- inadequate partnership planning;
- lack of oversight from senior managers.

Funding remains a central problem in providing for children with SEND. A National Audit Office (NAO) Report in 2019 stated that local authorities are increasingly overspending their budgets for supporting pupils with special needs: in 2017–2018 81.3 per cent of local authorities overspent. The main reasons for overspending according to the NAO is firstly that there are more pupils in special schools and that Alternative Provision rose by 20 per cent between 2014 and January 2018. Secondly, the Department for Education did not fully assess the likely financial consequences of the 2014 reforms.[73]

The government responded to the Education Committee's Report with an acknowledgement that the implementation of the 2014 reforms had not been uniform across the country. It also made a commitment to provide additional financial resources and to conduct an independent review of children's social care with the aim 'of better supporting, protecting and improving the outcomes of vulnerable children and young people'.[74]

Exclusions from school[75]

Being excluded from school damages a child's right to education and is intended to be a measure of last resort. Exclusions may be permanent or for a fixed term. All children of compulsory school age must be on the admission register of a school. Regulations provide that a pupil may be removed from the admission register on a number of grounds, ranging from attaining school leaving age, transferring to another school, being medically unfit, being detained for four months or more by order of a court. A child may also be deleted from the register on the basis that he or she 'has been permanently excluded from the school'.[76]

The number of both types of exclusion has been on the rise since 2014. The number of permanent exclusions from 2016 to 2017 was 7,720, up from 6,685 in the previous year. The most common reason for permanent exclusion to be given was persistent disruptive behaviour, accounting for 2,755 (35.7 per cent) of all permanent exclusions. Physical assault against another pupil or against an adult was the second largest category of exclusion (around 17 per cent), closely followed by verbal abuse and/or threatening behaviour against an adult. Other conduct leading to exclusions includes drug and alcohol-related behaviour, theft, damage, sexual misconduct, racist abuse, and bullying.[77] In relation to fixed-term exclusions, 108,640 were for persistent disruptive behaviour.

Eighty-three per cent of exclusions in 2016–2017 were from secondary schools. In the same year there were 361,865 fixed-period exclusions across all State-funded primary, secondary and special schools – corresponding to 'around 2,100 fixed-period exclusions per day'. Of these, 64,340 were exclusions from primary schools, 301,890 from secondary schools, and 14,635 from special schools. The average length of the exclusions was 2.1 days, with most (46.6 per cent) lasting only one day.[78]

Exclusions based on pupil characteristics revealed that over half of all exclusions occurred in year nine or above (aged 14 or above); 57.2 per cent of permanent exclusions and 52.6 per cent of fixed-term exclusions. The exclusion rate for boys is three times higher than that for girls. Pupils eligible for and claiming free school meals accounted for 40.0 per cent of all permanent exclusions and 36.7 per cent of all fixed-term exclusions. Pupils with identified Special Educational Needs (SEN) accounted for 46.7 per cent of permanent exclusions and 44.9 per cent of fixed-term exclusions. The permanent exclusion rate for pupils with SEN support was six times higher than the rate for pupils with no SEN support, and over five times higher than those with no SEN support. The primary need for over half the excluded pupils with SEND was recorded as 'social, emotional and mental health'.[79] Black Caribbean pupils had a permanent exclusion rate nearly three times higher than the school population as a whole while pupils of Asian ethnic groups had the lowest rates of both permanent and fixed-term exclusions.

In defence of exclusions, the government notes that 'good discipline in schools is essential to ensure that all pupils can benefit from the opportunities provided by education'.[80] The Select Committee of the House of Commons commented in 2019 that:

> An unfortunate and unintended consequence of the Government's strong focus on school standards has led to school environments and practices that have resulted in disadvantaged children being disproportionately excluded … There appears to be a lack of moral accountability on the part of many schools and no incentive to, or deterrent to not, retain pupils who could be classed as difficult or challenging.[81]

The rules on exclusion

As noted above, pupils may be excluded for a fixed period or permanently.[82] A pupil can lawfully be excluded for one or more periods of up to a maximum of 45 school days in one school year. Where a child is disruptive, say at lunch-time, he or she may be excluded for that specific period of time. A fixed-period exclusion may not be extended or converted into a permanent exclusion. In exceptional cases, a further fixed-term exclusion notice may be issued to begin immediately after the first period ends, or a permanent exclusion may be issued immediately after the end of the fixed period.[83]

Where a child is excluded permanently, local authorities are under a duty to arrange alternative educational provision (AP: see below) from the sixth day of exclusion. For children with fixed-term exclusion(s) on disciplinary grounds, the governing body of the school must make provision for full-time education.[84]

The Timpson Review of School Exclusion in 2018 accepts that exclusion is a necessary part of behaviour management in schools. However, the Review finds evidence that the outcomes for excluded children are 'often poor'. For example, of those reaching the end of Key Stage 4 (15- to 16-year-olds), only seven per cent of children who had been permanently excluded, and 18 per cent of children who had multiple fixed-term exclusions, went on the achieve good passes in English and Maths GCSEs. Of the children in Alternative Provision (AP), just 4.5 per cent achieved good passes in English and Maths in 2016/17. There is also a correlation between exclusion and involvement in criminal offences: in 2014, 23 per cent of children sentenced to less than 12 months in custody had previously been permanently excluded from their schools.

The Timpson Review also expressed concerns over the use of exclusions which disrupts a child's education and in the worst cases leaves a child without education. Timpson found that from 2016 to 2017, 95 pupils were excluded for 45 days and 80 were unlawfully excluded for more than 45 days. In the same year, 2,110 children received more than ten fixed-period exclusions. Short fixed-term exclusions do not require AP to be organised; hence leaving children without any education in these periods. The Review called on the DfE to consider revising the number of permitted exclusions, and/or to reconsider whether AP should be provided during these periods.

Exclusion has serious implications for children who may be drawn into gangs and/or criminal behaviour. Timpson reported that while there is a correlation between children participating in gangs and criminal behaviour, 'there is no evidence that exclusion is a direct cause for a child becoming involved with crime'. Of young offenders aged 16–17 sentenced in 2014, 23 per cent sentenced to less than 12 months in custody had been permanently excluded from school, and 16 per cent of those sentenced to more than 12 months' custody.[85] Ofsted reports that children who are excluded from school are twice as likely to carry a knife than children who are not excluded.[86] Writing in 2018, Ofsted reports that knife crime had increased by 22 per cent across England and Wales and by 36.7 per cent across London. Many schools now have a zero-tolerance policy of knife carrying in school and pupils will be automatically excluded on that basis. Ofsted heard evidence from parents that gangs were taking advantage of exclusions to get children involved in their gangs. While Ofsted acknowledges that while zero-tolerance policies can be 'extremely effective', schools need to do more to 'protect children from gang members who seek to exploit the rules to build their empires'. There is evidence that some head teachers refuse to acknowledge that knife crime affects their school: Ofsted states, 'this is depressing and shows that these schools have lost sight of their job in building children's resilience and teaching them how to stay safe'.

Challenging exclusions

There is a right to request the governing body of a school to consider reinstating a permanently excluded pupil. Where the governing board decides not to reinstate a child the parents can ask for the decision to be reviewed by an independent review panel.[87] The application for an independent review must be made within 15 days of receiving notice that the governing board will not reinstate a pupil. If there is a challenge to exclusion based on discrimination contrary to the Equality Act 2010, the application for review must be made within 15 days of the final decision of the SEND Tribunal or County Court.

The review must start within 15 days of the parents' application. The local authority or academy trust must arrange the venue, and the hearing must be in private. The review panel will be made up of three or five members comprising a lay member to chair the panel, current or former school governors, and head teachers (or those who have served as head teachers within the last five years). Irrespective of whether the school recognises that a pupil has SEND, all parents have the right to request the presence of an SEND expert at the review meeting. The independent review panel cannot order a governing board to reinstate the excluded pupil. It can, however, direct the board to reconsider the exclusion if it considers that the decision to exclude was flawed.

If parents consider that a disabled pupil has been excluded on the basis of discrimination contrary to the Equality Act 2010, they can take the case to the First-tier Tribunal (Special Educational Needs and Disability), or if the exclusion is discriminatory on other grounds the decision can be challenged in the County Court.

Provision of education for excluded children

Excluded pupils still have a right to education. During the first five days of exclusion, schools should set and mark work for pupils. Where a pupil has been excluded for consecutive fixed-term exclusions totalling more than five days, the local authority rather than the school must organise alternative full-time education from the sixth day.[88] Schools may make provision for 'exclusion' within the school, requiring the pupil to be taught separately from other pupils, with the advantage that the child is kept within the school environment rather than formally excluded. Most frequently, an excluded child will be placed in Alternative Provision.

Alternative Provision (AP)[89]

The Department for Education defines Alternative Provision as follows:

> Alternative provision is … education arranged by local authorities for pupils who, because of exclusion, illness or other reasons, would not otherwise receive suitable education; education arranged by schools for pupils on fixed-term exclusion; and pupils being directed by schools for off-site provision to improve their behaviour.[90]

The governing body of a school (but not a nursery school) has the power to require a pupil to attend educational provision outside the school at which he or she is registered for the purpose of improving his or her behaviour.[91] This placement can be either full-time or organised on a part-time basis so that the pupil can remain in his or her principal school. AP can also be tailored to meet the needs/interests of the child in a constructive and beneficial manner. Timpson cites an example of one secondary school which organised AP that offered gardening courses to support the good mental health of the child.[92] Others might arrange short-term work experience to run alongside education within the school.

However, there is inadequate data on the use of AP and its quality, and inadequate oversight by the DfE of AP arrangements. There is also the concern, raised with the Timpson Review, that AP is sometimes being used by schools to lower their number of recorded exclusions (which must be reported to the local authority). Additionally, there is concern that the lack of sufficient reporting and oversight means that there is no record of where some vulnerable children are, or whether they are even receiving a suitable education.[93]

There is evidence that 'informal exclusions' are operating where schools operate a part-time timetable for these children, the effect of which is to deny a child the full-time education to which he or she has a right. In evidence to the Timpson Review 'many parents and carers spoke of long-term arrangements spanning several years to which they had not consented and which amounted to their child not being offered a full-time education'.[94] Others spoke of pressure from schools to remove their child from the school, under the threat of permanent exclusion, resulting in them agreeing to homeschool their child without having the time and opportunity to consider whether or not this is the most suitable way forward. Timpson called for parents to be given sufficient time to reflect on removing their child, and for there to be a 'right to return' to ensure that their child has a way back into full-time education.[95]

'Managed' moves

The Timpson Review defined managed moves as being a:

> ... voluntary agreement made between schools, parents or carers for that pupil to change school. In many cases, managed moves are appropriate, well thought out and effective. Used well, they can be a good alternative to permanent exclusion. They can also be a way of removing a child from an immediate environment that may be heightening their vulnerability.

> However, there are cases of parents and carers who have been pressured into agreeing a managed move under the threat of an exclusion, and others where children have experienced a number of unsuccessful and uncoordinated managed moves.[96]

Off-rolling and gaming practices

Ofsted defines off-rolling and gaming as:

> ... the practice of removing a pupil from the school roll without using a permanent exclusion, when the removal is primarily in the best interests of the school rather than the best interests of the pupil. This includes pressuring a parent to remove their child from the school roll.
>
> While it may not always be unlawful, Ofsted believes off-rolling is never acceptable.
>
> Gaming covers any process when a school's actions or decisions regarding exclusion are made in favour of the school or academic league tables and is unlawful.[97]

CASE FOCUS: *ST OLAVE*

In 2017 St Olave's, a grammar school in London, sought to exclude 17 pupils who had failed to get B grades in their mock A level examinations. The policy of exclusion on academic grounds contravened the Education Act and Regulations and was therefore unlawful. The school's justification was that entrance to year 13 (their final school year) was discretionary. The affected families sought judicial review against the school's governing body and the local authority and a date was set for a hearing. However, in the face of media pressure and the prospect of legal action, the school reversed its policy and readmitted the students.

Children move schools for a variety of reasons, including leaving school to be homeschooled. They might also be registered with another school where they attend for particular subjects, or where a pupil has been directed to AP for reasons other than exclusion. As has been discussed above, children may also be excluded, perhaps permanently, and this is lawful provided the school has followed the legal requirements and guidance. None of these scenarios amount to off-rolling.

However, as noted above, once a child has been removed from the school roll, there is no right for them to return to that school. The Timpson Review on Exclusion calls on the DfE to review this rule with a view to introducing a 'right to return' to ensure that decisions made are always in the child's best interests – the guiding principle regulating those dealing with children and young people.[98]

Independent schools

An independent school is defined as:

> ... a school that provides full-time education for five or more pupils of compulsory school age, or for one or more pupils of that age who are looked after by a local authority or have a statement of SEN or an Education, Health and Care Plan, and which is not a maintained school or a non-maintained special school.[99]

In order to operate lawfully, all independent schools and other educational institutions must be registered by the Secretary of State for Education.[100] Regulations set out standards that must be satisfied in order to qualify for registration. These include:

- the quality of education provided;
- the spiritual, moral, social, and cultural development of pupils;

- the welfare, health, and safety of pupils;
- the suitability of staff, supply staff and proprietors, premises and accommodation at schools;
- the provision of information;
- the manner in which complaints are handled;
- the quality of leadership in and management of schools.[101]

The regulations do not apply to schools offering only religious instruction, even though they offer full-time education.

The Independent Schools Inspectorate (ISI) undertakes inspections of inde-pendent schools.[102] Where the required standards are not being met and there is a serious risk to pupils' welfare, schools will be required to produce, and imple-ment, an action plan to remedy the defects.[103] The school may appeal to the First-tier Tribunal against decisions of the ISI. The Tribunal may uphold the order, vary the order, or strike down the order.[104]

Taking a child out of school in term time

Parents have a legal duty to ensure that their children attend school regularly, and all schools (other than boarding schools) must maintain an attendance register.[105]

CASE FOCUS: *PLATT*[106]

Mr Platt had sought permission from the school to take his daughter out of school in term time for a seven day holiday. The school refused. On the child's return the local authority issued a fixed penalty notice which Mr Platt refused to pay, thereby committing an offence. He was prosecuted but the case was dismissed on the basis that, despite the holiday, the child had attended school 'regularly'. The case went to the Supreme Court which ruled that the term 'regularly' meant 'in accordance with the school rules', rather than any other interpretation. Accordingly Mr Platt had committed an offence and should have been convicted.

The case has not stopped parents taking their children out of school in term time. In the period 2018–2019 the number of fines issued rose to 333,400, up from 260,900 the previous year. The Department for Education says that 86 per cent of absences are due to holidays for which the penalties are low while the cost of holidays during school holidays is high compared with the cost during term time, encouraging parents to disrupt their children's schooling in breach of their duty.[107]

Unregistered schools

It is a criminal offence to run an independent school that is not registered.[108] In 2019 Ofsted published data revealing the scale of the problem of illegal schools in England:

> Ofsted estimates that there are as many as 6,000 children being educated in the unregistered settings it has inspected to date. These children are potentially at risk because there is no formal external oversight of safeguarding, health and safety or the quality of education provided.[109]

Between 1 January 2016 and 31 August 2019, Ofsted investigated a total of 618 'settings' and inspected 293, with some being inspected more than once. Settings vary in format. Some offer a general education, some offer AP, some are tuition centres, children's homes, sports clubs, language provision, and care farms – a setting offering therapeutic farming activities. In terms of faith groupings, there were inspections of 14 Christian, 19 Jewish, 39 Muslim settings. The settings were distributed fairly evenly over England, with the largest number, 142, being in London. Of the number inspected, 83 were issued with warning notices. Health and safety concerns were expressed in relation to 64 of the settings inspected; safeguarding concerns in relation to 83. There are loopholes in the regulation of such schools. To register a setting must provide full-time education, not defined in law, but under DfE guidance is 18 hours a week or more. Some settings are reported to operate for 17 hours and 50 minutes in order to avoid scrutiny.

Ofsted's Deputy Director in charge of the unregistered schools taskforce, Victor Shafiee has said:

> The problem here is first and foremost about safeguarding. Many of these places are unsafe – with poor facilities and hygiene, badly trained or untrained staff, who may not have had any employment checks made on them, and little care for children's health and well-being.[110]

Ofsted inspectors have the power to investigate unregistered schools, and if there is evidence that an offence has been committed will issue a warning notice to the school. Ofsted will also notify the Department for Education, and the relevant local authority which has a number of powers to safeguard children at risk of harm (see Chapter 2). The school may be also referred to the Crown Prosecution Service (CPS) with a view to prosecution. The CPS will only prosecute if there is sufficient evidence to make a prosecution likely to succeed and if it is in the public interest to do so. In addition, the consent of the Secretary of State required before a prosecution may proceed.[111]

Where an unregistered school is operating, local authorities have duties towards the children concerned. Local authorities are responsible for safeguarding and promoting the welfare of all children and young people in their area.[112] If they have reasonable cause to believe that a child is suffering, or likely to suffer significant harm there is a statutory duty to investigate.[113] Among the wide-ranging powers available to the local authority to protect the rights and well-being of children are applications to the courts for Emergency Protection Orders, Child Assessment Orders, and Care or Supervision Orders.[114] These are discussed in Chapter 6.

The liability of schools

Local authorities and schools are public bodies, and therefore have a duty under the Human Rights Act 1998, to protect the rights of children in their care. The right to life, freedom from abuse and inhuman treatment or torture, the right to respect for private and family life, and the right to freedom of expression must be protected.[115] In addition there must be no discrimination in the way in which rights are protected. A failure to protect these rights will cause the authority to act unlawfully.

There is a statutory duty to report abuse to the police. The failure of an authority to take action to prevent abuse, where there are reasonable grounds to believe that abuse is occurring, will also make the authority liable under the European Convention on Human Rights (on which see Chapter 1). For example, under the Female Genital Mutilation Act 2003 (discussed in Chapter 5), healthcare professionals, teachers and social workers have a duty to notify the police if a girl tells them that she is the victim of FGM, or if there are physical signs that FGM may have been carried out on the girl.[116] The notification may be oral or in writing and must be made within one month of becoming aware that FGM has been or may be carried out. Suspicions of other forms of abuse must also be reported in order to enable the local authority to carry out an assessment.[117]

CASE FOCUS: Z[118]

In Z four children had suffered horrendous neglect and abuse at the hands of their parents. Their abuse was brought to the local authority's attention in 1987. In spite of having a range of protective measures available to them, the local authority only took the children into emergency care in 1992. A consultant child consultant referred to their treatment as 'horrific experiences' and the Criminal Injuries Compensation Board found that the children had been subject to 'appalling neglect over an extended period and suffered physical and psychological injury directly attributable to a crime of violence'. The European Court of Human Rights ruled that there was 'no doubt as to the failure of the system to protect the children from serious, long-term neglect and abuse'. There were violations of Article 3 of the Convention (the right to freedom from torture, inhuman treatment, or punishment).[119] There was also a violation of Article 13 which guarantees an effective remedy before a national court.

A local education authority also has a duty of care towards its pupils, a breach of which will make the authority liable in negligence. Under the law of negligence, all people with a particular skill or profession:

- owe a duty of care to those who it can be foreseen will be harmed if due skill and care are not exercised;
- if the harm can be shown to have been caused by the lack of care;
- if it is just and reasonable to impose a duty of care in all the circumstances.

The liability will be vicarious: that is to say the local authority will be legally responsible for the negligence of its staff. This may include teachers or support staff such as educational psychologists. In the case of independent schools, the management of the school will be liable. The liability may be for a failure to diagnose a particular learning difficulty, or for mental, physical, or sexual abuse.

CASE FOCUS: *P*[120]

Pamela was born in 1973 and started school in 1978. By 1980 there were concerns over her lack of progress in school. She was seen by an educational psychologist and received psychotherapy. In 1985 she changed school and because of poor progress in reading and writing, was again seen by an educational psychologist and received extra tuition. None of the staff at either school suggested that Pamela might be dyslexic.

In 1990, after leaving school, Pamela was assessed at the Dyslexia Institute who reported that she was dyslexic and had a reading age of 7.9 years. She obtained a job in 1990 but was dismissed in 1991 as a result of her difficulties with literacy. Pamela was then unemployed.

In 1994 Pamela took legal action against the London Borough of Hillingdon alleging breach of statutory duty or, in the alternative, negligence on the basis that Hillingdon had failed to identify her needs and to exercise reasonable care in the detention, assessment diagnosis, and treatment of her learning difficulties/dyslexia.

The House of Lords (now the Supreme Court) ruled that the local authority was liable under common law negligence. The educational psychologist owed a duty of care to Pamela: she knew or ought to have known that her advice would be relied on. Dyslexia should have been diagnosed in 1985 and the psychologist 'had failed to exercise the degree of care and skill to be expected of an ordinary competent member of her profession'. That failure had caused harm to Pamela and damages would be awarded.

CASE FOCUS: *ST. WILLIAMS*[121]

St. Williams was a residential school for children in the care of the local authority. In 1993 and 2004 the headmaster was convicted of numerous counts of serious sexual offences against boys over a period of 20 years. The school was closed in 1994. Former pupils of the school made claims against managers of the school and the Institute of the Brothers of the Christian Schools whose members are lay brothers of the Catholic Church who taught at the school. The boys were particularly vulnerable, being 'virtual prisoners' at the school and, because of their backgrounds, unlikely to be believed if they made allegations. Were both the school and the Institute liable for the sexual abuse of the boys? Yes. It was 'fair, just and reasonable' for the Institute to share vicarious liability for the abuse.

Education in Scotland and Wales (in outline)

Very broadly speaking, although devolved to national administrations, education provision remains similar across the UK, with children being educated from the age of five to 18. Each country determines its own education structure, including the range of schools and the curriculum to be followed.

Scotland[122]

Education is the responsibility of 32 local education authorities. In place of the national curriculum followed in England and Wales, Scotland follows the Curriculum for Excellence (CfE) introduced in 2013. There are three core subjects: health and well-being, literacy, and numeracy. Aside from these, schools have a degree of freedom to structure their own curriculum. Scottish universities offer four- rather than three-year degrees. University education is free of tuition fees for students whose home is in Scotland, but not for students who come from England, Wales, or Northern Ireland.

Wales

Education is the responsibility of the Department for Education and Skills. With effect from 2022 all schools, except independent schools, will follow a new curriculum designed to reflect the needs of the digital age. A significant number of children all over Wales are taught wholly or largely through the medium of Welsh.

Northern Ireland

Education is the responsibility of the Department of Education. All schools follow the Northern Ireland national curriculum which is based on the English national curriculum, although this is under review. For historical reasons, the education system has been highly segregated on religious lines although the better integration of schools is being pursued. There are 27 Irish-medium schools.

Summary

Education is the fundamental right of every child, recognised under both international and national law. The extent to which every child receives the best possible education to meet his or her abilities and needs is difficult to evaluate. The distinction between private and State-funded education in terms of educational provision, facilities, and attainment in examinations remains stark. For children at State-funded schools, achieving their potential is dependent on many complex factors – not least the levels of investment by government. As has been seen above, local authorities struggle to provide the required levels of support for children with special needs – many overspending their budgets in a period of general financial constraints. Too many children find themselves, for the many reasons discussed, excluded from schools and the security of uninterrupted belonging to a school.

The coronavirus pandemic of 2019 to 2021 has brought to the fore the problem of poverty and its effect on children's education. With schools forced to close many children were denied access to their usual weekday free school lunch on which families depend. It took the intervention of Manchester United player Marcus Rashford to raise public awareness of the seriousness of the problem, forcing the government to change its policy and provide school lunches even when schools are closed. With schools closed, children are reliant on the provision of internet lessons which require access to computers/laptops and here again the problem of poverty has been highlighted: too many families simply lack the resources to provide the equipment needed by their children to maximise the benefit of education during the pandemic.

Notes

1 Article 18 is supplemented by Article 19 and both give substantial guidance as to how the right is to be given effect.
2 Elementary Education (School Attendance) Act 1893.
3 Education and Skills Act 2008.
4 ECHR, First Protocol, Article 2.
5 Education Act 1996, section 7.
6 ibid., section 14.
7 ibid., section 9.
8 ibid., section 437(1).
9 ibid., section 436A and Education (Pupil Registration) (England) Regulations 2006, as amended.

10 Education Act 1996, section 13A.
11 Ofsted, *Safeguarding Children,* 2005. www.safeguardingchildrenorg.uk/Safeguard ing-Childen/2005-report.
12 Children Act 1989, section 36 and Schedule 3.
13 Education Act 1996, Section 444(1A).
14 ibid., section 447(1).
15 Children Act 1989, Schedule 3, paragraph 12(1) and 13.
16 ibid., Schedule 3, paragraph 18.
17 Children Act, Schedule 3, para 14(2).
18 Defined in Education Act 2002, section 39.
19 School Standards and Framework Act 1998, section 104.
20 Formerly the Office for Standards in Education.
21 Under the Education (Schools) Act 1992. See also the Education and Inspections Act 2006. The same functions are carried out by the Education and Training Inspectorate in Northern Ireland, Education Scotland, and Estyn in Wales.
22 The School Governance (Constitution) (England) Regulation 2012.
23 School Standards and Framework Act 1998, sections 1 and 2.
24 See DfE: *Class size and education in England evidence report,* DfE-RR169.
25 The Office of Schools Adjudicator (OSA) is independent of the Department for Education Adjudicators are appointed by the Secretary of State for Education. The OSA rules on disputes about admissions, including appeals from local authority decisions on admissions.
26 *R (London Oratory School) v The School Adjudicator* [2015] EWHC 1012 (Admin).
27 Additional information may be obtained from a particular school's website.
28 Article 9.
29 *R (Begum) v Head Teacher and Governors of Denbigh High School* [2015] UKHL 15.
30 School Standards and Framework Act 1998, Schedule 19.
31 Education Act 2002, section 80(2)(a).
32 Education Act 1996, section 375.
33 School Standards and Framework Act 1998, section 71(3).
34 Department for Children, Schools and Families: *Religious education in English schools: Non-statutory guidance 2010.*
35 Education Act 1996, section 390.
36 Education Act 1996, section 391 and Religious Education (Meetings of Local Conferences and Councils) Regulations 1994, SI 1994/1304.
37 Munby LJ, in *Re G (Education: Religious Upbringing)* [2012] EWCA Civ 1233.
38 See also Chapter 2.
39 *Campbell and Cozens v United Kingdom* (1982) 4 EHRR 293. For an unsuccessful challenge to the ban see *R (Williamson) v Secretary of State for Education and Employment* [2005] UKHL 15.
40 Article 2 of Protocol 1.
41 Education (No) 2 Act 1986, section 47.
42 Education Act 1996, section 548.
43 Day Care and Child Minding (National Standards) (England) Regulations 2003, SI 2003/1996, paragraph 5.
44 Education and Inspections Act 2006, section 88. And see Department for Education Guidance, *Behaviour and discipline in schools: guidance for governing bodies,* 2013 and *Behaviour and discipline in schools: advice for head teachers and school staff,* 2016.
45 ibid., section 89.
46 ibid., sections 90 and 91.
47 ibid., section 92, 94.
48 Education Act 1996, section 550ZB(5).
49 Northern Ireland has its own anti-discrimination law.
50 Department for Education, *Bullying in England, April 2013 to March 2018,* November 2018.

51 Education Act 1996, section 7.
52 ibid., section 144.
53 ibid.
54 www.gov.uk/children-with-special-educational-needs/overview
55 Children and Families Act 2014, section 20.
56 Ofsted: *Annual Report of HM Inspector of Education, Children's Services and Skills 2018–19,* HC 28, 2019.
57 ibid., paragraph 231.
58 Children and Families Act 2014, Part 3.
59 Children and Families Act 2014, sections 22 and 23.
60 www.gov.uk/children-with-special-educational-needs/
61 Children and Families Act 2014, Part 3. The Independent Provider of Special Education Advice (IPSEA) provides a checklist of sections that an EHCP should have.
62 Children and Families Act 2014, sections 38–40.
63 Children and Families Act, section 37.
64 ibid., section 49.
65 ibid., section 44.
66 Education Act 1996, section 332ZA; www.gov.uk/courts-tribunals/first-tier-tribunal-special-educational-needs-and-disability
67 Children and Families Act 2014, section 51.
68 Ofsted: *Annual Report of HM Inspector of Education, Children's Services and Skills 2018–19,* HC 28, 2019.
69 https://publications.parliament.uk/pa/cm201919/cmselect/cmedu/20/2003.htm
70 *Special Education Needs and Disabilities*, paragraph 1.
71 ibid., paragraph 35.
72 ibid., paragraph 80.
73 National Audit Office, Report of the Comptroller and Auditor-General, Session 2017–19, HC 2636.
74 Government Response to the Committee's First Report of 2019, paragraph 21.
75 Education Act 2002, section 52.
76 Education Act 2002, sections 51A (England) and 52 (Wales).
77 Timpson review, page 97. See https://www.gov.uk/government/statistics/permanent-and-fixed-term-exclusions-in-england-2016-to-2017.
78 Department for Education: *Permanent and Fixed Term Exclusions in England 2016–2017,* July 2018.
79 Ofsted: Annual Report 2018–19, *supra,* paragraph 237.
80 Department for Education, *Exclusion from maintained schools, academies and pupil referral units in England,* 2016.
81 Education Select Committee, *Forgotten children: alternative provision and the scandal of ever increasing exclusions,* 2019.
82 Education Act 2002, section 52.
83 ibid.
84 Education and Inspections Act 2006, section 100.
85 Timpson Review, page 104.
86 https://educationinspection.blog.gov.uk/2018/11/12.knife-crime-a-shared-problem/
87 Education Act 2002, section 51A, and regulations made under this section.
88 Education and Inspections Act 2006, section 100; Education (Provision of Full-Time Education for Excluded Pupils) (England) (Amendment) Regulations 2014, amending the Education (Provision of Full-time Education for Excluded Pupils) (England) Regulations 2007.
89 https://www.gov.uk/government/uploads/system/uploads/attachment_data/file/268940/alternative provision statutory guidance pdf version.pdf
90 DfE, *Alternative Provision, Guidance for Local Authorities,* 2013, page 3.
91 Education Act 2002, section 29A.
92 *Timpson review of schools exclusions,* Cp 92, May 2019, page 98.

93 Review, page 99.
94 Review, page 100.
95 Review, page 102.
96 Review, page 97.
97 Owen, D. https://educationinspection.blog.gov.uk/2019/5/10/what-is-off-rolling-and-how-does-ofsted-look-at-it-on-inspection/
98 ibid., page 101.
99 Education Act 1996, sections 2, 4, 463.
100 Education and Skills Act 2008, Part 4. The standards required for registration do not apply to independent schools for children under the age of three years.
101 Education Act 2002, section 157.
102 ibid., section 164.
103 ibid., section 165.
104 ibid., sections 166 and 167.
105 Education Act 1996, sections 434(1)(3)(4) & (6) and 458(4) & (5) and Education (Pupil Registration) (England) Regulations, 2006 to 2016.
106 *Isle of Wight Council v Platt* [2017] UKSC 28.
107 *The Times*, 27 March 2020, page 24.
108 Education and Skills Act 2008, section 96(2).
109 Press Release, 12 April 2019. www.gov.uk/government/news/new-data-shows-illegal-schools-are-a-huge-nationwide-problem
110 UK Government Press Release, *New data shows illegal schools are a huge nationwide problem*, 12 April 2019.
111 ibid., section 134.
112 Children Act 1989, section 17.
113 Children Act 1989, section 47.
114 Children Act 1989, sections 44, 43, and 31, respectively.
115 European Convention on Human Rights and Fundamental Freedoms, Articles 2, 3, 8, and 10, respectively.
116 Female Genital Mutilation Act 2003, section 5B.
117 Children Act 2004, section 10; Children Act 1989, sections 17 and 47. See HM Government, *Working Together to Safeguard Children,* July 2018. See further Chapter 3.
118 [2001] ECHR 333; [2001] 2 FLR 612.
119 Paragraphs 74 to 75.
120 *Phelps v Hillingdon LBC* [2000] 4 All ER 504
121 *The Catholic Child Welfare Society v Various Claimants and the Institute of the Brothers of the Christian Schools* [2012] UKSC 56. See also *X (minors) v Bedfordshire County Council* [1995] 2 AC 633; *Barrett v Enfield LBC* [1999] 3 WLR 79; *W v Essex County Council* [2000] WLR 601.
    A 2021 report by the Education Policy Institute found that children from poorer homes were on average 'about' three grades behind their more affluent classmates. However, there are significant variations in the grade gap across the country, ranging from five A-level grades to none: *The Times,* 1 March 2021.
122 It shall be the right of every child of school age to be provided with school education by, or by virtue of arrangements made by, or entered into, by, an education authority: **Standards in Scotland's Schools Act 2000, section 1.**

5

FREEDOM FROM ABUSE

Introduction

This chapter covers a wide range of issues where the rights of children are violated. Each of these concerns the criminal activity of adults involving children. The first issue considered is child abuse within the family which is both difficult to identify and to eradicate. Two very different issues are then considered – forced marriage and Female Genital Mutilation (FGM). These are particularly problematic and sensitive issues for both society and the law. Under the law, both forced marriage and FGM are offences committed by adults, violating the rights of children. However, both of these offences are practices which are validated by the culture of the offenders. As a result, protecting children from these offences and working towards eliminating the practices are particularly problematic. Also discussed in this chapter is recruitment into drug trafficking, people trafficking and slavery for commercial and/or sexual exploitation, and the organised/institutional sexual exploitation of children, including internet abuse. Finally, the danger to children and their rights through extremism and radicalisation potentially leading to involvement in terrorism will be addressed.

Child abuse within the family

Every child has the right to protection from neglect or abuse and it is a criminal offence to neglect the abuse of a child.[1]

> State Parties shall take all appropriate legislative, administrative, social and education measures to protect the child from all forms of physical or mental violence, injury or abuse, neglect or negligent treatment, maltreatment or exploitation, including sexual abuse, while in the care of

DOI: 10.4324/9780429452710-5

parent(s), legal guardian(s) or any other person who has the care of the child.

UN Convention on the Rights of the Child, Article 19

Where a child is in need of care, which is not being provided by his or her parent(s), the local authority has a duty to provide for the child and where necessary seek an order from the court to take the child into its care. A local authority is under a duty to intervene where a child is at risk of 'significant harm', a term which remains undefined. In addition to the Children and Young Persons Act 1933 and the full range of offences under domestic criminal law, the European Convention on Human Rights (ECHR) Article 3, prohibits 'torture, inhuman and degrading treatment or punishment'. It is the duty of all State agencies to protect these ECHR rights and failure to do so will violate the ECHR. There is no shortage of law designed to protect children, but this does not, on too many occasions, prevent the violation of their rights. The intractable nature of child abuse was recognised in the 1985 Report into the death of Jasmine Beckford as follows:

> Some parents abuse, even kill their children. Throughout history, they always have, and they always will. What is new about child abuse has been the increased and still increasing public awareness of this socially unpalatable, endemic phenomenon. Realisation that the deliberate abuse of children not only occurs but is also by no means a rare occurrence is profoundly shocking both to the individual and to the body politic.[2]

Both worldwide and within the UK, the statistics on child abuse reveal appalling levels of violence within the family and against children. Globally, the World Health Organization (WHO) estimates that in the year ending June 2019, up to one billion children aged two to 17 years experienced physical, sexual, or emotional violence or neglect. The violence leads to death, severe injuries, and impairments to brain and nervous system development. Children exposed to violence are more likely to smoke, misuse alcohol and drugs, and have higher levels of anxiety, depression, other mental health problems, and be at risk of committing suicide.

Child abuse is a form of domestic violence and abuse. Domestic violence and abuse is defined as:

> Any incident or pattern of controlling, coercive or threatening behaviour, violence or abuse between those aged 16 or over who are or have been intimate partners or family members regardless of gender or sexuality. This can encompass but is not limited to the following types of abuse: psychological, physical, sexual, financial emotional.[3]

The current law relating to domestic violence is set out in a number of Acts of Parliament and for the most part is not specific to domestic violence but is contained in criminal, civil and family law provisions which apply to domestic abuse cases. The Domestic Abuse Act 2021 amends much of the existing law, but does not provide a comprehensive code. The 2021 Act defines domestic abuse by setting out the types of behaviours it covers.

Section 1 provides that:

Behaviour is 'abusive' if it contains any of the following:

(a) physical or sexual abuse;
(b) violent or threatening behaviour;
(c) controlling or coercive behaviour;
(d) economic abuse;
(e) psychological, emotional or other abuse;

and it does not matter whether the behaviour consists of a single incident or a course of conduct.

In relation to children, the Act provides that they are victims of abuse where they see, hear or experience the effects of abuse.

In England and Wales, where domestic abuse is occurring the Domestic Abuse Act 2021 provides that the police may issue a Domestic Abuse Protection Notice (DAPN), breach of which may result in arrest. The civil courts may issue a Domestic Abuse Protection Order (DAPO) on a free-standing application by the victim or other person with the permission of the court or in the course of other proceedings. The Act also provides that the police may also seek a DAPO following the issue of a DAPN. Breaching a DAPO is a criminal offence for which the offender may be arrested.

Local authorities are placed under a duty by the 2021 Act to provide accommodation for victims of domestic abuse and their children in refugees and/or other safe accommodation.

The Act creates the office of Domestic Abuse Commissioner and requires local authorities to cooperate with the Commissioner. The duties of the Commissioner include identifying children who are victims of domestic abuse.

Statistics from the Crime Survey for England and Wales for the year ending December 2019, estimated that one in five adults aged 18–74 experienced at least one form of child abuse, whether emotional abuse, physical abuse, sexual abuse, or witnessing domestic violence or abuse, before the age of 16 years (18.5 million people). As at March 2019, 49,570 children in England and 4,810 children in Wales were looked after by their local authority because of experience or risk of abuse or neglect. Furthermore, 52 per cent of adults who experienced abuse before the age of 16 also experienced domestic abuse later in life, compared with 13 per cent of those who did not experience abuse before the age of 16. The forms of abuse recorded included neglect, physical abuse, emotional abuse, and sexual abuse.

The police recorded 117,617 offences of child physical abuse in England and Wales in the year ending March 2019. The 2019 statistics reveal that physical abuse, most commonly inflicted by parents, resulted in 4,170 children in England being subject to a Child Protection Plan and 285 children in Wales were on the Child Protection Register. In the year ending March 2019 there were 93 child deaths by murder or manslaughter. In 2019 in England and Wales the police recorded 93,260 sexual offences against children.

Protecting children's rights to security and freedom from harm by eradicating child abuse remains a seemingly unobtainable goal. At the heart of the problem lie two too-often irreconcilable principles. The first is the official recognition that the family unit is the best place for children to develop and grow free from the interference of the State. The second is the need to protect the rights of children to freedom from abuse and harm within the family. The privacy of the family means that abuse is often difficult to identify and when it does come to light the rights of the child have already been violated. The law is reactive and its enforcement comes too late to guarantee the protection of children. There are also difficulties in getting sufficient evidence to secure a successful prosecution, and successful prosecutions leading to criminal convictions. Further, where the offender is removed from the home, this may cause further harm to the family. Victims frequently do not tell anyone when they have been abused: the Crime Survey states that one in seven adult victims who they called the National Association for People Abused in Childhood had not previously told anyone of their abuse. The Crime Survey records 'around' 227,500 identifiable child abuse offences, of which only one in 15 (four per cent) resulted in a charge or summons. The number of cases referred to the Crown Prosecution Service (CPS) fell by 22 per cent in 12 months to the end of March 2019. Those cases that were prosecuted resulted in convictions in four out of five, or 79 per cent, of cases. In 2018 approximately 50 per cent of convictions for child sexual abuse offences and 25 per cent of cruelty to and neglect of children resulted in immediate custodial sentences.

Increased public awareness of the problem of child abuse was brought about by the Cleveland Inquiry into child sexual abuse in 1985. Cleveland social services had a growing concern over child sex abuse in its area. It appointed a child abuse consultant. At about the same time a new consultant paediatrician started work in the area. Over a period of about five months, 125 children were diagnosed as sexually abused and removed from their homes, many of whom were admitted to hospital under Place of Safety Orders (now abolished) with little notice being given to their parents, while others were made wards of court (see Chapter 1).[4] The diagnoses were contested, with conflict arising between professionals, parents challenging the removals in the courts, a protest group being formed, and increasing media attention promoted by the local MP who supported the parents. In July 1985 the Health Minister announced a public inquiry was to be established. Chaired by Lord Justice Butler-Sloss, the inquiry reported in 1988.[5] The Cleveland crisis was a catalyst for reform. The Children Act 1989 provided powers for local authorities to remove children from their homes on an emergency basis, but only with an order of a court and where really necessary to protect a child (for further details see Chapter 6).

From time to time exceptionally appalling cases of neglect and abuse resulting in the death of a child come to light and a public inquiry is held to establish the truth behind the child's death. The list of such inquiries is depressingly long. One such case was that of Victoria Climbie.

CASE FOCUS: *VICTORIA CLIMBIE*

In 1998 Victoria Climbie, aged seven, was sent by her parents from the Ivory Coast to the UK in the hope of a better life for her. She was to be cared for by her great-aunt and her great-aunt's boyfriend. In 2000 Victoria died, 'bruised, deformed and malnourished' after sustained cruelty at the hands of her carers. In her short time in Britain, Victoria was known to three housing authorities, four social services departments, two child protection teams of the Metropolitan Police Service and had been admitted to two hospitals. Her great-aunt and boyfriend were convicted of murder.

An inquiry chaired by Lord Laming found that there had been a 'gross failure of the system' which was inexcusable. There was a lack of good practice and accountability. The agencies with responsibility for Victoria gave low priority to the task of protecting children; there had been no inter-agency cooperation, and none of them escaped criticism.[6] Lord Laming concluded that it was 'neither practical nor desirable to try to separate the support services for children and families from that of the service designed to investigate and protect children from deliberate harm'.

The institutional failures exposed in relation to Victoria Climbie's care led to reform. The Children Act 2004 requires local authorities to establish Children's Trusts providing children and their families with a full range of services both to protect children and to support the family as recommended by Lord Lamey. However, as further cases of child deaths came to light it was clear that law alone could not protect children from harm in the privacy of their family.

A very different violation of children's rights occurs when a child is forced into marriage against his or her will. Any ceremony of marriage which takes place while one of the parties lacks the legal capacity to consent, or is under duress, or is mistaken as to the true identity of the other party to the marriage will cause the marriage to be void or voidable, and if and when challenged may be declared so by a court of law. In recent years, the law has had to react to culturally sanctioned forced marriage, as discussed below.

A remaining controversy: corporal punishment in the home

One issue which remains contentious and unresolved in England (but not Scotland or Wales) relates to the right of a parent to discipline his or her child through the use of corporal punishment. Absent from the range of protective measures for children under the criminal law and the Children Act 1989 is a total prohibition on corporal punishment in the home. Corporal punishment is 'any punishment in which physical force is used and intended to cause some degree of pain or discomfort'. Whereas adults are protected in law from assault, children in England are not, provided that the assault does not amount to 'actual bodily harm' or 'cruelty'.[7]

The Council of Europe has stated that corporal punishment is the most widespread form of violence against children and a majority of the 47 States in the Council of Europe are now committed to abolishing it.[8] The European Convention on Human Rights (ECHR), Article 3, protects against torture, inhuman and degrading treatment and punishment and has proved relevant to the issue of corporal punishment.

CASE FOCUS: *TYRER*[9]

In 1972 on the Isle of Man, Tyrer, aged 15, was sentenced by a court to three strokes with a birch as punishment for an assault on a school prefect.

The European Court of Human Rights ruled that the punishment was humiliating and degrading and violated Article 3.

CASE FOCUS: *A*[10]

In 1990 A and his brother had been placed on the local authority's Child Protection Register on the basis of 'known physical abuse'. In 1993 A's head teacher reported to the Social Services Department that A, then aged nine, was being hit with a stick by his stepfather. The stepfather was charged with assault occasioning actual bodily harm: his defence was that this was 'reasonable chastisement' of a difficult boy. He was acquitted by the jury, on a majority verdict.

> The matter went to the European Court of Human Rights (ECtHR), alleging that the UK had failed to protect A from a violation of Article 3. The Court ruled that beating a child with a garden cane reached the level of severity to amount to a violation of Article 3. The defence of reasonable chastisement was rejected by the Court.

In relation to England, the government has taken the view that legislating to ban corporal punishment would be an intrusion into the privacy of family life, thereby downgrading children's rights to freedom from abuse.[11] The problem for those seeking to ban corporal punishment is that opinion polls in England consistently reveal opposition to a ban on smacking children. A total prohibition on corporal punishment could therefore be ineffective in stopping the practice.

However, some progress has been made. Since 1987 school teachers in State schools have been banned from administering corporal punishment to pupils.[12] In 1993 in response to a finding of a violation on Article 3 by the ECtHR, Parliament extended the ban to publicly funded children at independent schools (on Assisted Places Schemes for example). In 1993 the Education Act provided that corporal punishment could not be justified if it was 'inhuman or degrading'.[13] In 1998, the prohibition was extended to cover all schools, State and independent. The ban was extended to child minders and those providing day care in 2003.[14] But, while corporal punishment was banned in schools and nurseries, parents were left free to inflict physical punishment on their children. In 2004, Parliament provided that punishment which caused 'actual bodily harm' could not be used as a defence to criminal proceedings for assaults or cruelty to children, or in civil proceedings, on the basis that it constituted (lawful) reasonable punishment.[15] This still left parents free to inflict physical punishment, provided that it did not amount to actual bodily harm.

In 2019 Scotland became the first UK country to ban all forms of corporal punishment, by abolishing the defence of reasonable chastisement to charges of assault.[16] In Wales, the Assembly passed an Act in 2020 abolishing the defence of 'reasonable punishment' and will protect children from assaults by their parents.[17]

Forced marriage

A forced marriage is defined as being one in which person A is forced into marriage by person B (whether with B or another person) without A's full and free consent. Forced marriage is a global phenomenon recognised as an abuse of human rights and a child marriage is regarded by the United Nations as a form of forced marriage, on the basis that a child lacks the capacity to give consent to the marriage. The UN Office of the High Commissioner for Human Rights states that there are more than 650 million women alive today who were married as children and estimates that every year at least 12 million girls are married under the age of 18. In the least developed countries 40 per cent of girls are married before the age of 18 and 12 per cent before the age of 15.[18]

> Men and women of full age ... have the right to marry and to found a family. Marriage shall be entered into only with the free and full consent of the intending spouses.
>
> *UN Universal Declaration of Human Rights, Article 16(1) and (2)*

> Forced marriage is a criminal offence. A forced marriage is one in which one or both spouses do not (or, in the case of some adults with learning or physical disabilities or mental incapacity, cannot) consent to the marriage and violence, threats, or any other form of coercion is involved. Coercion may include emotional force, physical force or the threat of physical force, and, financial pressure.
>
> *Foreign and Commonwealth Office, Forced Marriage Unit Statistics 2017[19]*

In relation to children, under English law, a marriage is void if either party is under the age of 16.[20] A void marriage is one where no marriage has been created at all and there has been no change to a person's marital status. There is therefore no need to have it formally declared void (although if there is any doubt that might be desirable). Between the ages of 16 and 18, a marriage will be valid if there is parental consent to the marriage or a court of law has dispensed with the parent's objections.[21] As emphasised in the UN Declaration, and under domestic law, the freely given consent to marriage, by a competent person, is an essential prerequisite to a valid marriage. Valid consent is also a prerequisite to marriage in the eyes of the Christian, Jewish, Hindu, Muslim, and Sikh faiths. A marriage will be voidable – i.e. capable of being set aside (annulled) by a court because of a specific defect. The grounds on which a marriage will be voidable are set out in the Matrimonial Causes Act 1973;[22] the relevant ground here is that:

> ... either party to the marriage did not validly consent to it, whether in consequence *of duress*, mistake, unsoundness of mind or otherwise.[23,24]

CASE FOCUS: *SCOTT* (1886)[25]

A 22-year-old heiress was persuaded to take over the debts of a man who then threatened her with bankruptcy unless she married him. Having tricked her into a register office he then threatened to shoot her if she didn't go through

> with the ceremony. The marriage was never consummated and the marriage was set aside on the basis of lack of true consent through duress.

More recently, duress has also been found to invalidate consent to marriage in two cases where the parents had threatened to disown a young woman aged 21 and to cut off all financial support,[26] and where the parents applied such pressure on a young man to enter an arranged marriage that it amounted to force sufficient to invalidate his consent to marriage.[27]

In the United Kingdom, the Forced Marriage Unit (FMU) collates and publishes statistics and offers advice and support to those threatened with forced marriage. The FMU is a joint Home Office and Foreign and Commonwealth Office unit which operates both inside and outside the UK.

> In 2018 the FMU recorded 1,764 cases of possible forced marriage, an increase of 47% compared with 2017. Of these, 312 cases (17.7%) involved victims aged 15 and under; 262 cases (14.9%) involved victims aged 16–17 and 307 cases (17.4%) involved victims aged 18–21. Seventy-five per cent of cases involved women.
>
> Since 2011 the FMU has recorded cases relating to over 110 countries across Asia, the Middle East, Africa, Europe, and North America. In 2018 it handled cases relating to 74 countries. Those with the highest number of cases were:
>
> | | |
> |---|---|
> | Pakistan | 769 cases (44%) |
> | Bangladesh | 157 cases (9%) |
> | India | 110 cases (6%) |
> | Somalia | 46 cases (3%) |
> | Afghanistan | 44 cases (3%) |
> | Romania | 43 cases (2%). |

In the UK, forced marriage is a criminal offence, carrying a penalty of up to seven years' imprisonment.[28] In 2018 the FMU handled 119 cases (seven per cent) of which had no overseas element at all, demonstrating that forced marriage can and does take place within the UK. The law attempts to prevent forced marriage through Forced Marriage Protection Orders.

Forced Marriage Protection Orders

In order to prevent a forced marriage or to protect a person who has been forced into a marriage, an application can be made to a County Court or to the Family Division of the High Court for a Forced Marriage Protection Order (FMPO).[29] On who may apply see below. This is a civil (non-criminal) order, breach of which is a criminal offence carrying a maximum of five years' imprisonment.[30] While most orders exist to protect children, it is clear that an FMPO is also available to protect a mentally competent adult at risk of being forcibly married.[31] When an application is made for an FMPO, the court must consider all the circumstances of the case, 'including the need to secure the health, safety and well-being of the person to be protected'. When considering their well-being the court must have regard to the person's wishes and feelings to the extent that the court thinks it appropriate in light of the applicant's age and understanding.[32]

Although there is an upward trend, the number of FMPOs applied for and granted since their introduction in 2008 remains very low. In the period July–September 2019 there were 101 applications, of which 69 per cent of applicants were aged 17 and under. There were 140 orders made in that period: in many cases there are several orders made per application, or the orders are for extensions or variations of the orders for which no new application is necessary.[33]

An FMPO may contain a range of 'prohibitions, restrictions, or requirements' or 'other terms' as the court thinks necessary to protect the victim. The order can relate to conduct inside or outside the UK, and may relate to any person involved, or likely to become involved, in the forced marriage. 'Involvement' covers, 'aiding, abetting, counselling, procuring, encouraging or assisting another person to force, or attempt to force, a person to enter into a marriage' or 'conspiring to force, or attempt to force, a person to enter into a marriage'.[34] If there is a risk of violence from the person to whom the order is addressed the court must attach a power of arrest unless it is satisfied that there would be adequate protection without such a power. Where a power of arrest is attached a police officer who has reasonable cause to suspect that there is a breach of the order may arrest the person without a warrant.[35]

The victim herself (or himself),[36] a relevant third party (a local authority in England and Wales; the Chief Constable of the Police Service of Scotland)[37] and any other person with the permission of the court can apply for an FMPO. An order can be made without notifying the person from whom protection is needed (the respondent). This is an *ex parte* order and will be granted where it is 'just and convenient' to do so, usually when there is an urgent need for the order and the usual notice periods cannot be complied with.[38] The court can make an order for a set period or allow it to continue until it is challenged through an application for variation or discharge of the order.[39]

The terms of the Forced Marriage Act 2007[40] are extremely broad, giving little guidance to the courts as to how to interpret the Act or to the scope of their powers under the Act. Greater clarity has now been achieved through case law.

The Court of Appeal has set out a four-stage process to be followed in deciding whether to make an FMPO.[41]

Stage 1 requires the court to establish the facts of the case, placing the onus of the applicant to prove (on a balance of probabilities test) that the facts justify the making of an FMPO;

Stage 2 requires the court to decide, based on the facts established in stage 1, whether there is a need for an FMPO;

Stage 3 requires the court, based on the established facts, to weigh up the potential risk of a forced marriage and any protective factors which exist to prevent that happening;

Stage 4 requires that, if the court is satisfied that there is a sufficient risk to justify making an order, the court must then achieve an appropriate balance between protecting the potential victim from a violation of her right to freedom from torture, inhuman treatment, or punishment (Article 3 ECHR) and protecting her right to respect for her family and private life under Article 8 of the ECHR. In doing so the court should be aware of the high degree of flexibility in the legislation and should work towards making a 'bespoke order' tailored to fit the particular needs and circumstances of the case. There is no 'template': each order is unique to the circumstances.

CASE FOCUS: *G AND D*[42]

In 2007, two girls of Pakistani descent, then aged 12 and 14 were made British wards of court (on which see Chapter 1) on the basis that their parents intended to take them to Pakistan and force them to marry. Their two elder brothers, S and T, had already been forced to marry in Pakistan. The parent claimed that they wished G and D to go to Pakistan to attend an English-speaking school. This was held by the court to be a false claim: no arrangements had been made to choose a school and a letter, purportedly signed by the principal of a school, confirming that G and D had places at the school, proved to be a forgery.

The court considered the wishes and feelings of the two girls. They said they wished to go to Pakistan to meet their extended family. The court found that they had no understanding of forced marriage or its consequences and the court decided that the primary purpose of the visit to Pakistan was not education, but the forcible marriage of the two girls. There was a 'present real and substantial risk that G and D will be forced by their parents to marry against their wishes'. A Forced Marriage Protection Order was made.[43]

CASE FOCUS: A[44]

The applicant for a Forced Marriage Protection Order was A, in 2012 aged 20, who sought orders for herself and her six younger siblings, B, a girl, aged 18; C aged 16; D aged 15; E aged 10; F, a boy, aged 9; and G, a boy, aged 6.

A claimed that during a trip to Bangladesh her parents intended to force her to marry. She escaped with the assistance of the British High Commission and returned to England. Her parents then forced B to marry. B on returning to England managed to escape. A applied for an FMPO on the basis that her parents would force her other younger siblings to marry against their will.

The parents denied that B had been forcibly married. The court accepted the evidence of A and B and rejected that of the parents who, the court found, had lied. The court ruled that B had been forced into marriage and that there was a very strong likelihood that the parents would force their younger children into marriage as well.

A Forced Marriage Protection Order was made, without time limits. In addition the five younger children were to remain wards of court thereby preventing any decisions to be made without the approval of the court. As the younger children were at risk of significant harm, the local authority was ordered to prepare a report to be filed within three weeks with a view to the court making care and Supervision Orders in respect of the younger children. All passports and travel documents of the parents and children would be retained by the court.

Female Genital Mutilation (FGM)

Female Genital Mutilation (FGM) is defined as:

> ... procedures involving partial or total removal of the external female genitalia or other injury to the female genital organs whether for cultural or other non-therapeutic reasons.[45]

FGM is a criminal offence and a violation of a person's right to freedom from torture, inhuman treatment, or punishment which is protected by Article 3 of the European Convention on Human rights (ECHR) and other international human rights instruments.[46]

> [FGM] is a human rights issue, not only because of the unequal treatment of men and women, but also because the procedure will almost inevitably amount either to torture or to other cruel, inhuman or degrading treatment within the meaning, not only of Article 3 of the European Convention on Human Rights, but also of Article 1 or 16 of the Convention against Torture and Other Cruel, Inhuman, Degrading Treatment or Punishment,

Article 7 of the International Covenant on Civil and Political Rights, and
Article 37(a) of the Convention on the Rights of the Child.

> *Baroness Hale, Secretary of State for the Home*
> *Department v K [2006]* UKHL 46, paragraph 94

The UN Convention on the Rights of the Child provides that:

> State Parties shall take all appropriate legislative, administrative, social and
> educational measures to protect the child from all forms of physical or
> mental violence, injury or abuse, neglect or negligent treatment, maltreat-
> ment or exploitation, including sexual abuse, while in the care of parent(s),
> legal guardian(s) or any other person who has care of the child.
>
> *Article 19*

> State Parties shall take all effective and appropriate measures with a view to
> abolishing traditional practices prejudicial to the health of children.
>
> *Article 24.3*

FGM is gender-based violence with no medical justification or benefits and is
likely to take place without the consent of the victims, especially when prac-
tised on children. FGM has been labelled 'heinous and abhorrent, and its practice
impossible to justify', and 'a crime and its practice is repugnant and objectionable'.[47]

Accurate statistical evidence is difficult to acquire but UNICEF (the
United Nations International Children's Emergency Fund) estimates that over
200 million women alive today have suffered FGM.[48] Baroness Hale, in the case
cited above, explained that:

> … these procedures are irreversible and their effects last a lifetime. They are
> usually performed by traditional practitioners using crude instruments and
> without anaesthetic. Immediate complications include severe pain, shock,
> haemorrhage, tetanus or sepsis, urine retention, ulceration of the genital
> region and injury to adjacent tissue. Long term consequences include cysts and
> abscesses, keloid scar formation, damage to the urethra resulting in urinary
> incontinence, dyspareunia (painful sexual intercourse) and sexual dysfunc-
> tion. Infibulation can bring particularly severe consequences, and it may be
> necessary to cut open the skin to enable intercourse or childbirth to take place.
> It is likely that the risks of maternal death and stillbirth are greatly increased.[49]

In many parts of the world the practice remains widespread and resistant to
change. Within communities supportive of FGM it may be regarded as essential
to ensure the purity of girls and enhance their marriage prospects. Evidence
shows that the age at which FGM is performed varies between communities and
regions, with most girls suffering FGM between infancy and the age of 15.[50]

FGM is a deeply-ingrained cultural practice in at least 31 countries in Africa,
Asia, and the Middle East, and countries such as the UK and other western states

where there has been significant immigration from the countries where FGM is prevalent. The practice of FGM is often secret and there are real difficulties in identifying victims or potential victims and establishing sufficient evidence to take official action, whether designed to protect the child or to prosecute the offenders. There are cultural resistances to disclosing the practice of FGM. Family and community members are reluctant to report cases of girls at risk and girls might be reluctant to report parents as they are dependent on their family and community.[51] However, UNICEF reports that support for the practice is dwindling, with young girls less supportive of the practice than older women and that in many countries girls 'are at a much lower risk of being subjected to FGM than their mothers or grandmothers were'.[52] But as UNICEF notes, eliminating FGM requires strong political commitment and leadership and cannot be achieved by young people on their own.

UK FGM statistics

There were 5,391 recorded cases of FGM in England in 2016–17.[53] Of these, women and girls from Somalia accounted for 35 per cent of newly recorded cases. In 57 cases the FGM had been undertaken in the UK. The five to nine age groups was the most common age range at which FGM was performed. This amounts to 44 per cent, or 739 cases, of the total number of cases from any country.[54] In the period from October to December 2019 the NHS recorded 1,950 attendances of individual women and girls at NHS Trusts and GPs practices where FGM was identified.

In 2020, there were 6,615 women and girls reported to have attended at NHS trusts or GP surgeries where FGM was identified as a procedure undertaken. The figures are unreliable in so far as a variable number of NHS Trusts and GPs reported the statistics, the number of GPs being particularly low.

The law: the Female Genital Mutilation Act 2003

The first act to tackle FGM was the Prohibition of Female Circumcision Act 1985 which applied to the whole of the UK. The Act made FGM a criminal offence, punishable with up to five years' imprisonment. There were no successful prosecutions under the 1985 Act. The Act was replaced in England, Wales, and Northern Ireland by the Female Genital Mutilation Act 2003. In Scotland the relevant law is the Prohibition of Female Genital Mutilation (Scotland) Act 2005. This updated the law and created the offence of assisting a girl to carry out FGM on herself. It also created offences in relation to taking girls abroad for FGM. The penalty for FGM was increased from five to 14 years' imprisonment.[55] In 2015 the law was amended so that it is now an offence for a UK national or permanent resident to perform FGM abroad, assist a girl to perform it on herself, and assist a non-UK national or resident to carry out FGM outside the UK on a UK national or permanent resident.[56] The first, and only, successful prosecution in the UK took place in 2019 when a Ugandan mother was found guilty and sentenced to 11 years in prison.

The Female Genital Mutilation Act 2003 (hereafter the 2003 Act) creates both criminal offences in relation to FGM and civil orders to protect victims or potential victims. The principal elements of the law are as follows.

Protecting the identity of victims

The publication of any information that would be likely to lead to the identification of a victim of FGM is prohibited. The victim's anonymity is protected from the time an allegation is made and lasts for the victim's lifetime.[57] There are two exceptions to this anonymity. The first is where the trial of an accused person would be seriously prejudiced if the identity of the victim is withheld. The second is where withholding the victim's identity would be an unreasonable restriction on reporting of the proceedings and where it is in the public interest that the restriction be removed.

The duty to protect girls from the risk of FGM

Where a person has responsibility for a girl under the age of 16 – for example parents and other family members who are caring for a child – and has frequent contact with the girl, failing to protect the girl from FGM is now a criminal offence.[58] It carries a maximum penalty of seven years' imprisonment. It is a defence to show that he or she did not think that FGM would be committed, and couldn't reasonably be expected to be aware that there was such a risk.

The duty of professionals to report to the police

Healthcare workers, teachers, and social care workers have a duty to report to the police where they discover that FGM has been carried out on a girl under the age of 18.[59] They may become aware of this through being informed by the victim or they may observe physical symptoms which suggest that FGM has been carried out. The report may be made orally or in writing. There is a gap in the law, however, as having a reasonable suspicion that a girl is at risk of FGM does not require it to be reported. In the year to April 2020 some 6,590 patients (of all ages) had a procedure to treat FGM or were identified as having undergone it. Of these 205 were born in the UK.[60]

Where a local authority suspects that a girl has been harmed or is likely to be harmed by FGM it may apply for an Emergency Protection Order (on which see Chapter 6), or apply for a Female Genital Mutilation Protection Order.

Female Genital Mutilation Protection Orders (FGMPO)[61]

Female Genital Mutilation Protection Orders (FGMPOs) share many characteristics with Forced Marriage Protection Orders (FMPOs) discussed above.

The purpose of the FGMPO is both to protect a girl against the commission of FGM and to protect a girl who has been the victim of FGM. The order may contain 'such prohibitions, restrictions or requirements and such other terms' as the court considers appropriate to protect the victim. The order may relate to behaviour inside and outside England, Wales, and Northern Ireland (the equivalent Scottish Act has the same terms), and may involve any persons who may be involved in committing the offence of FGM. In particular an order may be made prohibiting aiding, abetting, counselling, procuring, encouraging, or assisting another person to commit, or attempt to commit an offence or conspiring to commit or attempt to commit the offence.[62] The order can be made for a fixed period or until it is varied or discharged by the court.

The number of applications for orders, and orders granted, remains very low. In the period between July 2019 and September 2019 there were only 71 orders made. Since their introduction in July 2015, there have been 489 orders made.[63]

The application process

The child or a relevant third party (a local authority) or any other person with the permission of the court may apply for an FGMPO. The court can make an order even where there is no application, but where the issue is raised in other family proceedings before the court (for example where an Emergency Protection Order is being made).[64] In urgent cases, an order may be made without notifying the person(s) against whom the order is to be made (an *ex parte* order).

If the victim, or the person who applied for the order, or any other person with the permission of the court, considers that the person to whom the order is directed has broken the order, she or he may apply to the court for a warrant for that person's arrest. A person who breaks the terms of the FGMPO is guilty of a criminal offence which carries a maximum penalty of up to five years' imprisonment.[65]

In deciding whether or not to make an FGMPO, the court considers a number of factors, both 'macro' and 'micro', which should be taken into account.[66] The macro factors include:

- what is the prevalence of FGM in the country to which a child might be taken?
- what are the societal expectations of FGM in the country?
- what is the prevalence of FGM in the region of the country to which a child might be taken?
- is FGM illegal in the country to which the child might be taken?
- if illegal, how effective are the authorities in the country in enforcing the prohibition on FGM?
- is there an extradition treaty between the UK and the country to which the child might be taken which would enable a prosecution to take place if the order prohibiting FGM was breached?

The micro factors include:

- is there a history of FGM in the child's family or the wider family to which the child will be exposed abroad?
- if so, on which generations of women has this been perpetrated?
- what are the attitudes of the mother and/or father to FGM generally, and/or in relation to their daughter?
- what is the power balance in the family?
- Is FGM regarded as a woman's issue or a man's issue within the family?
- what are the attitudes of the wider family to FGM?
- what safeguards can the family take to mitigate the risk of FGM?
- how well have the family co-operated with the authorities?
- what is the professional assessment of family relationships and of the capabilities of the parents?
- are there any other specific features of the case which make FGM more or less likely?

There are difficulties in protecting a child's right where an application for asylum has been made but rejected or there are other international dimensions to a case. For example:

CASE FOCUS: A[67]

There was clear evidence that A, then ten years old, was at risk of FGM if returned to her home country. The Home Secretary had rejected her mother's claim for asylum and the mother and daughter were at risk of being deported back to Bahrain where FGM was prevalent and their wider family were in favour of FGM being carried out. At a hearing in 2018, the judge transferred the case to the Family Division of the High Court, but ordered that the Home Secretary was prohibited from removing, instructing, or encouraging any other person to remove A from the country. When the matter was considered by the Family Division it was accepted that it had no power to give orders to the Home Secretary about immigration and asylum matters. All the Court could do was to ask the Home Secretary to reconsider his decision. The Court granted the FGMPO, but recognised that it would not protect A if she was returned to Bahrain.

CASE FOCUS: AD[68]

In 2017 an FGMPO was made to protect three girls from Country X, then aged 17, 15, and 13, who were at severe risk of being subjected to FGM if returned to their home country where their father and wider family remained. Their mother remained in the UK. The order contained travel restrictions preventing their return to Country X and neighbouring countries. In addition, Care Orders were made, although the girls were returned to their mother's care. In 2019 the Care Orders were discharged but the FGMPO continued as the girls remained at risk if they were returned to Country X. As the eldest girl was now 19 and considered by the Family Court to have a good understanding of the risks in her home country, the Court removed the travel restrictions relating to her and limited the travel restrictions in relation to her two sisters to the date when they each became 18.

CASE FOCUS: X[69]

When X was a few months old her mother, a British citizen resident in England, expressed concerns over her safety. The child's father was an Egyptian national who lived in Egypt and although he disapproved of FGM his wider family did not. In order to prevent X from being taken to Egypt where she would be at risk, a worldwide travel ban was imposed in an FGMPO. The ban was later challenged and a rehearing was ordered.

The matter returned to the High Court when X was three years old. The Court ruled that X could travel, with her mother, to Egypt for a one-week period in term time as an exception to the worldwide travel ban. The Court took undertakings from the mother, father, and maternal grandfather which laid out detailed rules for the trip: that X's passport would at all times be kept by her maternal grandmother, where they would stay, excluding them from entering an area where the paternal grandparents lived, the hours the father could visit X under supervision, that the mother would contact the local authority every 48 hours during the trip, and to make X available for a social work visit on their return. In total the mother and father gave over 30 separate undertakings to the Court in order to protect X from danger. Breach of such an undertaking is contempt of court and punishable by imprisonment.

Circumcision

In many respects male circumcision shares characteristics with FGM, being a physical assault by an adult on (usually) a child without his consent. However, rightly or wrongly, the law distinguishes between the two and circumcision is not unlawful in the UK. The issue is discussed in Chapter 3 where the legal differences between circumcision and FGM are explained.

Exploiting children[70]

Exploitation is a concept capable of several meanings. In the context of children and their rights, at its core is the idea that a child is wrongly (and unlawfully) subjected to control by another who exploits the child's relative powerlessness for personal gain. It is taking unfair advantage of their vulnerability in a way that violates their rights to autonomy and freedom and results in severe harm to the child.[71] Exploitation is categorised into five principal forms: labour exploitation (divided into labour and financial and criminal), domestic servitude, sexual exploitation, unknown exploitation, and exploitation for organ harvesting. In relation to adults, the most common form of exploitation is labour exploitation, whereas children are most commonly exploited for criminal purposes. There has been an increase in the criminal exploitation of children as a result of the activities of County Lines operations, discussed below.

County Lines[72]

County Lines is:

> ... the term used to describe gangs and organised crime networks involved in exporting drugs from one area (usually urban) into one or more other areas within the UK, using dedicated phone lines or other forms of 'deal lines'.[73]

As the National Crime Agency reports, County Lines gangs 'recruit, transport and exploit vulnerable individuals, including children, to carry out low-level criminal activity essential to their operations'.[74] The Children's Commissioner estimates that there are between 30,000 and 50,000 children being exploited by County Line gangs.

Although there remain significant gaps in intelligence, the creation of a National County Lines Coordination Centre (NCLCC) has enabled better data collection and understanding of the threats posed by County Lines gangs. The largest concentration of County Lines is in the area covered by the Metropolitan Police Service (approximately 15 per cent), followed by West Midlands Police (nine per cent), and Merseyside Police (seven per cent).

Heroin and crack cocaine are the most commonly supplied drugs distributed through County Lines. The 2018 data identifies victims as young as 11 years, with the majority being between 15 and 17 years old. Victims are usually recruited face to face or through social media. Gangs target vulnerable children, including children who are being looked after by a local authority, are poor, or have behavioural or developmental disorders, and those who have excluded from schools. Gangs also target children from stable backgrounds who might be having difficulties with parents and/or friends. Children are recruited from schools and further education establishments, from pupil referral units, special educational needs schools, foster homes, and homeless shelters. Crest Advisory, a police and criminal justice consultancy, reports that vulnerable children in care – especially those in unregulated private accommodation which are not subject to Ofsted inspections – are a prime target group for County Lines gangs. Furthermore, that gangs

> … may also coerce young people to engineer a situation, with or without parental collusion, where they are taken into local authority care with the explicit aim of using their placement as cover to work on a county line and/or recruit their peers for participation in county lines.[75]

The National Crime Agency reports that once recruited victims are made compliant through grooming and various coercive methods. These include debt bondage, threats of kidnap and serious violence against the victims and their families. Sexual abuse has also been used as a means of controlling (mostly) female victims.

Writing in *The Times* the then Children's Commissioner Anne Longfield wrote in 2020 that:

> The problem of 'county lines' gangs often involves one of these groups of teenagers – those expelled from school, recruited from pupil referral centres, many of them needing mental health support but not getting it. Eventually they tip into the care system or the criminal justice system. The police tell me that these teens are in need of social care support rather than police intervention. Partly as a result, the number of teenagers coming into care has risen sharply to try to protect them from criminal gangs.[76]

In May 2020 it was announced that 130 County Lines networks were shut down, and drugs worth more than £3 million seized by the police. One hundred and forty children were identified as linked to the drugs trade and more than 650 arrests were made. The operations involved the British Transport Police and the Metropolitan Police, Merseyside Police, and West Midlands Police.[77]

Modern slavery and trafficking: see also the protection of refugee children discussed in Chapter 6

Modern slavery 'encompasses slavery, servitude, forced and compulsory labour and human trafficking'.[78]

> State Parties shall take all appropriate national, bilateral and multilateral measures to prevent the abduction of, the sale of or traffic in children for any purpose or in any form.
>
> *UN Convention on the Rights of the Child,*
> *Article 35*[79]

No one shall be held in slavery or servitude and no one shall be required to perform forced or compulsory labour.

European Convention on Human Rights, Article 4[80]

Slavery and trafficking is a global problem, and, as the Anti-Slavery Commissioner comments, one which has a very different character from the slave trade eradicated in the nineteenth century:[81]

When William Wilberforce was fighting to outlaw the slave trade, the abuse was taking place in plain sight, slave owners were well-known wealthy people and the trade in slaves was highly visible. Today, slavery is illegal, the goods and services produced by long and complex supply chains – it is hidden in plain sight.

Strategic Plan 2019–2020[82]

In 2013 in the UK alone there were estimated to be between 10,000 and 13,000 potential victims of modern slavery. In 2018 4,577 offences of modern slavery were recorded by the police across the UK, a 45 per cent increase over the previous year.[83] There is increased operational activity across the police forces, and in July 2019 there were 1,479 live police operations. It remains the case, however, that the scale of modern slavery is still not understood. In 2020 the Centre for Social Justice (CSJ)[84] estimated that there could be 'at least 100,000 victims in the UK, with the actual number likely to be even greater'.[85]

Prosecution levels for slavery and trafficking, remain – compared with the increased police activity – relatively low. In the year ending March 2019 there were 322 prosecutions for modern slavery, resulting in 219 convictions. The Anti-Slavery Commissioner reports that although the maximum penalty for offences has been raised from 14 years to life imprisonment, there have been cases where sentences for human trafficking have been lower than for drug trafficking.[86] This fails to reflect the seriousness of the offence and the Commissioner is working with the Sentencing Council to produce guidelines which better reflect the gravity of the offence.[87] Successful prosecutions in 2018 included two London gang members who trafficked a girl to Wales to deal heroin and crack cocaine and received ten and nine years' imprisonment and a drug dealer who used three children aged between 14 and 15 to deal crack cocaine and heroin while they lived in substandard accommodation, transporting the children, drugs, and money, and maintaining contact between customers and suppliers. He was jailed for 14 years.[88]

The offence of trafficking is extra-territorial, that is to say, the offence is committed regardless of the country in which the trafficking is facilitated or arranged. In relation to trafficking, the consent of the victim to travel, whether they are an adult or a child, is irrelevant. The Modern Slavery Act creates a presumption relating to age.[89] Where the age of a victim of trafficking is uncertain, it is presumed that he or she is a child. This enables immediate assistance, support, and protection to be given. Section 45 of the Modern Slavery Act 2015 also provides for a defence for victims of slavery and trafficking. Where a child commits an act which amounts to an offence, he or she is not guilty of that offence if it has been committed as a direct result of their being a victim of slavery or exploitation. This is subject to the proviso that a reasonable person having the child's characteristics would, under the same circumstances, have committed the offence. This defence reflects the understanding that the legal system has regarding the power of slave traffickers over their victims and the powerlessness of those under their control. Where a prosecution of a victim of trafficking is undertaken, that may amount to a breach of Article 4 (protection against slavery) and Article 6 of the European Convention (ECHR) – the right to fair trial, as the following case reveals. Note that the case relates to proceedings prior to the section 45 defence being in force.

CASE FOCUS: *VCL AND AN*[90]

When minors, VCL and AN (both Vietnamese nationals) were discovered work-ing on a cannabis farm and prosecuted for drugs offences. They were sen-tenced to 20 and 18 months' detention. Both were subsequently identified as being victims of trafficking. On appeal to the Court of Appeal their sentences were reduced, but the prosecution upheld as justified.

VCL and AN applied to the Court of Human Rights, alleging violations of Article 4 (protection from slavery) and Article 6. The Court of Human Rights stated that once the authorities were aware, or ought to be aware, that an individual might be a victim of trafficking, it was essential that they were assessed promptly by 'individuals trained and qualified to deal with victims of trafficking'. Once that assessment had been made, it was the duty of the State to protect the individual. The Court of Appeal had not considered the State's duty under Article 4 (which had been breached) and the proceedings as a whole were a violation of Article 6.

The Anti-Slavery Commissioner reports that there have been 'recent successes' in using the offence of trafficking in cases where children have been exploited within County Lines operations (on which see above). However, in 2020 there were 1,371 referrals to the National Referral Mechanism (below) of children involved in County Lines operations. This was an increase from 1,039 referrals in 2019. Boys accounted for 81 per cent of referrals.[91] To assist and protect child vic-tims, there are Independent Child Trafficking Guardians. Among other things, the guardians can apply for legal aid for the child and instruct lawyers on behalf of the child.

The National Referral Mechanism (NRM)

The Home Office's National Referral Mechanism (NRM) is a specialist organi-sation established to receive referrals from bodies such as the police and local authorities and to investigate and support victims of slavery.[92] Referrals can only be made to the NRM from 'first responders', an extensive list which includes the National Crime Agency, police, and the UK Border Force. In the end of year summary for 2019, 10,627 potential victims of modern slavery were referred to the NRM, a 52 per cent increase from 2018. Forty-three per cent (4,566) of all referrals were for children.[93] That percentage increased in 2020, with children making up 57 per cent of all slavery referrals. The number of overall referrals of potential victims remained a depressing 10,613.

Once a child is referred to the NRM, a decision will be made within five working days as to whether there are reasonable grounds for believing that the child has been trafficked. If the authority reaches a conclusion that he or she has been, there is then a 45-day period in which a full assessment can be made. During this time there can be no action taken to detain or to remove the child. Within the 45-day period, a decision will be made – a 'conclusive grounds decision' – on whether the person is a victim of trafficking. The test to be used is whether, on the balance of probabilities, it is more likely than not that the person is a victim of trafficking. Where the authority concludes that a person has been trafficked, support will be given by the Salvation Army.

The Centre for Social Justice (CSJ) states that the NRM 'has many flaws'. The system is 'slow and bureaucratic' and the NRM struggling to cope with the increased volume of referrals. The CSJ calls for 'a complete overhaul' of the system. It also calls on the government to improve the system of victim support. This could be achieved by passing the Modern Slavery (Victim Support) Bill 2019–2021 which, in relation to children, provides that local authorities have a duty to safeguard and promote the welfare of a child looked after by them and in particular has a duty to consider the risk of a child being re-trafficked and to take steps to accommodate the child to lessen that risk.[94]

The Anti-Slavery Commissioner

There is an Independent Anti-Slavery Commissioner who works with police forces and other agencies to improve their ability to recognise and support victims.[95] She has a UK-wide remit to encourage good practice in the prevention, detection, investigation, and prosecution of slavery and human trafficking offences.

In her Strategic Plan 2019–2021, the Commissioner, Dame Sara Thornton, has stated that her priorities were to:

- improve victim care and support;
- support law enforcement;
- raise public awareness;
- and get value from research.

The Commissioner records that there are complaints about poor police identification of victims of modern slavery, and the ability of non-specialist officers to offer the right support and advice. The Home Office records that in a 38-month period that there were 4,107 potential victims who declined support – nearly half of whom had been referred by police forces. There are also problems with victims waiting years for decisions on their asylum claims, and where asylum is refused, victims can be sent back to high-risk situations. Clearly much remains to be done to protect the rights of vulnerable victims of modern slavery.

The 2020 report by the Centre for Social Justice (CSJ) makes a number of recommendations for reform of the system. Among these are the need for an urgent inquiry into the increasing exploitation; giving charities a 'strategic role' in partnering with police; passing the Modern Slavery (Victim Support) Bill to provide better support and protection; the need to transform police activity to dismantle criminal networks and prosecute more traffickers; and the prioritisation of international action and coordination to dismantle criminal networks.

Child Sexual Exploitation (CSE)[96]

The protection of children from sexual abuse within the family is discussed above. The powers of local authorities to intervene to protect vulnerable children are discussed in Chapter 6. Here attention turns to the organised criminal sexual exploitation of children, discussed firstly with reference to the Rotherham scandal of abuse between the 1980s and 2010s and secondly to the Independent Inquiry into Child Sexual Abuse established in 2015.

> Child sexual exploitation is a form of child sexual abuse. It occurs where an individual or group takes advantage of an imbalance of power to coerce, manipulate, or deceive a child or young person under the age of 18 into sexual activity (a) in exchange for something the victim needs or wants, and/or (b) for the financial advantage or increased status of the perpetrator or facilitator. The victim may have been sexually exploited even if the sexual activity appears consensual. Child sexual exploitation does not always involve physical contact; it can also occur through the use of technology.
>
> *Department for Education Guidance Child Sexual Exploitation, 2017*

> State Parties shall take all appropriate legislative, administrative, social and education measures to protect the child from all forms of physical or mental violence, injury or abuse, neglect or negligent treatment, maltreatment or exploitation, including sexual abuse.
>
> *UN Convention on the Rights of the Child, Article 19*

State Parties undertake to protect the child from all forms of sexual exploitation and sexual abuse. For these purposes, State Parties shall in particular take all appropriate national, bilateral and multilateral measures to prevent:

(a) the inducement or coercion of a child to engage in any unlawful sexual activity;

(b) the exploitative use of children in prostitution of other unlawful sexual practices;

(c) the exploitative use of children in pornographic performances and materials.

UN Convention on the Rights of the Child, Article 34

The Rotherham scandal

Over the years there have been several inquiries into the organised sexual exploitation of children in the UK. Of these, the Rotherham scandal – because of its duration, scale, and serious abuse – attracted the most in-depth examination.

The rights of approximately 1,400 girls aged 11–16, in Rotherham, Yorkshire, were violated from the late 1980s to the 2010s. Writing in *The Times* in 2012, Andrew Norfolk reported that there was widespread organised sexual abuse taking place in Rotherham and that the council and police had known about it for over ten years. In 2013 the House of Commons' Home Affairs Committee opened an inquiry. Rotherham Council commissioned an independent inquiry, led by Professor Alexis Jay, which reported in 2014.[97] The inquiry looked at the situation in the period from 1997 to 2013. The Jay Report states that in 'just over a third of cases, children affected by sexual exploitation were previously known to services because of child protection and neglect'. From the beginning there was growing evidence that the abuse was taking place, but the police and council effectively ignored the problem. The police gave no priority to allegations of CSE and treated victims with 'contempt'. Senior Council officers 'disbelieved' the data and reports of sexual exploitation linked to drugs and guns in the borough were ignored. The victims identified the perpetrators as 'Asian', but the Council did nothing to address this with the Pakistani community, fearing that this would lead to charges of racism.

In 2014 the National Crime Agency (NCA) launched Operation Stovewood to investigate the allegations of organised abuse in Rotherham: the largest law enforcement investigation into Child Sexual Exploitation and abuse in the UK. By 2015 the NCA had identified 300 suspects. Its inquiry was expected to last eight years at a cost of over £30 million. As of March 2019 its investigations had led to 20 new prosecutions and prison sentences totalling around 250 years.

In response to the Jay Report the Department for Communities and Local Government commissioned a further inquiry led by Louise Casey CB. The Casey Report 2015 found that Rotherham Council was not 'fit for purpose'.[98]

Rotherham's Children's Services were 'failing, with a lack of clarity over priorities, repeated missed deadlines for the assessment of children in need of care and protection, poor decision-making, drift and delay'. The investigation found that:

- the council was in denial about serious and ongoing safeguarding failures;
- an archaic culture of sexism, bullying, and discomfort around race;
- a failure to address past weaknesses, in particular in Children's Social Care;
- weak and ineffectual arrangements for taxi licensing which leave the public at risk;
- ineffectual leadership and management, including political leadership;
- no shared vision, a partial management team, and ineffective liaison with partners.

The Leader of the Council resigned, the Director of Children's Services resigned, the Police and Crime Commissioner for South Yorkshire resigned, and the government sent in a team of five commissioners to take over the running of the Council.[99]

The Independent Inquiry into Child Sexual Abuse 2015–2022[100]

Growing concerns over reports of child sexual abuse in various institutions such as the BBC, the NHS, local authorities, children's homes and schools, and failures by the police and Crown Prosecution Service (CPS) to prosecute offenders led to the establishment in 2015 of an independent statutory inquiry chaired by Professor Alexis Jay OBE.[101] The inquiry covers England and Wales, but where material identified relates to Northern Ireland and/or Scotland this will be passed to the relevant authorities. The Inquiry notes that there are estimates that one child in every 20 in the UK has been sexually abused and that in 2014 police statistics show that there were over 28,000 recorded sexual offences where the victim was aged under 16.

The purpose of the Inquiry is:

> To consider the extent to which State and non-State institutions have failed in their duty of care to protect children from sexual abuse and exploitation, to consider the extent to which those failings have since been addressed; to identify further action needed to address any failings identified; to consider the steps which it is necessary for State and non-State institutions to take in order to protect children from such abuse in future; and to publish a report with recommendations.

The Inquiry has looked at State and non-State institutions, including government departments, Parliament, churches, the police, political parties, and the armed services. It was concerned, among other things, to establish the extent to which child victims were known to local authorities such as the police, schools, and/or the NHS and whether the 'relevant authorities effectively identified the risk of Child Sexual Exploitation and took action to prevent it'. It was also concerned to evaluate whether there are 'effective strategies' now implemented to prevent future exploitation and to monitor the safety of vulnerable children, including missing children (on whom see Chapter 6). The Inquiry has liaised with Operation Hydrant, the national police investigation into more than 1,400 investigations of non-recent sexual abuse of children. It has also liaised with other inquiries into abuse in Australia, Jersey, Northern Ireland, and Scotland.

As of December 2020 the Inquiry had undertaken 15 separate investigations and heard evidence from more than 600 witnesses. Among the many reports is one into the failings of the Roman Catholic Church to protect chid victims of abuse. Between 1970 and 2015 there had been over 900 complaints involving over 3,000 alleged instances of child sexual abuse in England and Wales. Inquiries were conducted into the Church's leading schools: Ampleforth Abbey and School, Downside Abbey and School and Ealing Abbey, and St Benedict's School, in each of which substantial instances of abuse were revealed and perpetrators jailed. The Report finds that the Church prioritised its own reputation over the welfare of children for decades and that it had failed to support victims and protected perpetrators.[102] Despite repeated requests, neither the Holy See nor the Apostolic Nuncio co-operated with the Inquiry, an attitude at odds with Pope Francis' statement in 2019 calling for 'concrete and effective action that involves everyone in the Church'.[103]

Internet abuse

The sexual exploitation of children on the internet is a global phenomenon, and in recent years combating it has become a major aspect of police work. The Protection of Children Act 1998 makes it a criminal offence to take indecent images of children.[104] The Coroners and Justice Act 2009 makes possession of such images unlawful.[105] The offence carries a potential three-year custodial sentence. The Communications Act (CA) 2003 makes it a criminal offence to send message that are grossly offensive or of an indecent, obscene, or menacing character. The Malicious Communications Act (MCA) 1988 makes it an offence to send indecent or grossly offensive material or false information with the intention of causing distress or anxiety. There is no shortage of law, but it is clearly defective in policing harmful internet activity.[106] In January 2020 the NSPCC estimated that 25,300 child abuse images and sexual grooming offences were recorded by the police since March 2019. On the basis of recorded crime data, the NSPCC estimates that an average of one online abuse offence against a child was recorded every 16 minutes in England and Wales.

In the UK the Internet Watch Foundation (IWF) is responsible for identifying and removing child abuse content from the internet. The IWF is funded by service providers, mobile network operators, software and hardware manufacturers, and others. It provides a hotline to report illegal content and assesses the content on behalf of the law enforcement agencies. The IWF also works with service providers to help avoid abuse of their systems by those seeking to exploit children through illegal child sex abuse images and works with the police, security services, and the Crown Prosecution Service (CPS) to seek illegal content online. In its Annual Report IWF recorded that 89 per cent of images analysed in 2019 were hosted in Europe, with 71 per cent hosted in the Netherlands. Whereas the UK has a relatively robust system of identification and removal of images of child abuse, in the Netherlands there are greater internet freedoms and rights and it is necessary to get a court order to remove content. The Independent Inquiry into Child Sexual Abuse (IICSA) states that the IWF has 'made remarkable progress in removing child sexual abuse material from web addresses that are hosted in the UK'.

However, it remains the case that indecent images of children can still be accessed in 'only three clicks' and the IICSA calls on internet companies to do more to pre-screen material before it is uploaded on to their systems. The IICSA is also critical of internet companies in relation to the online grooming of children. Furthermore, internet companies are criticised for not fully understanding the scale of the problem of live screening on their platforms, and states that 'more needs to be done' than employing existing technologies many of which will not work where communications are encrypted.

Reform of the law is imminent. In 2019 the government published an Online Harms White Paper. The Law Commission (the body responsible for recommending law reform) concluded a consultation in 2020 and will report in 2021. The Independent Inquiry into Child Sexual Abuse has also published proposals on internet regulation. A Draft Online Harms Bill was published in May 2021.

The Law Commission has provisionally proposed a new criminal offence to replace existing offences.[107,108] The Commission considered that the current law, while covering a wide range of online communications, does not focus on the harms caused by online abuse. The law also fails to address adequately the offences of cyber-flashing (the transmission of images or video recordings of genitalia) or pile-on harassment (the coordinated attack on an individual). The proposed new offence would focus on the likely emotional or psychological harm caused to the recipient of communications, making communications criminal where harm is likely to be caused. At the same time, the Commission aims to protect freedom of expression as required by the common law and Article 10 of the ECHR.[109]

In debate in December 2020, the Secretary of State for Culture, Media and Sport (DCMS), Oliver Dowden, outlined the government's approach to regulation to be included in the new Act.[110] The government intends to impose on online companies a duty of care to their users. This will be overseen by Ofcom and failure to comply with their duty will make companies liable for fines totalling up to £18 million or ten per cent of their global turnover, whichever is the higher. In addition, if Parliament agrees, senior managers will face criminal sanctions for the failures of their company. Companies will be required to remove illegal content and Ofcom could be given power to compel internet service providers to block devices from connecting to offending services. The first priority in the new regime will be child sexual abuse, terrorism, and posts that incite violence and hatred. The DCMS and the Home Office have jointly published a draft Code of Practice on online Child Sexual Exploitation and abuse. Oliver Dowden described the proposals as making this 'the toughest and most comprehensive online safety regime in the world'.

Extremism and radicalisation

The UK Government's 2015 Prevent Strategy defines radicalisation as follows: 'Radicalisation' refers to the process by which a person comes to support terrorism[111] and extremist ideologies associated with terrorist groups.[112]

> 'Extremism' is the vocal or active opposition to fundamental British values, including democracy, the rule of law, individual liberty and mutual respect and tolerance of different faiths and beliefs. We also include in our definition of extremism calls for the death of members of our armed forces, whether in this country or overseas. Terrorist groups very often draw on extremist ideas developed by extremist organisations.[113]

The UK Government's counter-terrorism strategy is CONTEST of which the Prevent strategy is a part. According to the Government Guidance, the Prevent strategy has three specific objectives:

- to respond to the ideological challenge of terrorism and the threat we face from those who promote it;
- to prevent people from being drawn into terrorism and ensure that they are given appropriate advice and support;
- to work with sectors and institutions where there are risks of radicalisation that we need to address.

Public bodies are under a duty to 'have due regard to the need to prevent people from being drawn into terrorism', including non-violent terrorism.[114] The bodies include local authorities, prisons and young offenders institutions, all schools, colleges and universities, the National Health Service, and the police. Preventing people becoming involved in terrorism 'requires challenge to extremist ideas where they are used to legitimise terrorism and are shared by terrorist groups'. The Prevent strategy is aimed at all kinds of terrorist threats to the UK. Particularly prominent are the threats caused by terrorist organisations in Syria and Iraq and Al Qa'ida groups and also threats posed by extreme right-wing views: the 'white supremacist ideology'.

The success of the Prevent strategy depends on adequate training of staff to ensure awareness of the risks involved in extremist ideology and inter-agency cooperation. The Home Office has overall responsibility for issuing guidance on the strategy. The Extremism Analysis Unit (EAU) is a Home Office unit which researches extremism in the UK and overseas. The Home Office is also responsible for drawing together data from the agencies involved.

CASE FOCUS: *DR BUTT*[115]

A legal challenge to Home Office Prevent Guidance centred on the identification by the Extremism Analysis Unit (EAU) of Dr Salman Butt – the editor of *Islam21C*, a website dedicated to 'articulating Islamic beliefs in the 21st century' – as a 'hate speaker'. Dr Butt claimed that the collection and retention of data of his views was incompatible with Article 8 of the ECHR (the right to respect for privacy, etc.), and that the Higher Education Prevent Duty Guidance (HEPDG) was incompatible with Article 10 ECHR (freedom of speech). The Guidance stated that when considering whether to host a particular speaker, a higher education institution has to 'have regard to the need to prevent people from being drawn into terrorism'. However, higher education bodies are also under a duty to 'pay particular regard' to the duty to ensure freedom of speech.[116] If there is a perceived risk of people being drawn into terrorism, the institution should refuse to allow a speaker a platform unless the risk could be mitigated by either strong chairing of the meeting and by having speakers with opposing views on the platform. The Court of Appeal dismissed Dr Butt's appeal relating to the collection of data by the EAU, but allowed his appeal in relation to the Secretary of State's guidance relating to freedom of speech: that part of the guidance was unlawful and quashed (declared invalid). This was because the Secretary of State had failed to balance the risk that was posed by a particular speaker against the mitigating factors (i.e. chairing, platforming opposing views) and he had therefore not discharged his duty of balance under the Act. The challenge on Article 10 was dismissed: there was no evidence that the Secretary of State had actually prevented Dr Butt from speaking at universities.

Channel is the Government's programme for identifying and protecting children and adults from being drawn into terrorism.[117] A key part of the Channel strategy is early identification of potentially vulnerable children and adults and supporting them before they become victim to extremism and radicalisation and from there into involvement with terrorism. This requires inter-agency cooperation, with the police coordinating activity by requesting information from public bodies, assessing the vulnerability of people at risk, and presenting this to a local multi-agency panel with a view to developing a support plan for an individual. The Channel programme overlaps with the safeguarding duties of local authorities to protect children from harm (on safeguarding see Chapter 1).

Assessing the vulnerability of individuals to being drawn into terrorism focuses on three factors: *engagement* with a group, cause or ideology; *intent to cause harm* and *capability to cause harm*. Indicators of engagement include:

- spending time with suspected extremists;
- changing personal style of dress or appearance to fit in with the group;
- day-to-day behaviour becoming increasingly focused on extremist ideology;
- loss of interest in friends or activities;
- possession of materials or symbols associated with an extremist cause (e.g. a Nazi swastika);
- attempts to recruit others to a group or cause;
- communications which suggest identification with a group or cause.

Indicators as to intention include:

- clearly identifying another group as threatening what they stand for;
- using insulting or derogatory language or labels for another group;
- speaking about the imminence of harm from the other group and the importance of action now;
- expressing attitudes that justify offending on behalf of the group, cause, or ideology;
- condoning or supporting violence or harm towards others;
- plotting or conspiring with others.

Indicators as to capability of causing harm or contributing to terrorist acts include:

- having a history of violence;
- being criminally versatile and using criminal networks to support extremist goals;
- having occupational skills that enable acts of terrorism;
- having technical expertise, e.g. IT skills, that can be deployed in terrorist acts.

Channel is a voluntary programme and therefore requires the consent of participants: for children this requires the consent of parents or carers. Consent is required at two stages: for the sharing of information between agencies and in advance of support measures being put in place. Where parental consent is not given for participation in the support programme, consideration must be given to whether the child is a 'child in need' (Children Act 1989, section 17) of local authority support, and/or whether the child is at risk of significant harm (Children Act 1989, section 31(9)). In either case social services must be involved and statutory assessments made with a view to protecting the child under a care or Supervision Order.[118]

For all the good intentions of the Prevent programme and Channel, it has to be recognised that there are serious criticisms which have been expressed by parliamentarians, community groups, and NGOs. The mention of 'British values' in the definition of extremism has attracted the accusation from Muslim commentators and rights groups that it is 'racist'. Muslim communities have repeatedly claimed that they are disproportionately targeted and that this violates their rights. The strategy is also criticised for having an adverse impact on freedom of speech and religion. Rights Watch UK claims that Prevent has led to 'a systematic breach of children's human rights in the school setting', leading to 'violations of the right to education, the right to freedom of expression, the right to freedom of religion, the right to privacy, the right to freedom from discrimination' and the fundamental principle that actions taken in relation to children must treat the child's best interests as a primary consideration.[119]

The reliance on teachers, health workers, and social workers to identify those vulnerable to extremism and make referrals to Channel has been described as having a 'negative impact' on the fragile trust between communities and public services and has led to calls for it to be scrapped.[120] It has also allegedly led to a significant increase in the number of referrals to Prevent. In 2017–2018 over 7,000 people, including children, were referred, 95 per cent of whom did not require action under the Channel programme.

The Government is under a statutory duty to establish an independent review of its strategy for supporting those vulnerable to being drawn into terrorism.[121] In 2019, the Government appointed Lord Carlile as the reviewer, but was forced to drop him after allegations that Lord Carlile had a well-recorded bias in favour of the Prevent programme and Rights Watch (UK) threatened legal action. He was replaced by Jonathan Hall QC. The Review was published in March 2021.

Several cases of alleged harm caused to children through radicalisation have reached the courts. The issue most frequently comes before the courts within the context of care proceedings under the Children Act 1989.[122] The process through which the courts work in reaching decisions over the child's welfare within the context of radicalisation was set out in a case in 2017.[123] The principles to be applied are as follows:

- the burden of proving the facts pleaded before the court rests with the local authority;
- the standard of proof is the balance of probabilities: there is no room for a finding that 'something might have happened';
- findings of fact must be based on evidence not on speculation;
- in deciding whether an authority has discharged the burden of proof the court looks at a wide range of matters, including the credibility of witnesses and inferences that can be drawn from the evidence;
- suspicion is not enough: any findings of fact made by the court must be based on evidence;

- the evidence of parents and carers is of utmost importance and the court must have a clear view of their reliability and credibility;
- in relation to proceedings brought under the Children Act the court must be satisfied that the criteria for making an order is made out and bear in mind that the child's welfare is the paramount consideration.

The approach of the courts is revealed in the following cases.

CASE FOCUS: C, D, AND E[124]

The North-East Counter Terrorism Unit were inquiring into activities of the parents of three children. The children had been taken into care as a result of their parents' extremist ideology but returned home pending a further decision about their welfare. The father was arrested for involvement in racial hatred. A search of the family home disclosed Jihadi activity and association with terrorist organisations. Both parents were arrested and the mother charged with cruelty or neglect exposing the children to danger (section 1 Children and Young Persons Act 1933). The family took a trip to Folkestone. The parents said they were taking a family holiday, but the factual evidence pointed to their real intention being to travel to Isis-controlled territory in Syria or Iraq.

Prior to a further court hearing to decide the children's future, the children were allowed home. The parents were electronically tagged, a contract was agreed with the local authority over the care of the children, the terms of which were to be monitored by the local authority.

CASE FOCUS: Y[125]

Care proceedings brought by a local authority involved three children, J, a girl aged 16, and two boys aged 14 and 10, allegedly at risk of radicalisation by their father. They had been intercepted at Harwich Ferry Port, suspected of travelling to Syria and Islamic State. The children had said that they did not wish to leave the family home or be separated from one another. However, the judge found that the attitudes, belief systems, and behaviours in the family meant that the 'effect of radicalisation was 'so pervasive'; and the dangers of further infection of views so great that an individual incident (Harwich) could not affect the outcome. The treatment of the children, the delight in the infliction of pain (the youngest child had been forced to eat raw chilli) was a cause of extreme concern.' With a 'heavy heart' a Care Order was granted.

CASE FOCUS: *A*[126]

There were four children, aged 17, 12, 9, and 7. On returning from a holiday in Turkey in 2018 they were searched under terrorism legislation.[127] Days later the police searched the family home and a computer, tablet, memory stick, and mobile phones were removed. Examination of these revealed images glorifying Islamic State (IS) and encouraging terrorism. The local authority nevertheless concluded that the children were not at risk of significant harm and recommended the intervention of the Prevent programme. Four months later Prevent made a referral to the local authority, on the basis that the police intended to arrest the parents on terrorism charges. On the local authority's application Interim Care Orders were granted.

All four children were at risk of continuing significant harm to their physical and emotional well-being attributable to the care of their parents. The mother was a strong supporter of terrorism and the use of murder and violence in support of IS. The father also supported terrorism and stated that he wished to become a suicide bomber. The children were all exposed to extremist images of violence, hatred, and murder. Care Orders were granted, and the local authority given permission to apply for the confiscation of the eldest child's passport until she reached the age of 18, or travelled with the family with the approval of the local authority.

Summary

Although diverse in nature, all of the issues discussed above have one common feature: that of the vulnerability of children and their relative powerlessness compared with adults intent on harming them, whether through criminality or ingrained cultural beliefs which violate their rights.

The law responds to challenges as they arise, providing new remedies for victims and creating new criminal offences to both deter and punish offenders. Nevertheless, there are real difficulties in eradicating the assaults on children's rights. The law recognises that the family is the key building block of society and that children are best brought up by their parents free of legal intervention unless there are serious grounds on which to intervene. Where the problem arises within the family, it is unrealistic to expect a child to complain against his or her own parents or siblings. Even if a child has the knowledge and courage to complain, to do so will risk his or her long-term security within the family and/or place his or her family member(s) at risk of legal sanctions with unknown consequences for the child and his or her family.

Where a child's rights are violated through the actions of non-family agents the problems are no less intractable. All children are potentially vulnerable to being targeted by criminals intent on using them for financial or other advantages. Parents, schools, local authority welfare agencies, and the police all have a duty to play a role in safeguarding children's well-being and rights. Too often, as various examples discussed in this chapter have illustrated, children can become victims and serious harm caused before the protective agencies become aware of their plight and step in to offer protection and, where necessary, to prosecute the offenders.

Notes

1 Children and Young Persons Act 1933, section 1.
2 London Borough of Brent, *A Child in Trust*, 1985.
3 Home Office, March 2013; see Domestic Abuse Act 2021, section 1.
4 Now abolished.
5 London: HMSO, Cm 412; CM 413.
6 Lord Laming, *The Victoria Climbie Inquiry Report*, 2003, CM 5730, paragraphs 1.18; 1.31.
7 Children and Young Persons Act 1933, section 1.
8 www.coe.int/en/web/children/corporal-punishment#("12441097":[1])
9 *Tyrer v United Kingdom* [1978] 2 EHRR 1.
10 *A v United Kingdom* [1998] ECHR 85.
11 DfES (2007b), paragraph 55.
12 Education (No 2) Act 1986, section 47.
13 Education Act 1993, section 293.
14 Day Care and Child Minding (National Standards) (England) regulations 2003, SI 2003/1996, paragraph 5.
15 Children Act 2004, section 58.
16 Children (Equal Protection from Assault) (Scotland) Act 2019. The Act comes into force in 2022.
17 Children (Abolition of Defence of Reasonable Punishment) (Wales) Act 2020.
18 www.ohchr.org/EN/Issues/Woman/WRGS/Pages/ChildMarriage.aspx   In 2017 the International Labour Organisation recognised forced marriage as a form of slavery.
19 By contrast, an arranged marriage is one organised by families where both parties consent to the union but can still refuse to marry if they choose to.
20 Marriage Act 1949, section 2; Matrimonial Causes Act 1973, section 11(a)(ii).
21 ibid., section 2.
22 In Scotland lack of consent because of duress makes a marriage void: Family Law (Scotland) Act 2006, section 2.
23 Matrimonial Causes Act 1973, section 12(1)(c). In Scotland, the Family Law (Scotland) Act 2006, section 2 amending the Marriage (Scotland) Act 1977.
24 Although the requirement of valid consent is a feature of many faiths, the grounds for void and voidable marriage under English law reflect the traditional influence of the Christian faith.
25 *Scott v Sebright* (1886) 12 PD 21.
26 *Mahmood v Mahmood* [1993] SLT 589.
27 *Mahmud v Mahmud* [1994] SLT 599.
28 Anti-social Behaviour, Crime and Policing Act 2014, section 121.
29 Forced Marriage (Civil Protection) Act 2007, section 1, amending Family Law Act 1996. In Scotland, the Forced Marriage etc. (Protection and Jurisdiction) (Scotland) Act 2011.

30 Family Law Act 1996, section 63CA.
31 *Re K (Forced Marriage: Passport Order)* [2020] EWCA Civ 190: an FMPO was granted to protect a mentally competent 35-year-old.
32 Family Law Act 1996, section 63A.
33 Ministry of Justice, Family Court Quarterly Statistics, July to September 2019, page 13.
34 ibid., section 63B.
35 ibid., section 63I.
36 ibid., section 63C.
37 Family Law Act 1996 (Forced Marriage) (Relevant Third Party) Order 2009; Forced Marriage etc (Protection and Jurisdiction) (Scotland) Act 2011 (Relevant Third Party) Order 2017.
38 ibid., section 63D.
39 ibid., section 63F and 63G.
40 Which amended the Family Law Act 1996.
41 *re K (Forced Marriage: Passport Order)* [2020] EWCA Civ 190.
42 *G and D (Risk of forced marriage: Forced Marriage Protection Order)* [2010] NI Fam 6 (26 March 2010).
43 Under the Northern Ireland Forced Marriage (Civil Protection) Act 2007.
44 *Re A, B, C, D, E, F and G (Minors)* [2012] EWHC 435 (Fam).
45 Joint Statement: WHO, UNICEF, and UN Population Fund, *Female Genital Mutilation*, 1997.
46 Article 1 or 16 Convention Against Torture and Other Cruel, Inhuman or Degrading Treatment, or Punishment, Article 7 International Covenant on Civil and Political Rights, Article 37a UNCRC.
47 Mr Justice Newton, in *A* [2020] EWHC 3323 (Fam), paragraphs 21 and 22.
48 UNICEF UK: *Unleashing Youth Power: A Decade of Accelerating Actions Towards Zero Tolerance FGM.* 2020.
49 Baroness Hale, *Secretary of State for the Home Department v K; Fornah v Secretary of State for the Home Department* [2006] UKHL 46, paragraphs 92, 93.
50 UNICEF, *Female Genital Mutilation/Cutting.* Executive Summary, 2013a.
51 Leye, E and Middleburg, A, *FGM and Children's Rights* in Routledge International Handbook of Children's Rights Studies, 2017, p 295.
52 UNICEF UK, supra note xiv.
53 NHS Digital.
54 NHS Digital Annual Statistics.
55 In Scotland the equivalent law is now the Prohibition of Female Genital Mutilation (Scotland) Act 2005.
56 Serious Crime Act 2015, sections 70 to 75, amending the 2003 Act.
57 ibid., section 71, inserting section 4A into the 2003 Act.
58 Serious Crime Act 2015, section 72, inserting new section 3A into the 2003 Act.
59 ibid., section 74, inserting new section 5B into the 2003 Act.
60 NHS Digital, Annual Report: The Times 24 July 2020.
61 ibid., section 73, inserting new section 5A into the 2003 Act 2003. For further detail see the 2003 Act, Schedule 2.
62 Female Genital Mutilation Act 2003, section 1.
63 Ministry of Justice, Family Court Quarterly Statistics, July 2019 to September 2019, page 13.
64 ibid., section 2.
65 ibid., section 4.
66 *Re X (FGMPO No 2)* [2019] EWHC 1990 (Fam).

67 *A (Female Genital Mutilation Protection Order Application)* [2020] EWHC 323 (Fam).
68 *Oxfordshire County Council v AD and Others* [2019] EWFC B66 (17.12.2019)
69 *Re X (Female Genital Mutilation Protection Order No 2)* [2019] EWHC 1990 (Fam).
70 See the UN Office on Drugs and Crime, *The Concept of Exploitation in the Trafficking of Persons Protocol* 2015; and the UN Convention against Transnational Organised Crime, 2003, ratified by the UK in 2006.
71 See also Honderich, T, ed., The Oxford Companion to Philosophy, Oxford: OUP, 2nd edn., 2005.
72 Other categories of exploitation are labour exploitation, domestic servitude, sexual exploitation, unknown exploitation, and organ harvesting: Home Office, National Referral Mechanism Statistics 2019.
73 UK Government, *Working Together to Safeguard Children*, 2018.
74 National Crime Agency, Intelligence Assessment: *County Lines Drug Supply, Vulnerability and Harm 2018*, January 2019.
75 The Crest Report, cited in *The Times*, 24 July 2020.
76 16 January 2020.
77 *The Times*: 29 May 2020.
78 HM Government, *Modern Slavery Strategy*, 2014, paragraph 1.2.
79 See also the Council of Europe Convention on Action Against Trafficking Human Beings 2005.
80 The Modern Slavery Act 2015, the Human Trafficking and Exploitation (Scotland) Act 2015, and Human Trafficking and Exploitation (Criminal Justice and Support for Victims) Act (Northern Ireland) 2015 govern this area of the law.
81 See the Slave Trade Act 1807 and the Slavery Abolition Act 1833.
82 Page 19, paragraph 3.4.1.
83 In October 2019, 39 people trafficked from Vietnam died in a refrigerated container and in 2017 and 2018 there were over 1,400 Vietnamese trafficking victims referred to the National Referral Mechanism (see below).
84 *It Still Happens*: Fighting UK Slavery in the 2020s, July 2020.
85 *It Still Happens,* 2020, Executive Summary.
86 Strategic Report, 2019–2021, paragraph 2.3.5.
87 See the Centre for Social Justice Report, *It Still Happens Here: Fighting UK Slavery in the 2020s*, 2020.
88 Max Hill QC, DPP, Speech to Heads of Prosecution Agencies Conference in Uganda, 15–17 April 2019: *Emerging Areas of Child abuse.*
89 Modern Slavery Act 2015, section 51.
90 *VCL and AN v United Kingdom* (2021) ECtHR 16 February 2021; Times LR 17 March 2021.
91 *The Times*, 19 March 2021.
92 Established in 2009 following ratification of the Council of Europe Convention on Action against Trafficking in Human Beings (ECAT).
93 Albania and Vietnam feature high on the list of countries from which victims are trafficked.
94 Modern Slavery (Victim Support) Bill, clause 3 amending the Children Act 1989, section 22.
95 In 2018, the Anti-Slavery Commissioner, Kevin Hyland, resigned, complaining of government interference in his work. He had publicly criticised police forces for failing to tackle enslaved Vietnamese teenagers and young people trafficked into the UK to work in illegal cannabis farms: a criticism rejected by the Home

Office as 'disproportionate': Amelia Gentleman, *The Guardian,* 28 October 2019.

96 The National Crime Agency reports that it and UK police arrest around 500 child sex offenders each month and in 2018 560 children referred for trafficking for sexual exploitation.

97 Alexis Jay OBE, *Independent Inquiry into Child Sexual Exploitation in Rotherham 1997 to 2013,* 2014.

98 Louise Casey CB, *Report of the Inspection of Rotherham MBC,* London: Department for Communities and Local Government, 2015, HC 1050. See also the House Of Commons Home Affairs Committee Report, *Child Sexual Exploitation and the response to localised grooming: follow up,* 6th Report, 2014–15, HC 203.

99 Under the Local Government Act 1999.

100 www.iicsa.org.uk

101 Established under the Inquiries Act 2005.

102 In 2020 Ampleforth College failed an Ofsted inspection for failure to take 'all reasonable, timely and appropriate action to safeguard pupils'. The Education Secretary announced that with effect from December 2020 Ampleforth was banned from taking new pupils, a prohibition likely to lead to the closure of the College.

103 10 November, 2920, www.iicsa.org.uk/publications/investigations/roman-cath olic-church

104 Protection of Children Act 1989, section 1(1)(a).

105 Coroners and Justice Act 2009, section 62.

106 See also the Criminal Justice Act 1988, section 160; Sexual Offences Act 2003, sections 10, 12, 14, 15.

107 Malicious Communication Act 1988 and Communication Act 2003, section 127(1).

108 And a new offence covering the sending of knowingly false communications.

109 See: The Law Commission, *Harmful Online Communications: The Criminal Offences – A Consultation Paper; Harmful Online Communications: The Criminal Offences – Summary of the Consultation Paper.*

110 Hansard, 15 December 2020, Col 686 ff.

111 Terrorism is defined in the Terrorism Act 2000, section 1. It is a criminal offence to belong to, support, or display support for a proscribed (prohibited) organisation.

112 Prevent Duty Guidance for England and Wales, 2015.

113 Statutory Duty for Channel panel members and partners of local panels, 2015.

114 Counter-Terrorism and Security Act 2015, section 26 and Schedule 6.

115 *Butt v Secretary of State for the Home Department* [2019] EWCA Civ 256.

116 Counter-Terrorism and Security Act 2015, section 26.

117 HM Government: *Channel Duty Guidance: Protecting vulnerable people from being drawn into terrorism,* 2015.

118 Under the Children Act 1989, section 17 or section 47.

119 Rights Watch UK: *Preventing Education: Human Rights and UK Counter-Terrorism Policy in Schools,* 2016.

120 UN Special Rapporteur Fionnuala Ní Aoláin.

121 Counter-terrorism and Border Security Act 2015, section 20.

122 Section 31, on which see above.

123 In *A Local Authority v HB* [2017] EWHC 1437 (Fam), cited in *A Local Authority v A Mother* [2018] EWHC 2056 (Fam), paragraphs 66 to 69.

124 *Re C, D and E* [2016] EWHC 3088 (Fam).

125 *Re Y (Children) (Radicalisation)* [2016] EWHC 3827 (Fam).
126 *A City Council v A Mother and A Father (Care Proceedings: Radicalisation)* [2019] EWHC 3076 (Fam).
127 Terrorism Act 2000, Schedule 7.

6

PROTECTING VULNERABLE CHILDREN

Introduction

In this chapter we discuss the role of the State in protecting children's rights when they are in need of care, protection, and support. Responsibility for child protection and children's services is devolved to each of the four nations of the UK. In England the responsibility for child protection policy and guidance lies with the Department for Education (DfE), while responsibility for administering the system rests with local authorities. In Wales, the Social Services and Well-being (Wales) Act 2014 regulates child protection whilst in Northern Ireland, the Northern Ireland Executive, through the Department of Health, has that responsibility. In Scotland the Children and Young People (Scotland) Act 2014 governs child protection and the Scottish Government sets out policy, legislation, and guidance on how the system should work.[1] The principal focus in this chapter is on the English system.

As discussed in Chapter 1 and elsewhere, the governing principle in reaching decisions over the care and upbringing of children is their welfare. Local authorities are also under a duty to safeguard children: a duty which runs alongside the welfare principle. To reiterate:

> It is the general duty of every local authority to safeguard and promote the welfare of children within their area who are in need, and as far as is consistent with that duty, to promote the upbringing of such children by their families by providing a range and level of services appropriate to those children's needs.
>
> *Children Act 1989, section 17*

The duty to protect children must be viewed in light of the right of families to the protection of their private and family life, as guaranteed by Article 8 of the

DOI: 10.4324/9780429452710-6

European Convention on Human Rights ECHR). Any interference with the right to family life must, under Article 8, be in accordance with law. This, in turn, requires that any action interfering with family life, must be 'necessary' and proportionate to the circumstances of the case. These requirements were central to the case below.

CASE FOCUS: *HAASE*[2]

Mrs H had 12 children, seven from her first marriage, five from her second. Relations between her and her husband deteriorated and he sought a divorce. In the course of legal proceedings, a report was drawn up by an expert which was highly critical of the children's care. The (German) Youth Office applied for an interim injunction removing parental rights over some of the children on the basis that the parents had failed to give the children adequate care and education and were unreasonably harsh with the children. The order being granted, the children were taken from the family, including the removal of a new-born from hospital. The separation of the children from their family was supplemented by an order that the whereabouts of the children were to be kept from the parents and prohibiting any access to them. An appeal against the orders was dismissed without a hearing.[3]

The issue went to the European Court of Human Rights. The Court stated that 'there were serious doubts' whether the German courts had respected the importance of parental rights...and whether they had sufficiently taken into account the principle of proportionality. The orders had

> ... led to a drastic change of the living conditions of all the persons concerned and constituted an interference with the parental rights of a particular high intensity. However, no inquiries had been made.. before taking the decision. No reasons were given justifying the urgency of the matter (at paragraph 30).

Moreover, 'taking suddenly six children from their respective schools, kindergarten and from home and placing them in unidentified foster homes, and forbidding all contact with the [parents], went beyond the exigencies of the situation and cannot be accepted as proportionate'. There was a violation of Article 8.

The duties of local authorities[4]

Note: Local authority powers and the orders that courts can make is a complex and detailed area of the law. What follows is no more than an overview of the different local authority duties and powers and the orders a court can make in relation to children.

There were 655,630 new referrals of children to local authorities in the year ending March 2018 and 404,710 of these were children in need of care and protection.[5] The principal law relating to the State's role in children's safety and well-being in England and Wales is the Children Act 1989 (see further Chapter 1) and in Scotland the Children (Scotland) Act 1995. The Children Act does not regulate all aspects of child law but it is comprehensive in relation to the courts' powers to make orders relating to the care and upbringing of children including regulating arrangements for children when parents separate or divorce.

Where parents cannot fulfil their obligations and protect the rights of the child, the State – in the form of the local authority – must step in and care for and protect the child. In 2018 there were 75,420 children being looked after by local authorities due to abuse or neglect, a 40 per cent increase on the previous year. Neglect is the most cited category of abuse for Child Protection Plans (CPP) which related to 25,330 children at the end of March 2019. Neglect is defined by the government as:

> … the persistent failure to meet a child's basic physical and/or psychological needs, likely to result in the serious impairment of the child's health or development.[6]

Neglect is difficult to measure: whereas physical neglect may be obvious, emotional or psychological neglect is not. The Crime Survey for England and Wales estimated that one in 100 adults suffered neglect before the age of 16, amounting to 481,000 or 1.2 per cent of the population. Of those, 70 per cent also suffered emotional abuse.[7]

Every child has the right to grow up free from abuse or neglect. This is reflected in the criminal law in the following manner:

> If any person who has attained the age of sixteen years and has responsibility for any child or young person under that age, wilfully assaults, ill-treats (whether physically or otherwise), neglects, abandons, or exposes him or causes or procures him to be assaulted etc. in a manner likely to cause him unnecessary suffering or injuring to health (whether of a physical or psychological nature), that person shall be guilty of an offence.
>
> *Children and Young Persons Act 1933, section 1(1)*

Children in need

The Children Act defines a child as being in need if:

- he or she is unlikely to achieve or maintain, or to have the opportunity of achieving or maintaining, a reasonable standard of health or development without the provision for him of services by a local authority;

- his or her health or development is likely to be significantly impaired, or further impaired, without the provision of such services; or
- he or she is disabled.[8]

Referrals

Anyone may make a referral to the local authority if they have concerns over a child's well-being. All practitioners who may have concerns about a child's welfare should make a referral to the local authority social care team, which has primary responsibility for safeguarding children. Practitioners should include any information they have on the child's developmental needs, the capacity of parents and carers to meet those needs, and any external factors which might affect a child's welfare.[9]

The duty to provide services for children in need

In addition to any other duties imposed by the Children Act, local authorities are under a duty to safeguard and promote the welfare of children in need and to promote the upbringing of children by their families. In order to achieve this, it is the duty of local authorities to provide 'a range and level of services appropriate to those children's needs'.[10]

The duty to investigate: Children Act, section 47

The Children Act 1989 places a duty on local authorities to investigate and to decide whether it needs to take action to ensure the safety and well-being of the child. Where an authority has reasonable cause to believe that a child in their area is suffering, or is likely to suffer, significant harm, or where the authority already has obtained an Emergency Protection Order (on which see below) it must carry out an investigation.[11] Following this investigation, the local authority may hold a Child Protection Conference, bringing together family members, the child (if appropriate on the basis of age and understanding), and professionals involved with the family (doctors and other health workers, teachers, and police officers). The person chairing the conference may exclude a person if there is a suspicion of their involvement in any domestic violence. A parent may request that someone else attend in order to support them, and may have a solicitor present if that is felt necessary. The child concerned may attend, but is not required to attend, and if attending may have a solicitor present.

Where a child is considered to be suffering from harm, or likely to be suffering from harm, the outcome of the Child Protection Conference will be a child protection plan (CPP) and the child's name will be entered on the Child Protection Register. The CPP will set out ways in which the child can be protected and the responsibilities of those involved in the child's care and set a date for a Child Protection Review Conference. These will take place every three to six months. The plan will end when the child reaches the age of 18, leaves the country permanently, or the local authority decides that the child is no longer at risk of significant harm. If parents do not comply with the plan, the local authority may consider applying for court orders (on which see below).

Care plans: Children Act, section 31A

When a local authority identifies a child who is in need of care, it must draw up a care plan for the child.[12] The objective of the plan is to set out arrangements to protect the welfare of the child. The plan is prepared by a social worker in consultation with the child, his or her parents, and anyone who is not a parent but who has been looking after the child.

A key aspect of the care plan is to establish arrangements for the upbringing of the child, providing stability and permanence, the 'permanence plan'. Once the problems which led him or her to come into care have been settled this may be achieved by returning the child to his or her birth family. A court considering an application for a Care or Supervision Order must consider the arrangements made under the plan. The plan should give details of the child's needs, his or her wishes and feelings, and whether any intended placement with foster parents is intended to be short- or long-term. The plan must also set out the arrangements for contact with parents and other family members (the child's health and education needs should also be covered).[13]

The duty to provide accommodation: the Children Act 1989 section 20[14]

Every local authority must provide accommodation for any child in need who appears to require accommodation as a result of the following situations:

- there is no one with parental responsibility for their care;
- he or she is lost or has been abandoned;
- the person who has been caring for him or her is temporarily or permanently unable to provide accommodation.

Local authorities must also provide accommodation for children in need aged 16 and whose welfare will be 'seriously prejudiced' if accommodation is not provided for him or her. The local authority may also provide accommodation for any child in need even though there is someone with parental responsibility who is able to provide accommodation for him or her, if this would safeguard or promote the child's welfare. The authority may not, however, provide accommodation if there is a person with parental responsibility who is willing and able to provide accommodation (or arrange other suitable accommodation) objects.[15] The person with parental responsibility may remove the child from voluntary accommodation at any time. However, if the child is aged 16 and agrees to being accommodated by the authority, this will override any parental objections and the right to remove the child from the accommodation. Local authorities must also provide accommodation for children who have been taken into police protection (on which see below).[16]

CASE FOCUS: W[17]

A 12-year-old boy, one of eight siblings, was caught shoplifting. The police visited his home and found it to be in an unhygienic and dangerous state unfit for habitation by children. The police removed the children to suitable accommodation for a maximum of 72 hours.[18] The local authority organised foster placements. The parents signed a 'Safeguarding Agreement' by which they agreed to the children remaining with foster parents for the time being. They were not informed of their right to object to the children's continued accommodation after 72 hours, or of their right to remove them at any time.[19] The parents later gave formal notice that they withdrew their consent to the accommodation and the children were returned. Criminal proceedings against the parents were dropped, and they then took proceedings claiming that there had been no lawful basis for the accommodation of the children (because of their lack of consent) and a breach of their right to respect for family life (Article 8 ECHR). The case went to the Supreme Court.

The Supreme Court unanimously rejected the parents' appeal. The parents did not object to the council providing accommodation, nor did they request the immediate return of the children. The lawfulness of the section 20 accommodation depended on whether the parents had made an unequivocal request for the children to be returned. They had not, therefore there was a lawful basis for the children's continued accommodation.[20]

Before arranging the accommodation, the local authority must – to the extent that it is consistent with the child's welfare – consider the wishes and feelings of the child concerned. In order to safeguard and promote the child's welfare, the authority must appoint at least one qualified local authority employee to take responsibility, and where decisions are to be made in relation to the child, the authority must consider the wishes of the child, his or her parents, and anyone else with parental responsibility for the child.

There is a duty to arrange accommodation for looked-after children with foster parents or in children's homes within the authority's area. However, the right of a child to be accommodated within his or her area is qualified by the duty imposed on local authorities being to take steps 'as far as practicable'. In other words it is not an absolute right, and as the data shows, too often children are accommodated not just out of area, but many miles from home. On this see below, page 171.

Court orders

Child Assessment Orders (CAOs): Children Act, section 43[21]

A Child Assessment Order is an order of the court authorising a local authority to make an assessment of a child's health and development with a view to deciding whether further action should be taken to protect the rights of the child. Where a local authority (or other authorised person, i.e. the NSPCC and its officers) has concerns over the welfare of a child it may apply to the court for a Child Assessment Order. The court will grant this only if it is satisfied that:

- the authority has reasonable grounds to suspect that the child is suffering, or is likely to suffer, significant harm;
- an assessment of the child's health and development and the way he or she has been treated is necessary to enable the authority to decide whether or not he or she is suffering, or likely to suffer, significant harm; and
- it is unlikely that a satisfactory assessment will be made unless an order is made.

The CAO must state the date on which the assessment is to begin, and may last for only seven days after that date. While in force the CAO requires any person who has the child in his or her care to produce the child and comply with any directions given by the court. If it is necessary for the child to be kept away from home for the purpose of an assessment, the court must authorise this and the period for which he or she may be kept away from home. The court also gives directions as to the contact he or she is allowed to have with others while away from home. A CAO may authorise a medical or psychiatric examination or assessment. If the child is old enough to make an informed decision (a question for the court to decide), he or she may refuse to submit to such a medical or psychiatric examination.

The court can treat an application for a CAO as an application for an Emergency Protection Order. Where the court considers that there are grounds for making an Emergency Protection Order (see below) it may not also make a Child Assessment Order.[22]

Emergency Protection Orders (EPOs): Children Act, section 44[23]

An Emergency Protection Order (EPO) is a court order authorising the immediate removal of a child from his or home in order to protect him or her from danger. Given that being removed from home is a frightening and confusing experience for a child, an EPO will only be granted if it is really necessary for urgent action to be taken in order to protect the child.

In order to make an EPO the court must be satisfied that there is reasonable cause to believe that the child is suffering, or is likely to suffer, significant harm unless he or she is removed from his or her home. An EPO may only be made on the application of a local authority where enquiries are being made[24] and the enquiries are being frustrated by access to the child being unreasonably refused and the authority considers that access to the child is a matter of urgency. Where the applicant is an 'authorised person' – the NSPCC and its officers – the same grounds must be satisfied, with the difference that a section 47 investigation is not underway, but the person is making enquiries as to the child's welfare.

Unless extended by the court an EPO lasts for eight days. While the order is in force, it requires the person having care of the child to comply with any request to produce him or her and it authorises the removal of the child to local authority accommodation. The EPO operates to prevent the child's removal from a hospital or any other place where he or she was accommodated immediately before the EPO was made. The court may give directions as to contact between the child and others, and any necessary medical, psychiatric, or other assessment of the child. It is a criminal offence to intentionally obstruct a person authorised to remove a child, or prevent his or her removal to a place of safety.

Where an EPO is made and the court considers that harm to the child will be prevented by ordering the exclusion of another person living in the property, the court may require that person to leave the property, not to enter the property, and/or order that he or she be excluded from a defined area in which the home is situated. Where an EPO contains an exclusion requirement the court may attach a power of arrest to the order. This power of arrest authorises a police officer to arrest without warrant any person the officer believes to be in breach of the exclusion requirement.[25]

Taking a child into police protection: Children Act, section 46

Supplementing local authority powers and providing a short-term emergency solution, where a police officer 'has reasonable cause to believe' that a child would be likely to suffer significant harm, he or she may remove the child to 'suitable accommodation', or take whatever steps are necessary to ensure that the child is not removed from a hospital or other place where he or she is being accommodated. This provides a breathing space for enquiries to be made concerning the child's safety and well-being. There is a duty to inform the local authority, parents, or others with whom the child was living that he or she has been taken into police protection. No child may be kept in police protection for more than 72 hours. When the police enquiry is complete, the child must be released from police protection, unless the officer considers there is still reasonable cause to believe that the child would suffer significant harm if released.

The power to remove a child from police protection may be exercised even when an EPO is in existence. This will normally not be necessary but should the conditions for removing a child exist, the police power is not excluded by the existence of an EPO and the action of the police in removing a child will be lawful.[26] However, where the police know that an EPO exists, a child should only be removed if there are compelling reasons to do so.

Care and Supervision Orders: Children Act, section 31[27]

A Care Order is an order of the court authorising a local authority to take a child into its care and to keep him or her there while the order remains in force. A Care Order gives parental responsibility to the authority, to be shared with the parents of the child, enabling the authority to take all decisions relating to the child's care and upbringing. However, protecting the rights of parents and the integrity of the family unit, the authority may only exercise parental responsibility if it is necessary to do so to safeguard or promote the child's welfare.[28]

Any local authority, or an officer of the NSPCC, may apply to the court for a Care or Supervision Order. A Care or Supervision Order may only be made by the court if it is satisfied:

- that the child concerned is suffering, or is likely to suffer, significant harm; and
- that the harm, or likelihood of harm, is attributable to – the care being given to the child not being what it would be reasonable to expect a parent to give to him or her or that the child is beyond parental control.

A court must not make the order unless it considers that doing so would be better than making no order at all (the 'no order' principle).[29] Consistent with all child care decisions, in deciding whether to make an order, the child's welfare is the paramount consideration.

In every case there is a need to establish whether the care provided for the child has crossed the threshold from reasonable care into care causing significant harm. As Baroness Hale explained in *Re B* (2013), when applying the law the court should bear in mind:

- that the court's task is not to improve on nature or even to secure that every child has a happy and fulfilled life, but to be satisfied that the statutory threshold has been crossed;
- when deciding whether the threshold is crossed the court should identify, as precisely as possible, the nature of the harm which the child is suffering or is likely to suffer. This is particularly important where the child has not yet suffered any, or any significant, harm and where the harm which is feared is the impairment of intellectual, emotional, social, or behavioural development;
- significant harm is harm which is 'considerable, noteworthy or important'. The court should identify why and in what respects the harm is significant.

Again, this may be particularly important where the harm in question is the impairment of intellectual, emotional, social, or behavioural development which has not yet happened;

- the harm must be attributable to a lack, or likely lack, of reasonable parental care, not simply to the characters and personalities of both the child and her parents. So once again, the court should identify the respects in which parental care is falling, or is likely to fall, short of what it would be reasonable to expect;
- finally, where harm has not yet been suffered, the court must consider the degree of likelihood that it will be suffered in the future. This will entail considering the degree of likelihood that the parents' future behaviour will amount to a lack of reasonable parental care. It will also entail considering the relationship between the significance of the harm feared and the likelihood that it will occur. Simply to state that there is a 'risk' is not enough. The court has to be satisfied, by relevant and sufficient evidence, that the harm is likely.[30]

While the child is in care, the local authority has a duty to ensure reasonable contact for the child with his parents, guardians, or others with parental responsibility, unless the authority considers that refusing contact is necessary to do so to safeguard the child's welfare. Any refusal may last only seven days. While the child is in care, parents, guardians, and others with parental responsibility may apply to the court for contact with the child, and a local authority may apply to the court to authorise the refusal of contact.

While the child is subject to a Care Order, the authority must respect the religion in which he or she has been brought up. The authority cannot consent or refuse to consent to adoption of the child. No one, while the order is in force, may change his or her surname or take him or her out of the UK, without the written permission of every person who has responsibility for the child.

Supervision Orders: Children Act, section 31

A Supervision Order is an order of the court placing a child under the supervision of the authority but it does not affect the parents' responsibilities. On an application for a Care Order the court may make a Supervision Order rather than a Care Order, and where an application is made for a Supervision Order the court may make a Care Order.

A Supervision Order may require the child to comply with various directions. These may include the requirement to live at a specified place, to meet with his or her supervisor, and to participate in activities specified in the directions. An order may also require the supervised child to undergo medical or psychiatric examinations. Supervision Orders normally run for a 12-month period, which may be extended on an application to the court, but may not run for longer than three years.[31]

Education Supervision Orders: Children Act, section 36 – see Chapter 4

Adoption[32]

Adoption today is a legal means of providing a child with a permanent family and home. It has existed (albeit in a very different form) since Roman times but remained unregulated by law in the UK until 1926.[33] Adoption is the most permanent form of order a court can make in relation to the care and upbringing of a child and confers parental responsibility on the adoptive parents and extinguishes that of the natural parent. The nature of adoption has changed over the years. Professor Stephen Cretney explains the differing forms of adoption at the beginning of the twentieth century as follows:[34]

> … the term 'adoption' in relation to children was used in three different senses. First it was used to describe the situation in which a child was taken into the home of a person other than the child's parent, and brought up to a greater or lesser extent as the child of the adopter…Secondly, there was the situation in which 'adoption' was simulated: an unmarried pregnant woman would arrange for her child to be delivered in a private lying-in home, the owner of which would be paid a lump sum in exchange for arranging the child's 'adoption'. The child would then be removed to 'the worst class of baby-farming house' where it would usually be neglected and die.[35] Thirdly, there was the so-called Poor Law Adoption in which the Poor Law guardians assumed by resolution all the child's parents' rights and powers in respect of the child's upbringing, and would arrange for the child to be 'adopted'.

Before contraception and abortion became readily available, adoption represented a means of providing families for young babies born outside marriage. Cretney records that in 1968 half the children adopted were less than one year old: by the end of the century 'this proportion had fallen to four per cent'.[36] The election of the Labour government in 1997 saw a change in government policy: the emphasis was to be on using adoption as a means of reducing the number of children being cared for by local authorities. Since that time, adoption has been a valuable process for providing permanent families for older children who are being looked after by local authorities and have no prospect of being reunited with their natural families.

For most of the 20th century adoption was run by private adoption agencies rather than local authorities. Every local authority must now maintain an adoption service.[37] An Adoption Order protects a child's rights through providing the child with permanence and security for the child within his or her new family. While adoption used to be 'closed' in that all links with the birth parents were severed, there is now a right not only to know one's genetic origins but also, where appropriate and in the child's best interests, a right to maintain contact with the natural parents.[38]

An Adoption Order can only be made with the consent of the birth mother, unless the court considers that consent is being unreasonably withheld. As was made clear in *Re W* (1971) a reasonable mother must consider the welfare of her child when coming to a decision on whether or not to consent.[39] In those circumstances, where the mother is unable to give adequate care to the child, for whatever reason, it is difficult for the mother to be reasonable in refusing consent to adoption. The court may decide that the welfare of the child requires her consent to be dispensed with.[40]

The law provides that from the age of 18, the adopted person has the right to obtain information from the adoption agency which will enable him or her to obtain a certified copy of his or her birth certificate. He or she also has the right to receive a copy of the Adoption Order from the court.[41] The European Court of Human Rights (ECtHR), interpreting Article 8 (the right to respect for private and family life) has upheld the right of a child to obtain the necessary information from public agencies which enables him or her to understand his or her origins, and for any uncertainties over his or her identity to be eliminated without delay.[42]

Particularly for an older child, contact with his or her natural parent(s) and other relatives may be beneficial, and he or she may apply to the court for a Contact Order.[43] However, opinions on the value of post-adoption contact are divided and there is no general rule. Where siblings have been separated by adoption contact has been ordered.[44] In other cases, the rights of the adopting parents to protection from interference must be considered alongside the claim of the natural parent(s) and or the child. If the matter goes to court, the decision will turn in the court's assessment and application of the welfare test. Face-to-face contact with the natural parents is rare, and more likely to take place through photographs and letters sent via an adoption agency.

Special Guardianship Orders (SGOs)[45]

Special Guardianship Orders (SGOs) were introduced in 2002 as an available alternative to adoption.[46] An SGO gives parental responsibility to the person appointed, while not removing parental responsibility from the child's natural parent(s). The advantages of SGOs are said to be:

- that an SGO gives the guardian clear responsibility for all aspects of caring for the child or young person, and for making the decisions to do with their upbringing. It also means that the child will no longer be in the care of the council;
- the SGO provides a firm foundation on which to build a lifelong permanent relationship between the carer and the child or young person;

- it preserves the legal link between the child or young person and their birth family;
- it can be accompanied by proper access to a full range of support services including, where appropriate, financial support.[47]

A special guardian must be over the age of 18 and not be a parent of the child. The law specifies categories of eligible applicants, which include local authority foster parents with whom the child has lived for one year, and relatives with whom the child has lived for one year. The local authority must be given three months' notice of the intention of an individual to apply for an SGO, and, having investigated the suitability of the applicant, prepare a report for the court.[48] If an application is made for an SGO, the court may make the Order in any family proceedings in which the welfare of the child is being considered, but may make an SGO where no application has been made. While the SGO remains in force, no person may change the child's surname or remove the child from the UK without the consent of all those having parental responsibility, or the permission of the court (although the SG may do so for a period less than three months). The court may vary or discharge the SGO. While the SGO is in force, the local authority must provide support services for the SG. These include counselling advice and information, therapy, respite care, and financial support.[49]

Adoption or special guardianship?

The introduction of Special Guardianship Orders (SGOs) has provided a useful alternative to adoption. Whereas adoption transfers parental responsibility away from the natural parents, the SGO gives to the guardian parental responsibility without removing it from the natural parent. From the child's perspective, it provides him or her with a permanent and secure home while not severing all links with his or her natural parents. The government's White Paper 2000 explained that:

> Adoption is not always appropriate for children who cannot return to their birth parents. Some older children do not wish to be legally separated from their birth families. Adoption may not be best for some children being cared for on a permanent basis by members of their wider birth family. Some minority ethnic communities have religious and cultural difficulties with adoption, as it is set out in law. Unaccompanied asylum-seeking children may also need secure, permanent homes, but have strong attachments to their families abroad. All these children deserve the same chance as any other to enjoy the benefits of a legally secure stable permanent placement that promotes a supportive, lifelong relationship with their carers, where the court decides that is in their best interests.[50]

CASE FOCUS: S[51]

S was born in 2000. The local authority had concerns over domestic violence and the parents' drug use and chaotic lifestyle. Aged three, S was placed with a foster parent, DO, on a voluntary basis. Care proceedings commenced, and S was formally placed with DO. S's father's cousin wanted to take care of S and she was transferred to his care aged 4 years 8 months. That placement broke down and S was returned to DO.

The local authority's long-term care plan was for S to be adopted and in 2005 DO applied to adopt her. DO and S's birth mother were on good terms and DO had no objection to S having contact with her mother. S wanted to continue to live with DO, but maintain contact with her mother. DO sought adoption so that there would be no further litigation and disruption of her family life with S.

The judge made a Special Guardianship Order, rather than an Adoption Order and DO appealed. The Court of Appeal upheld the judge's decision. The SGO would provide long-term emotional and physical security which DO would provide. If things did go wrong, the courts would be there to deal with them, and the Court of Appeal stressed that the availability of judicial continuity was of particular importance.

Evaluating the system

In 2016, the House of Commons Committee of Public Accounts inquired into the child protection services.[52] The Committee found that children were at risk of harm as a result of the variability in the quality and consistency of help and protection services. Ofsted reported that 80 per cent of authorities it had inspected since 2013 were not providing services rated as 'good' to help or protect children. The National Audit Office reports that average spending on social work in 2014 to 2015 ranged from an estimated spend of £340 per child in need in one authority to £4,970 per child in need in another, but neither the Department for Education nor the local authorities understood why spending varied.[53]

The Children's Commissioner has been particularly critical of looked-after children being sent 'out of area'. In 2019 the Commissioner wrote that:

> There are over 30,000 looked after children living 'out of area' in England. This is 41 per cent of all children in care and has risen by 13 per cent since 2014. Over 11,000 of these children are more than 20 miles from what they would call home, with over 2,000 further than a hundred miles away.[54]

The Commissioner states that children living far from home 'are likely to have more complicated and fragmented histories'; that 52 per cent living out of area have SEN and 24 per cent have social, emotional, and mental health needs. They are also at greater risk of going missing and that they are vulnerable to exploitation by criminal gangs. One girl, in care over 100 miles from home, commented that 'I feel like a parcel getting moved around all the time, getting opened up and sent back and moved on to somewhere else'.

Missing children[55]

Children who go missing or run away from home are at risk of harm and falling outside the web of care and support which is every child's right. The UK Missing Persons Unit[56] Report for 2020 records that 68,944 children were reported to the police as missing. While 90 per cent are found within 48 hours, nine per cent are not. Missing children are at particular risk of sexual exploitation or exploitation by criminal gangs or engaging in drug and alcohol abuse. At an international level, the Global Missing Children's Network connects signatory countries, enables information and images of missing children to be shared, and assists in investigations into missing children.

The duty to safeguard and promote the well-being of children includes planning to prevent children from going missing and protecting them when they are found. The Local Safeguarding Children Board also has a role to play and should ensure that all relevant agencies and service providers work together to prevent children going missing. An Ofsted Report of 2013 highlighted a number of concerns over the way local authorities work in relation to missing children. In particular, in relation to looked-after children, there was an acknowledged risk of children going missing when they were moved from one foster home placement to another and lacked the stability of a secure family life. The problems are exacerbated when – due to a lack of suitable local accommodation – children are placed a long way from their homes.

Local authorities must have a runaway and missing from home and care (RMFHC) protocol, agreed with the police and other agencies. The protocol should set out who has the principal responsibility for missing children, a framework for assessing risk when a child goes missing and what response each agency will offer in relation to different degrees of risk and identifying who will support the family of the missing child.

When a child returns or is found, 'safe and well checks' are carried out by the police. The purpose of the checks is to establish where the child has been, and with whom, and whether he or she has suffered harm. There should also be an interview with a trained independent person with a view to uncovering why the child went missing, the risks he or she has been exposed to, and ways in which the risk of the child going missing again can be minimised.

The liability of local authorities

Local authorities are accountable to law for the exercise of their duties, or failure to act, in a number of ways. Where a local authority has responsibility for a child as a result of a Care Order, for example, and places the child or children with foster parents,[57] the local authority may be vicariously liable for any abuse of the child by the foster parents. In effect, the foster parents are 'standing in the shoes' of the local authority and carrying out the care functions of the authority.

CASE FOCUS: A[58]

A had been in the care of a local authority from the ages of seven to 18. The local authority placed her for a time in the care of two sets of foster parents. In the first placement A was physically and emotionally abused by the wife and in the second she was sexually abused by the husband.

The local authority had recruited and trained the foster parents and supervised the fostering. Placing children with foster parents created a relationship of trust between foster parents and the child where close control could not be exercised by the local authority: this made the children particularly vulnerable. There was no danger that holding the authority liable in negligence would deter local authorities from placing children in care with foster parents. For these reasons the Supreme Court held the local authority vicariously liable for the acts of the foster parents.

As discussed in Chapter 1, the Human Rights Act 1998 brought about fundamental change to domestic law by enabling ECHR rights to be enforced in the local courts. In force from 2000, the Act incorporates European Convention Rights into domestic law, and provides for remedies. Failure by state agencies to protect Convention rights is unlawful. In relation to children the relevant provisions are Articles 2 and 3 (the right to life and freedom from torture, inhuman and degrading treatment, and punishment) and Article 8 (right to respect for private and family life). The failure to provide 'an effective remedy' (Article 13 ECHR) is also unlawful.

Where, for example, a local authority fails to protect victims of violence and social services should have been aware that there was a history of sexual and physical abuse there will be a breach of Article 3 (the right to freedom from torture, inhuman treatment, and punishment). If the State fails to provide a satisfactory remedy to the problem there may also be a violation of Article 13 of the ECHR which guarantees a right to an effective remedy as illustrated by the case below.

CASE FOCUS: E[59]

In 1996 to 1997 four children were abused by a man who was living with their mother. The man had been arrested and charged and pleaded guilty. He was placed on probation and returned home. He was later found guilty on other charges and given a two-year suspended prison sentence. The Criminal Injuries Compensation Scheme awarded £25,000 in damages. The victims asked the local government ombudsman to investigate their allegations that the local authority had been negligent and guilty of maladministration. The ombudsman said that he had no jurisdiction to investigate their claims.

The Court of Human Rights ruled that there had been a violation of Article 3 a violation of Article 13. Social services knew or ought to have known of the abuse but failed to take any steps to prevent further abuse taking place. The Court awarded €16,000 to each of three applicants and €32,000 to the fourth.

In the past the domestic courts had refused to accept that local authorities owed a common law duty of care under the law of negligence to protect children from harm. In *X v Bedfordshire County Council* (1995),[60] for example, the House of Lords (now the Supreme Court) explicitly rejected a duty of care, stating that it would not be just and reasonable to impose such a duty. The effect of this case was that children could not sue a local authority in negligence nor could they sue for breach of statutory duty. Children failed by the State, their rights violated, had no remedy.

However, in 2001 the European Court of Human Rights (ECtHR) undermined the exemption of local authorities from the law of negligence and actions for breach of statutory duty. In *Z v United Kingdom* (2001)[61] the abuse of children had been brought to the local authority's attention in 1987. It was not until 1992, however, at the insistence of the mother, that the children were taken into emergency care. Between 1987 and 1992 they had suffered appalling neglect and 'horrific experiences' leading to physical and psychological injuries. The ECtHR acknowledged the difficulties faced by local authorities but nevertheless ruled that the authority had failed to protect the children from serious, long-term neglect, and abuse. There was a violation of Article 3 ECHR. There was also a violation of Article 13. The victims had no available means of challenging the local authority's failures, and no means of seeking compensation for the damage suffered as a result.[62]

Two recent cases show how the European Court of Human Rights has interpreted the Convention right to respect for private and family life (Article 8).

CASE FOCUS: *HERNEHULT V NORWAY* (2020),[63]

Doubts had been expressed over whether there had been justification for a local authority taking three children into emergency care and then placing them with foster parents under a Care Order. The authority had proceeded on the basis that the placement of the children would be prolonged. Contact with the natural parents was restricted to four times a year for one-and-a-half hours each time. The parents were forbidden to speak Romanian (their native language) with the children. The effect of all this was that the children would become settled with the foster parents and further alienated from the parents. The primary duty of social services is to make decisions and to act in the best interests of the child. One aspect of this duty is, wherever possible, to exercise powers in a way that will facilitate the reunion of children with their families. That duty had not been complied with: social services had made assumptions which amounted to an unjustified, unlawful, infringement of the parents' rights to family life under Article 8.

CASE FOCUS: *PEDERSEN V NORWAY* (2020)[64]

X was taken into care as a result of his parents' mental health issues. Social services had assumed that there would be a long-term placement of X with foster parents, leading to his adoption. No attempt had been made to establish whether his family were now capable of caring for him and nothing had been done to facilitate reunion with his family. An 'open' Adoption Order was made, but contact with his parents was restricted to two hours twice a year. The authorities had failed in their positive duty to work towards reuniting X with his parents, and the ECtHR ruled there had been a violation of Article 8.

Protecting child refugees

A *refugee* is defined as a person who:

> Owing to a well-founded fear of being persecuted for reasons of race, religion, nationality, membership of a particular social group, or political opinion, is outside the country of his nationality and is unable to or, owing to such fear, is unwilling to avail himself of the protection of that country.[65]

Asylum is defined as the protection given to a refugee by the State to which he or she travels as a refugee.

> State Parties shall take appropriate measures to ensure that a child who is seeking refugee status or who is considered a refugee in accordance with applicable international or domestic law and procedures shall, whether accompanied or unaccompanied by his or her parents or by any other

person, receive appropriate protection and humanitarian assistance in the enjoyment of applicable rights set forth in the present Convention and in other international human rights or humanitarian instruments to which the said States are Parties.

UN Convention on the Rights of the Child,
Article 22.1[66]

The right to claim asylum is an international human right. Following the Second World War when countless numbers of people were uprooted from their homes and homeland, the 1951 UN Convention Relating to the Status of Refugees (the Geneva Convention) was signed, and in 1967 a separate Protocol Relating to the Status of Refugees agreed. The Convention now has 145 signatories. The central or core principle of the Convention is *non-refoulement:* that there must be no return to a country where a refugee would face threats to life and freedom.

In addition to the Geneva Convention, there is the Dublin III Regulation under which family unity and the best interests of the child are key considerations. This is EU legislation which establishes criteria for determining which EU Member State is responsible for examining an asylum claim made in the EU.[67] It also provides mechanisms for reuniting separated asylum-seeking family members in the UK.[68] Having left the EU in 2020, the UK Government introduced regulations[69] to ensure continuity in immigration law until new legislation is passed by Parliament. However, with effect from January 2021, Dublin III no longer applies in the UK. The government has made a commitment to review routes of entry for asylum seekers, including unaccompanied children, seeking to join relatives in the UK.

Globally in 2019 over 68.5 million people were forced from their homes and there were nearly 25.4 million refugees, over half of whom were under the age of 18. The UN High Commission for Refugees (UNHCR) records that in the year June 2018 to June 2019, there were 32,693 applications for asylum in the UK, 25 per cent of which (4,563) were for children.[70,71] The UK was under a duty to accept and support unaccompanied children from other EU countries in response to the humanitarian crisis brought about by the mass migration of unaccompanied asylum-seeking children from the Middle East and North Africa as a result of the conflicts in Syria and Sudan.[72] In 2018, the countries from which most refugees (of all ages) came into the UK were Iran, Iraq, Albania, Eritrea, and Pakistan. The countries receiving the highest number of asylum applications in 2018 were Germany (161,900) and France (114,500).

Immigration and asylum in the UK is regulated under the Immigration Acts and the associated Immigration Rules. The Immigration Acts apply to the whole of the UK, but responsibility for caring for and safeguarding child asylum seekers is devolved to the nations. The law and practice of immigration is also influenced by both the UN Convention on the Rights of the Child and the European Convention on Human Rights (ECHR), on both of which see Chapter 1.[73]

In the UK in 2019 there were 3,651 asylum applications from unaccompanied children. An unaccompanied child is one who:

- is under the age of 18 years when the asylum application is submitted;
- is applying for asylum in their own right;
- is separated from both parents and is not being cared for by an adult who in law or by custom has responsibility to do so.

A child under the age of 18 has the right to claim asylum and to have that claim considered separately from any other person. Immigration officials must give priority to handling the cases of unaccompanied children.[74] Local authorities have an important role to play in supporting refugees and over 300 authorities participate in the community resettlement scheme. Unaccompanied asylum-seeking children are 'children in need' (see above). This means that local authorities are under a general duty to safeguard and promote the welfare of children in their area who need accommodation. A child under the age of 16 will usually be placed with foster parents. For those over 16, they may be placed in 'other arrangements' which may be shared accommodation or lodgings which are not regulated in the same way as foster homes or children's homes. Home Office guidance states that Bed and Breakfast (B&B) accommodation is 'not suitable' for any child, even on an emergency basis, as it does not cater for their protection or welfare needs.

The Home Office policy objectives for processing children who claim asylum in their own right, which closely reflect the CRC, are to ensure that:

- immigration, asylum, nationality, and customs functions are discharged having regard to the need to safeguard and promote the welfare of children who are in the UK, including that the best interests of the child are a primary consideration at all times;
- the welfare of the child is paramount at all times when the child is being cared for by appropriate adults or agencies with safeguarding responsibilities being met;
- protection is given swiftly to those who need it;
- information about the asylum claim is collected in an appropriate way with decisions made promptly and communicated to the child in a way that acknowledges their age, maturity, and particular vulnerabilities;
- staff are constantly alert to any signs that the child is at risk of harm or abuse or may have been trafficked – if staff have any doubts whatsoever about such a potential risk to a child, they must refer the case immediately to a senior manager (minimum Chief Immigration Officer or Higher Executive Officer);
- children who have been trafficked or who are at risk with regard to modern slavery are identified as early as possible, are provided with the necessary support, and are referred to the National Referral Mechanism (NRM, on which see Chapter 5).[75]

In many instances, refugees arrive in the UK without any documentation to establish their identity.[76] Therefore, those dealing with a claim for asylum must firstly determine whether the person seeking asylum is a child. It used to be the case that in deciding this question, if an immigration officer had a 'reasonable belief' that a child appeared to be 'substantially' over the age of 18, he or she was to be treated as an adult. This rule was successfully challenged in the case below, removing a potential or actual injustice damaging to the rights of the child.

CASE FOCUS: *A*[77]

A, aged 16, was an unaccompanied Sudanese boy who arrived in the UK in 2014. He reported to the local police, seeking asylum. There were doubts about his age and he was assessed to be an adult and detained in an adult asylum detention centre. In judicial review proceedings the Home Office's policy regarding age was held to be unlawful. The court ruled that the question of age was not to be determined according to the 'reasonable belief' of an immigration officer, but as a matter of objective fact. For the government it was argued that A's case was 'profoundly troubling for the efficient running of a fair immigration system'. The judge was unimpressed with this argument: he was not concerned with the efficiency or otherwise of the system, but with the rights of a child. The Home Office's policy was unlawful.

The presumption now where there is doubt as to age, is that the person is a child.

In the first instance an unaccompanied child asylum seeker will be granted temporary leave to remain in the UK for a period of 30 months or until he or she is 17-and-a-half years old. Temporary leave may come to an end sooner if any of the requirements for leave cease to be met or there has been a misrepresentation or omission of facts, including the use of false documents, which were decisive for the grant of leave.[78] The requirements for temporary leave include:

- the child being under the age of 17-and-a-half years;
- there being no adequate reception arrangements in the country to which they would be returned if leave is not granted;
- there are no reasonable grounds for regarding the applicant as a danger to the security of the UK;
- the applicant has not been convicted of a particularly serious crime and is not a danger to the community of the UK;
- the applicant is not, at the date of their application, subject to a deportation order or a decision to make a deportation order.

Where a child makes a claim for asylum the Home Office is under a duty to try to trace any family of the child.[79] A person must also be appointed to assist the child in the processing of his or her application. When considering a child's application for asylum, the circumstances of his or her family are particularly important. The child may have experienced personal persecution, or be aware of the persecution of family members even though he or she may not have been harmed. Where the child is separated from his or her family, it is not automatically assumed that contact with the family is in the child's best interests. It may be that contact is not in his or her best interests if the family has been involved in practices such as Female Genital Mutilation (FGM) or forced marriage (on which see Chapter 5).

The standard of proof for children is the same as for adults: is there a reasonable degree of likelihood that they have a well-founded fear of being persecuted? The phrase 'well-founded fear of being persecuted' involves both an objective and subjective element. The 'fear' is subjective: does this child actually fear persecution? The fear being 'well-founded' is objective: looking at all the evidence, is the claim credible? Assessing the credibility of a child's claim is more complex than assessing an adult's. Officials must take into account the child's understanding and what is reasonable for a child to know given their age, maturity, education, etc. In particular, they must have regard to:

- the child's age and maturity at the time of the event and at the time of the interview;
- the mental or emotional trauma experienced by the child;
- educational level;
- fear or mistrust of authorities;
- feelings of shame, painful memories, particularly those of a sexual nature.

Officials are also advised that children may be subjected to specific forms of persecution, and that age may be a central factor in the harm inflicted or feared. Child-specific persecution may include:

- forcible or underage recruitment into military service;
- family or domestic violence;
- infanticide;
- forced or underage marriage;
- discrimination against street children;
- Female Genital Mutilation (FGM);
- forced labour;
- Child Sexual Exploitation;
- images of child abuse;
- trafficking;
- children born outside of strict family planning laws and policies.

The child's fear of persecution must fall within one of the five grounds in the 1951 Refugee Convention, namely that the fear of persecution 'for reasons of race, religion, nationality, membership of a particular social group or political opinion'. Where the child satisfies the criteria, he or she should be given refugee status.[80] However, under the Immigration Act 1971, the Secretary of State also has a wide discretion to grant Leave to Enter or Leave to Remain outside the immigration rules. Where Convention (ECHR) rights are in issue, particularly Article 3 (prohibition against torture inhuman and degrading treatment or punishment) or Article 8 (right to respect for private and family life), these may prove decisive in supporting an asylum seeker's claim because under the Human Rights Act 1998 a public authority (the Secretary of State) has a duty to protect Convention rights and will act unlawfully if he or she fails to do so.

The UK Border Agency which has primary responsibility for administering the immigration rules is under a duty to act according to the following principles:

- every child matters even if they are someone subject to immigration control;
- in accordance with the UNCRC the best interests of the child will be a primary consideration (although not necessarily the only consideration) when taking decisions affecting children;
- ethnic identity, language, religion, faith, gender, and disability are taken into account when working with a child and their family;
- children should be consulted and the wishes and feelings of children taken into account wherever practicable when decisions affecting them are made, even though it will not always be possible to reach decisions with which the child will agree. In instances where parents and carers are present they will have primary responsibility for the children's concerns;
- children should have their applications dealt with in a timely way that minimises the uncertainty that they may experience.[81]

The decision-making process has three potential outcomes: refugee status; humanitarian protection; discretionary leave to remain. It must first be decided whether refugee status should be granted, or if not, whether Humanitarian Protection (HP) should be granted and or whether permission to remain should be granted under human rights law or on a discretionary basis.

Under the immigration rules, refugee status will be granted to an asylum seeker if the Secretary of State is satisfied that:

(i)   they are in the UK or have arrived at a port of entry into the UK;

(ii) they are refugees (as formally defined in the Regulations);

(iii) there are no reasonable grounds for regarding them as a danger to the security of the UK;

(iv) having been convicted of a serious crime, they do not constitute a danger to the community of the UK;

(v)   refusing the application would result in them being required to go in breach of the Geneva Convention, to a country in which their life or freedom would be threatened on account of their race religion, nationality, political opinion, or membership of a particular social group.

If a child does not qualify for refugee status, he or she may be given HP, or granted discretionary leave to remain in the UK. Humanitarian protection may be granted where substantial grounds have been shown that if returned to his or her country of origin, he or she would face a real risk of suffering serious harm and as a result is unable or unwilling to return to that country.[82] Unlike those seeking asylum, the risk of harm does not have to be for a specific reason such as race, religion, or political opinion. Humanitarian protection will be refused if there are serious reasons for considering that he or she has committed serious crimes or been involved in encouraging others to commit such crimes.

Humanitarian protection carries many of the same benefits as refugee status. There will be a grant of five years leave to remain in the UK, but where there are exceptional circumstances, a longer period of leave may be granted. There are, however, differences which make asylum preferable to HP. These are that:

- refugees can apply for a Convention Travel Document which entitles them to entry to all Refugee Convention countries. Those with HP may apply for a Certificate of Travel, for which they need evidence that they have been refused a passport in their country of origin;
- in relation to access to higher education, refugees are treated as home students. Those with HP cannot be treated as home students until they have been ordinarily resident in England for three years (although Scotland, Wales, and Northern Ireland do not make this distinction);
- the Immigration Act[83] provides that refugees shall not be prosecuted for illegal entry to the UK: this does not apply to those with HP;
- if the Home Office seeks to revoke refugee status it must notify the UN High Commissioner for Refugees, but there is no duty to do so for those with HP.

Where neither refugee status nor HP has been granted an unaccompanied asylum seeking child may still be eligible for limited leave to remain. The requirements to be met are that he or she:

- is an unaccompanied asylum-seeking child under the age of 17-and-a-half years throughout the duration of leave to be granted in this capacity;
- must have applied for asylum and been granted neither refugee status or HP;
- there are no adequate reception arrangements in the country to which they would be returned if leave to remain was not granted;
- there are no reasonable grounds for regarding his or her as a danger to the security of the UK;
- if convicted of a particularly serious crime, he or she does not constitute a danger to the community of the UK;
- is not subject, at the date of the application, the subject of a deportation order or a decision to make a deportation order.[84]

In all asylum and HP cases caseworkers must observe the statutory guidance in *Every Child Matters – Change for Children*.[85] As discussed earlier, the key principle is the duty to have regard to the need to safeguard and promote the welfare of children.[86] Usually, the child's welfare will be best served by remaining in the UK. Local authorities must be aware of the outcome of the case so that social workers can prepare a pathway plan to facilitate the long-term residency of the child. If there are concerns over the child's welfare or need for protection, the local safeguarding team must be notified. Leave to remain includes the right to work and study and gain access to the NHS and benefits. After the period of limited right to remain, the refugee may apply for settlement.

There is a presumption that once a person is recognised as a refugee or in need of HP and their term of leave to remain expires they will proceed to settlement in the UK by applying for indefinite leave to remain. Settlement means that the individual has permission to stay in the UK permanently, free of immigration control. An application for settlement can be refused when a person:

- is liable to deportation or administrative removal;
- has obtained leave by deception;
- ceases to be a refugee or person in need of HP because of their own actions;
- fails to meet the requirements of the immigration rules for settlement as a refugee or person with HP.

Where refugee status or humanitarian protection has been denied there is a right to appeal to the Immigration and Asylum Tribunal.[87] The grounds for an appeal are that:

- removal from the UK would breach the UK's obligations under the Refugee Convention;
- removal would breach the UK's obligations in relation to persons eligible for humanitarian protection;
- removal would be unlawful under the Human rights Act, section 6 (duty of public authority not to act contrary to Convention rights).

If a child fails to achieve refugee status, HP, or leave to remain he or she may be removed from the UK. Pending deportation, he or she must not be detained in an adult Immigration Removal Centre. If it is necessary to detain a child, this should be in exceptional circumstances and for the shortest possible time with appropriate care being provided. Home Office Guidance makes clear that an unaccompanied child must not be detained other than for the purpose of enabling the child to be 'properly and safely escorted' to their point of departure.[88]

However, the courts have made it clear that although they may make orders to protect a child under the jurisdiction of the family courts and the wardship jurisdiction (see Chapter 1) and grant an order to protect a child from FGM (see Chapter 5), none of these orders can limit the exercise by the Secretary of State in relation to immigration controls. The relationship between these differing jurisdictions was explained in the case below.

CASE FOCUS: *A*[89]

A was a case in which the Home Secretary intended to deport a mother and child and at the time an application was before the courts for a Female Genital Mutilation Protection Order. One of the key questions before the court was whether a court, exercising its powers under the family or other jurisdiction, had the power to prevent/restrain the Home Secretary from exercising his immigration powers. The Home Secretary argued that he could not be bound by an FGMPO and that it had been made without jurisdiction.

The judge stated that 'the Secretary of State and the family courts are each operating a different and entirely distinct jurisdiction that has separately been entrusted to them by Parliament. Whilst... the two jurisdictions may be complementary, they are wholly separate with no potential for any structural crossover. Notwithstanding the probable engagement of Article 3 [the pro-hibition against torture, inhuman treatment, etc.], there is simply no juris-dictional space in the structure that has been created by Parliament in which the family court can reach across and directly interfere in the exercise by the Secretary of States exclusive powers with respect to the control of immigration and asylum'.

The court requested that the Home Secretary delayed enforcement of her immigration powers until the conclusion of the FGMA application and to reconsider her decision in light of the risk assessment in relation to the child.

As in *A* above, Article 3 of the ECHR comes into play to protect an individual from being returned to his or her country of origin where he or she is at risk of death, torture, inhuman treatment, or punishment at the hands of the State and its agents. In addition to Article 3 of the ECHR, Article 8 – the right to respect for privacy and family life – may have a role to play in immigration decisions, although the courts have made it clear in relation to adults that a very strong case would have to be made out for a claim based on Article 8 rights to succeed in deportation cases. One instance in which Article 8 has played a decisive role is in relation to the right to family reunification. Family reunification is the process whereby a person who has been given the right to remain in the UK may apply to have his or her family members join him or her in the UK. The immigration rules provide that adults may apply to have their dependent children join them, but there is no mention of the right of a child refugee to apply to have his or her parents and/or siblings come to the UK. This exclusion was considered in the case below.

CASE FOCUS: *M*[90]

M, then aged 16, arrived in the UK as an unaccompanied minor in 2012. He was refused asylum and successfully appealed. He was then given five years limited leave to remain in the UK, a period due to expire in April 2018. M wished to have his mother and brother join him in the UK, and used Article 8 in support of his application. The Entry Clearance Officer (ECO, the alter ego of the Secretary of State in Abu Dhabi) referred to the immigration rules, and refused his application on the basis that the rules were designed for dependent partners and children of sponsors (those applying), not for parents and siblings. On appeal, the tribunal recognised that there was no substantive right for M to have his family join him. The tribunal also stated that it had to balance M's claim against the public interest. Two aspects of public interest were in play: that of maintaining an effective system of immigration control and that of safeguarding children. The judge referred to the absence of authority or evidence in relation to either aspect of the public interest. However, he noted that there was some recent increase in the number of unaccompanied children. Taking everything into account the judge concluded that the decision of the ECO disproportionately interfered with M's right to respect for family life and allowed M's appeal.

Asylum support for families

The majority of adult asylum seekers do not have the right to work and must rely on State support.[91] Housing is provided, but there is no choice in the housing and the UNHCR claims that refugees are often housed in 'hard to let' properties. The government says that it is unlikely that housing will be in London or the south-east of England. Evidence heard by the Home Affairs Committee relating to housing found poor quality, dirty and damp accommodation, unsafe neighbourhoods, separation from family members through dispersal, financial pressures, and anxiety caused by the asylum process.

In 2020 cash support for adults in 2020 amounted to £37.75 per person, per week for food, sanitation and clothing. A pregnant mother will receive an extra £3 a week, a baby under one year old qualified for an extra £5 per week, and a child aged one to three an extra £3 per week. Benefits include free NHS healthcare, free prescriptions, free dental care, free eyesight tests, and help paying for glasses. Children aged five to 17 are obliged to be in school: state schools are free and children may be eligible for free school meals.[92] Nevertheless, according to the Children's Society, the levels of support for asylum seekers are usually much lower than those provided through the mainstream benefits system. The Parliamentary Inquiry into Asylum Support for Children and Young People 2013 to 2014 found that the current levels of support were too low to meet the essential living needs of children.

If asylum has been refused, the asylum seeker will be provided with somewhere to live and £35.39 per person on a payment card for food clothing and toiletries. If the offer of accommodation is refused, there will be no payment card and no money. 'Section 4' support is 'not fit for children' according to the House of Commons Home Affairs Committee Inquiry in 2013–2014.[93] From 2013 to 2014 there were around 800 children receiving section 4 support, designed according to the government to be an 'austere regime' of temporary support for failed asylum seekers. The Committee stated that section 4 support is not designed for children, does not have their best interests in mind, and does not meet their needs.[94] The Committee 'heard powerful evidence of the reality of living on as little as £5 per day, as parents are forced to skip meals to feed their children and are unable to buy them warm clothing in the winter'.

Conclusion

As has been discussed in this chapter there are a number of situations which cause a child to become in need of the care, protection, and support of the State. Where children come to the attention of the authorities and intervention is deemed necessary to protect a child, the relevant law is designed to facilitate that protection but at the same time wherever possible to respect and preserve a child's right to family life. Where a child has been the victim of abuse and or violence at the hands of family members alternative solutions outside the natural family must be sought. Fostering, guardianship, and adoption provide differing levels of permanence and security for a child.

In relation to refugee children, the law provides a framework for accepting and settling often traumatised children within the UK. The extent to which State agencies – especially local authorities – can provide adequate care and support depends less on the law than on sufficient investment in the services for children.

Notes

1 Each local authority in Scotland has a Child Protection Committee (CPC) which is responsible for multi-agency child protection policy, procedure, guidance, and practice. The CPCs work with social services, health services, and the police to protect children.
2 *Haase v Germany* [2004] ECHR 142.

3 An initial appeal to the Federal Constitutional Court was dismissed although subsequently the order of the Lower Court was quashed. However the Lower Court's decision meant that the separation of the children from their parents continued.
4 In 2019 the National Audit Office reported that £8.8bn was spent on children's services and that 91 per cent of local authorities had overspent their budgets on children's social care in that year.
5 Between 2010–2011 and 2017–2018 there was a 26 per cent increase in the number of children subject to a child protection plan.
6 HM Government, *Working Together to Safeguard Children*, 2018.
7 In 2016–2017 there were 54,846 sexual offences against children, up by 17 per cent since 2015–2016.
8 Children Act 1989, section 17(10).
9 HM Government: *Working Together to Safeguard Children*, July 2018.
10 Children Act 1989, section 17(1).
11 ibid., section 47.
12 ibid., section 31A.
13 DfE, *Children Act 1989 Guidance and Regulations, Vol 2*. 2015.
14 Children Act 1989, section 20; Social Services and Well-being (Wales) Act 2014.
15 ibid., section 20(7).
16 ibid., section 21.
17 *Williams v London Borough of Hackney* [2018] UKSC 37.
18 Exercising powers under section 46 Children Act 1989.
19 Children Act 1989, section 20(7) and (8).
20 The Court of Appeal had held that the interference with the Article 8 right was lawful and that issue was not pursued in the Supreme Court.
21 Children Act 1989, section 43.
22 ibid., section 43(3) (4).
23 ibid., sections 44–45.
24 Under section 47, the duty to investigate.
25 ibid., section 44A.
26 *Langley v Liverpool City Council* [2005] EWCA Civ 1173.
27 Children Act 1989, section 31.
28 ibid., section 33.
29 Children Act 1989, section 1(5).
30 *Re B (a Child)* [2013] UKSC 33.
31 Children Act 1989, Schedule 3, Part I.
32 The principal Act regulating adoption is the Adoption and Children Act 2002.
33 See now the Adoption and Children Act 2002.
34 Cretney, S, *Family Law in the Twentieth Century: A History*, Oxford University Press, 2003, page 596.
35 Cretney notes here that this form of adoption at the time was 'often a cover for child trafficking – either for paedophiles or for financial gain'.
36 Cretney, S, *Family Law in the Twentieth Century: A History*, Oxford University Press, 2003, page 597.
37 Adoption and Children Act 2002, section 2(1).
38 See Triseliotis, J, *In Search of Origins,* Routledge and Kegan Paul, 1973.
39 *Re W* [1971] AC 682.
40 Adoption and Children Act 2002, section 52(1)(b).
41 ibid., section 60.
42 *Gaskin v United Kingdom* (1989) 12 EHRR 36.
43 Adoption and Children Act 2002, section 26.
44 *Re P* [2008] EWCA Civ 535.
45 Children Act 1989, section 14A–F.
46 Under the Adoption and Children Act 2002, now section 14A–F Children Act 1989.

47 HM Government White Paper, *Adoption: a new approach,* Cm 5017 2000.
48 Children Act 1989, section 14A(6)(b).
49 Children Act 1989; Special Guardianship Regulations 2005.
50 HM Government, *Adoption: a new approach,* Cm 5017, 2000.
51 *Re S (A Child)* [2007] EWCS Civ 54.
52 House of Commons' 31st Report of 2016–2017, HC 713 2016.
53 ibid.
54 Children's Commissioner: *Pass the parcel: children posted around the care system,* December 2019.
55 See Department for Education, *Statutory guidance on children who run away or go missing from home or care,* 2014.
56 The unit is part of the National Crime Agency.
57 Under the Child Care Act 1980.
58 *Armes v Nottinghamshire County Council* [2017] UKSC 60.
59 *E v United Kingdom* [2002] ECHR 763.
60 [1995] 2 AC 633.
61 [2001] ECHR 333.
62 See also *TP and KM v United Kingdom* [2002] 34 EHRR 3.
63 [2020] ECHR 214.
64 [2020] ECHR
65 Convention Relating to the Status of Refugees, 1951, Article 1.
66 See also the Human rights Act 1998, Dublin Regulation (Regulation EU No 604/2013, Borders, Citizenship and Immigration Act 2009.
67 Regulation (EU) No 604/2013 and Council of June 26, 2013.
68 In May 2020 the UK Government announced that it has successfully completed the transfer of 478 unaccompanied asylum-seeking children under Dublin III. In total in the year ending March 2020 the UK granted protection to over 7,320 children and since 2010, through the different pathway schemes, more than 44,900 children.
69 The Immigration, Nationality and Asylum (EU Exit) Regulations 2019, 2019 SI No 745.
70 In 2002 84,000 applications were made: the highest on record.
71 See Home Office: *UNHCR 2018, Global Trends Report.*
72 Immigration Act 2016, section 67.
73 From 2020 the UK has introduced a new Global Resettlement Scheme consolidating three existing UK programmes: the Vulnerable Persons' Resettlement Scheme (VPRS), the Vulnerable Children's Resettlement Scheme (VCRS), and the Gateway Protection Programme.
74 Immigration Rules, Part 11, paragraphs 349 and 350.
75 Home Office, *Children's Asylum Claims,* Version 3.0, 15 August 2019.
76 It is a criminal offence to enter a country illegally. The Immigration and Asylum Act 1999 provides a number of defences to charges of illegal entry.
77 *R (AA) v Secretary of State for the Home Department* [2016] EWHC 1453 (Admin).
78 Immigration Rules, paragraph 352ZC.
79 Asylum Seekers (Reception Conditions) Regulations 2005, regulation 6.
80 Immigration Rules, paragraph 334.
81 *Every Child Matters,* 2009, paragraph 2.7.
82 ibid., paragraph 339C.
83 Immigration and Asylum Act 1991, section 31.
84 Immigration Rules, Guidance, paragraph 352ZC.
85 UK Border Agency and Department for Children, Schools and Families, November 2009.
86 Borders, Citizenship and Immigration Act 2009 section 55; in Scotland the Protection of Children (Scotland) Act 2007 and Children (Scotland) Act 1995; in Northern Ireland the Children (Northern Ireland) Order 1995 and Safeguarding Vulnerable

Groups (Northern Ireland) Order 2007; for Wales see cymru.gov.uk/pubs/circulars /2007/nafwc1207en.pdf?lang=en.

87 Nationality, Immigration and Asylum Act 2002, section 82.

88 Detention must be in a place of safety as defined in the Children and Young Persons Act 1933; the Children (Scotland) Act 1995; the Children (Northern Ireland) Order 1995.

89 *Re A (A Child: Female Genital Mutilation: Asylum)* [2019] EWHC 2475 (Fam).

90 *AT (Article 8 ECHR – Child Refugee – Family Reunification – Eritrea)* [2016] UKUT 227 (IAC).

91 Support for asylum seekers is regulated under the Immigration and Asylum Act 1999.

92 The statutory framework for asylum support is section 4 and section 95 of the Immigration and Asylum Act 1999. For children in need, section 17 of the Children Act 19989 imposes a duty on local authorities to provide. The interrelationship between social services legislation and asylum support legislation has been described as a 'monstrous labyrinth' (see *R (VC) v Newcastle City Council* [2011] EWHC 2673).

93 House of Commons' Home Affairs Committee: *Parliamentary Inquiry on Asylum Support for Children and Young Persons,* 2013–2014.

94 ibid., paragraph 25.

7

CHILDREN AND THE CRIMINAL JUSTICE SYSTEM

Introduction

This chapter focuses on the rights of children in the criminal justice system in England and Wales. The Scottish system, which takes a very different approach to youth justice, is discussed at the end of the chapter.

> Every court in dealing with a child or young person who is brought before it, either as an offender or otherwise, shall have regard to the welfare of the child or young person.
>
> *Children and Young Persons Act 1933, section 44(1)*

The rights of children under the English criminal justice system have in the past come under significant criticism for failing to give adequate recognition to children's age and vulnerability. Within any youth justice system, there are two competing models: the welfare model and the punishment (or 'justice') model. The welfare model emphasises treating children who have come into conflict with the law in a manner sensitive to their age and vulnerability and is designed to prevent them from reoffending. Where, as in most of continental Europe, the age of criminal responsibility is set at between the ages of 14 and 18, the welfare approach will ensure that most children and young persons in conflict with the law will be dealt with outside the criminal justice system. In England and Wales, by contrast, where the age of criminal responsibility is set – controversially – at ten, the focus has traditionally been on protecting society from antisocial behaviour or low-level crime by children and young people by dealing with any offending conduct through the court system and punishment.

At the end of the 20th century, however, a major change in the approach to youth justice was ushered in, moving away from punishment and towards

DOI: 10.4324/9780429452710-7

measures designed to prevent children and young people from offending, and keeping those who do offend out of the formal criminal justice system. From 1998 the stated aim of the youth justice system in the UK has been: 'to prevent offending or reoffending by children and young persons'.[1] People and agencies engaged in the youth justice system are under a general duty to have regard to that aim. In addition, all agencies dealing with children must act in the interests of the child.

As discussed previously in this book, the law provides differing interpretations of children and young persons. A child, for most purposes, is a person under the age of 18, the age of majority in the United Kingdom.[2] In the youth justice system a 'young person' is defined as 'a person who has attained the age of 14 and is under the age of 18'.[3] However, as children acquire capacity for different purposes at different ages, measures or procedures which may be appropriate for a 15-year-old may be highly inappropriate for a younger child. Therefore, in order to protect the rights of every child it is essential that when reaching decisions, courts and other State agencies are sensitive to the age and level of maturity of each child.

Central to the youth justice system in England and Wales is the Youth Offending System comprising Youth Offending Teams and Panels. Youth Offending Teams (YOTs) are part of a local authority and separate from the courts.[4] They are made up of education and health authority staff, social workers, drug and alcohol referral teams, housing officers, police officers, and probation officers. Each YOT has a manager who is responsible for coordinating the work of the youth justice services. Their task is to devise local community programmes, in the form of a youth justice plan, designed to deter criminal behaviour.

A Youth Offending Panel (YOP) is made up of two volunteers from the local area, plus a professional from the YOT. Where the Youth Court makes a Referral Order (on which see below), it determines the length of the order and leaves it to the YOP to decide on the programme of required behaviour. Where a child is arrested a member of the YOP will talk to the child and advise him or her on rights and procedures.

Youth justice is an area of law and practice which is greatly influenced by international provisions, principally the UN Convention on the Rights of the Child (CRC) 1989, the UN Standard Minimum Rules of the Administration of Juvenile Justice ('the Beijing Rules'), and the European Convention on Human Rights (ECHR). Neither the CRC nor the Beijing Rules are enforceable under English law, but they nevertheless represent the international standards to be respected and/or worked towards by people working with children and young people. Rights under the ECHR, however, are enforceable before the domestic courts,[5] and a breach of these rights is unlawful. The following ECHR provisions are central to youth justice:

- Article 3: the prohibition against torture, inhuman or degrading treatment, or punishment;

- Article 5: the right to liberty;
- Article 6: the right to fair trial;
- Article 8: the right to respect for privacy and family life.

The Age of Criminal Responsibility (ACR)

The age of criminal responsibility in England, Wales, and Northern Ireland is ten;[6] in Scotland it is 12;[7,8] and is lower than in most of continental Europe. In France the age is 13; in Austria, Germany, Italy, and Spain it is 14. In Scandinavian countries the age is 15, while in Belgium and Luxembourg it is set at 18 years.

In England, Wales, and Northern Ireland children under the age of ten are presumed to be incapable of committing an offence: they lack the 'capacity' necessary for criminal responsibility. Over the age of ten, however, children may be held responsible for any criminal offences they commit. The UN Committee on the Rights of the Child has concluded that an ACR below the age of 12 is 'internationally unacceptable'.[9] To date, the UK Government has refused to raise the age from ten to 12.[10]

Wherever it is set, having a fixed age is arbitrary. A fixed, and low, age of criminal responsibility also contrasts sharply with the approach taken in relation to decision-making by children and young people over other areas of their lives. For example, as discussed in Chapter 3, in relation to decisions over medical treatment and whether a child should be allowed to make a binding decision, the key question is whether the child has sufficient maturity to understand the nature of the treatment and its consequences. Derived from the case of *Gillick v West Norfolk and Wisbech Area Health Authority* (1986)[11] 'Gillick competence' provides for flexibility in decision-making, distinguishing between competence and lack of competence in a subtle and sensitive manner and allowing the 'competent child' to determine his or her treatment. The age of criminal responsibility removes any flexibility from the system. Whether children's rights will be protected within the criminal justice system therefore depends upon the way in which the police and the courts deal with children who come into conflict with the law through antisocial behaviour or committing offences. This is discussed below.

In England and Wales, children between the ages of ten and 18 can be arrested and taken to court to answer for an alleged offence. They are, however, treated differently from adults, and will generally be dealt with in Youth Courts. If convicted of a serious offence he or she will be sent to secure units set up for children and young people rather than to an adult prison. From the age of 18 young people are treated as adults, but if convicted of an offence which is punishable by imprisonment he or she will be sent to a unit that holds only those aged 18 to 25, rather than a prison holding adult offenders.

Establishing a minimum age of criminal responsibility below which a child cannot be prosecuted does not, however, mean that a child under that age who breaks the law will be totally exempt from action by the State. Where a child behaves in a way which would be criminal if he or she were over the age of ten, he or she may become subject to a Parenting Order (PO) or a Child Safety Order (CSO).[12] If a child who has not been involved in any criminal or antisocial behaviour but is identified as being at risk of significant harm as a result of parental failure to provide adequate care or a child is beyond parental control, a Care Order or Supervision Order may be sought by a local authority (these are discussed in Chapter 6).[13]

In the following section we look firstly at the rights of children over the age of criminal responsibility who are diverted out of the criminal justice system and secondly those who are prosecuted.

Preventing children from offending

Child Safety Orders[14]

If a child under the age of ten has either acted in a way which – but for his or her age – would be a criminal offence, or has acted in a way that has caused or is likely to cause harassment, alarm, or distress to someone who does not live in the same household, a local authority may apply to the family court for a Child Safety Order (CSO).

A CSO may be granted to ensure that a child receives 'care, protection and support' and 'is subject to 'proper control', in order to prevent a repetition of the kind of behaviour for which the order was granted. The CSO will place the child under the supervision of a social worker or member of the Youth Offending Team for a maximum period of 12 months, and requires the child to comply with any requirements specified in the CSO. While the aim of CSOs is to prevent children from 'slipping into a life of crime' and they are civil in nature (as opposed to criminal) they nevertheless have overtones of the punitive criminal justice system rather than one aimed at support for the child. Where the child has caused the loss of or damage to property the court may (on the application of the local authority), make a Parental Compensation Order requiring a parent or guardian to pay up to a maximum of £5,000 in compensation.[15]

Parenting Orders[16]

Parenting Orders supplement Child Safety Orders. Where a Child Safety Order and/or a Parental Compensation Order is made, or a child fails to comply with the terms of the CSO, is truanting from school, or is convicted of an offence, the court may grant a Parenting Order. The aim of Parenting Order is to provide guidance and support to a parent or carer with the aim of preventing a child from repeating the conduct which led to the CSO being applied: in other words, the PO is a means of ensuring compliance with the terms of the CSO.

Parents and/or carers must be willing to cooperate with the PO and the Order normally requires attendance by the parent or carer at a counselling or guidance programme for a period not exceeding three months and includes such conditions as the court considers will help prevent the child from offending or truanting. It is an offence, punishable by a fine, without reasonable excuse, to breach the requirements of a Parenting Order.

Diverting children out of the criminal justice system

Youth cautions[17]

Youth cautions may be given to children aged ten to 17 who have committed an offence as an alternative to prosecution. They are a means of avoiding a trial which carries the prospect of a criminal conviction. Youth cautions may be given:

- for any offence (but see further below) where the offender admits an offence;
- there is sufficient evidence for a realistic prospect of conviction at trial; but
- it is not in the public interest to prosecute.

The police are responsible for deciding whether a caution is the appropriate remedy. They should work closely with the Youth Offending Team (YOT) who will carry out an assessment of the child. The caution can be given for any offence which is triable summarily, i.e. may be tried before the Magistrates' Court or Youth Court; or triable either way, i.e. may be tried before the Magistrates' Court, Youth Court, or the Crown Court. It is not usually available for indictable offences, i.e. more serious offences which may only be tried before the Crown Court, unless the Crown Prosecution Service agrees to the giving of the caution.

The youth caution carries the advantage that it will be 'spent' once it is administered. It will therefore not be disclosed and will not affect the child's employment prospects or eligibility for insurance. As with Referral Orders discussed below, it will however remain a matter of record and may become relevant if the child reoffends. There are also limited exceptions to non-disclosure, such as employment with children, the sick and vulnerable, or situations where financial honesty is essential. A conditional youth caution, rather obviously, is one that includes conditions and is imposed for a period of time, such as three or 12 months (depending on the age of the child). The conditions may require the child to pay a financial penalty, or attend a particular place for a specified number of hours. If the conditions are breached, without any reasonable excuse, criminal proceedings may follow.

Any youth caution or conditional youth caution must be given in the presence of an 'appropriate adult'.[18] This may be a parent or guardian, a local authority social worker or person working for a voluntary organisation, or other responsible adult who is not connected to the police.

Civil injunctions[19]

Civil injunctions and Criminal Behaviour Orders have replaced Antisocial Behaviour Orders (ASBOs) to deal with antisocial behaviour in England, Wales, and Northern Ireland. ASBOs are still used in Scotland.[20] Civil injunctions are designed to deter antisocial behaviour whereas Criminal Behaviour Orders (on which see below, page 205) may only be issued following conviction of an offence.

Where there is low-level antisocial behaviour, such as causing a nuisance and annoyance, the local council, police (including British Transport Police), NHS Protect, private registered providers of social housing, Transport for London, and the Environment Agency can apply for an injunction to prevent the behaviour recurring. The person applying for the injunction against a person under the age of 18 must, before making the application, consult the local Youth Offending Team about the application.[21]

Antisocial behaviour is defined as:

(a) conduct that has caused, or is likely to cause, harassment, alarm, or distress to any person;
(b) conduct capable to causing nuisance or annoyance to a person in relation to that person's occupation of residential premises;[22]
(c) conduct capable of causing housing-related nuisance or annoyance to any person.

An injunction is a civil (non-criminal) order which can be granted by the Youth Court against a child aged between ten and 18. The court must be satisfied that an individual has engaged in, or threatens to engage in, conduct capable of causing nuisance and annoyance.[23] The civil standard of proof applies, namely that the court is satisfied 'on the balance of probabilities' that the child has engaged in antisocial behaviour. The court must also consider that it is 'just and convenient' to grant the injunction. The injunction may prohibit specified conduct and may also require the person to do anything described in the injunction. Where the injunction is granted against a child, the duration of the injunction can be no more than 12 months.

Where the injunction is breached the person(s) who applied for the injunction may apply for the young offender to be brought back to court with a view to either a Supervision Order[24] or in relation to a young person over the age of 14, a detention order being imposed. The court may only grant the order if it is satisfied 'beyond reasonable doubt' (the criminal standard of proof), that there has been a breach of the injunction. The person applying for the order must, before making the application, consult the area Youth Offending Team.

The Court granting the injunction may attach a power of arrest where the antisocial behaviour includes the threat of violence against others, or there is a significant risk of harm to others from his or her conduct. Where a power of arrest has been attached, the police may arrest the person without warrant if there is 'reasonable cause to believe' that the injunction has been breached.[25] If the injunction was granted by the Youth Court and the child is still under 18, he or she must be brought before the Youth Court within 24 hours.[26] If the injunction was granted by the Youth Court, but the young person has now reached the age of 18, he or she must appear before the County Court within 24 hours of the arrest. Breach of an injunction may lead to a Supervision Order being imposed.[27]

The person who applied for the injunction or the person subject to the injunction may apply for the variation or discharge of the injunction. An appeal against a decision of the Youth Court may be made to the Crown Court.

Statistics on youth crime

The **Annual Youth Justice Statistics for England and Wales** for the year ending March 2019,[28] reveal the following:

- there were 11,900 first-time entrants into the Youth Justice System (YJS), a reduction of 85 per cent since the year ending March 2009, and an 18 per cent fall in the year ending March 2018;
- there were 60,208 arrests of children;[29]
- there were 8,552 cautions given to children by the police;
- 27,352 children were proceeded against in court;
- 19,316 sentences were given to children at court; of which
    12,810 were community sentences;
    1,287 were custodial sentences (5,219 'other sentences');
    21,700 children were cautioned or sentenced, a fall of 83 per cent over the last ten years, and a 19 per cent fall in the last year (to end March 2018);
- 4,500 knife and offensive weapon offences were committed by children, a fall of 31 per cent over the last ten years;
- the average custodial sentence length has increased over the last ten years, from 11.4 to 17.7 months;
- the number of children held in custody on remand has increased by 12 per cent in the last year to just over 240 children and accounted for 28 per cent of all children in youth custody;
- the average monthly population in youth custody was 859; this is a reduction of 70 per cent from ten years ago when there was an average of 2,900 children in custody, and a fall of four per cent in the past year;

- of the 11,000 (approximately) remands given to children, 83 per cent were remands on bail; 11 per cent were to youth detention accommodation and six per cent were community remands with intervention;
- the ten to 14 age group made up five per cent of the youth custody population; 95 per cent being aged 15–17 years;
- boys made up 97 per cent of the custody population, girls three per cent;
- the proportion of White children in youth custody has fallen from 72 per cent to 51 per cent;
- the proportion of children from a Black ethnic background has increased and is now 28 per cent of the custody population;
- children from Mixed or Asian and other ethnic backgrounds has increased in proportion from 12 per cent and nine per cent, respectively;
- 65 per cent of children in custody were in an establishment less than 50 miles from their homes while 11 per cent were in an establishment 100 miles from home;
- the reoffending rate of children and young people decreased by 2.5 per cent over the previous year, but remained higher than in 2008 (when it was 37.1 per cent).

Arrest, remand, and prosecution

> No child shall be deprived of his or her liberty unlawfully or arbitrarily. The arrest, detention, or imprisonment of a child ... shall be used only as a measure of last resort and for the shortest appropriate period of time.
>
> *UN Convention on the Rights of the Child, Article 37(b)*

Arrest

If any person (of any age) is stopped and questioned by the police, there is no duty to cooperate with the police. If a police officer has a reasonable suspicion that an offence has been committed, the correct course of action is to arrest the suspect.

CASE FOCUS: *KENLIN V GARDINER*[30]

Two boys aged 14 were innocently contacting others to notify them about a rugby match. Two police constables, in plain clothes, became suspicious and approached the boys, showing their warrant cards. The boys, not believing they were policemen, moved away, at which point the officer grabbed one of them. A scuffle ensued and one of the boys hit and kicked at the officer in order to get away. The boys were charged with assaulting a police officer in the execution of his duty and convicted.[31] On appeal, their convictions were quashed. The boys had been assaulted by the officer who tried to detain them and were acting in self-defence.

Where a child or young person is arrested, he or she has the same rights as an adult but with the additional requirement that all those dealing with the child must consider the interests of the child and his or her needs.[32] Furthermore, as the case below shows, when a child is held in custody by the police he or she must be treated as a child, not as an adult.

CASE FOCUS: *HC*[33]

In 2013, HC, then aged 17, was arrested on suspicion of stealing a mobile phone. He asked that his mother be informed but that was not allowed. He was kept in custody for more than 11 hours during which time his mother was not allowed to speak to him, and he had refused to see a solicitor. He was later released and no charges were ever brought. At the time, the Police and Criminal Evidence Act 1984, and the Code of Practice, provided that 17-year-olds should be treated in the same way as adults, and an officer could lawfully refuse to contact a nominated person if doing so 'would hinder the recovery of property …'. Had HC been treated as a child he would have had an unqualified right to have someone informed and to have assistance during the custody procedures.

In judicial review proceedings against the Home Secretary, the High Court ruled that 17-year-olds must be treated as children when in custody. The judge cited the UN Convention on the Rights of the Child which provides that children separated from their parents have the right to have their parents informed of their whereabouts and to have contact with them. Mr Justice Moses said:

> This case demonstrates how vulnerable a 17-year-old may be. Treated as an adult, he receives no explanation as to how important it is to obtain the assistance of a lawyer. Many 17-year-olds do not believe they need any guidance at all.
>
> It is difficult to image a more striking case where the rights of both child and parent under Article 8 [Article 8: the right to respect for private and family life] are engaged than when a child is in custody on suspicion of committing a serious offence and needs help from someone with whom he is familiar and whom he trusts in redressing the imbalance between child and authority.

The Home Secretary had violated Article 8 and the Code was declared to be unlawful on the basis that it failed to distinguish between adults and children.

Legal advice and legal aid

Where a child is to be interviewed, unless the child asks for legal advice, he or she must be informed of the right to talk with a solicitor on the telephone and to have a solicitor present during the interview. There is a right to have an appropriate adult present at interview, and that adult may request legal advice if the child has not done so. There is a right to be represented in court.

Remand on bail

There is a presumption that a defendant has a right to bail.[34] Bail is the term for the conditions attached to the release of a person who has been charged with an offence in order to ensure that he or she will attend court at the required time. Following arrest and charge, a child is entitled to be released from police detention either with bail or without bail: he or she is 'remanded' to appear in court at a future date.[35] Bail may be granted by the police following an arrest, or may be granted by a court when the matter comes before the court. If bail is refused by the police, or a court refuses to consider an application for bail, that decision may be challenged through judicial review proceedings.[36]

CASE FOCUS: *B*[37]

B was charged with attempted burglary and going equipped to steal. He appeared in court and remanded into custody on the basis that there was a substantial risk that he would commit further offences if granted bail, and/or interfere with witnesses (when arrested he was on bail for an alleged offence of aggravated burglary for which he was later found guilty). Four further applications for bail were refused, the court holding that there were no new considerations to be taken into account.

B sought judicial review, arguing that the court's refusal to consider his applications for bail was unlawful. The court found that in refusing to consider the substance of his bail application, the court had erred. The court then turned to section 44 of the Children and Young Persons Act 1933: the welfare principle, ruling that even if the previous court had decided that there were no new arguments in favour of the defendant, the court should have taken into account the welfare of a child or young person and that required it to consider the new bail applications afresh.

There are exceptions to the right to be released. Immediate release may be delayed for the purposes of determining a child's identity or in relation to offences involving Class A drugs to enable a sample to be taken. Samples may only be taken from those aged 14 and over and require the presence of an appropriate adult. Release will be denied where the charge is murder and may be denied in order to prevent further offences being committed or where it is considered to be necessary for the protection of the child. In relation to children, there is the additional requirement that the custody officer must also have reasonable grounds for believing that detention is in his or her interests.

Remand in custody

Where it is considered that there is a risk of a child reoffending, or absconding, bail may be refused and the child remanded in custody. When a child is detained an appropriate adult must be contacted as soon as possible, and attend within two hours of the request being made, in order to minimise the length of time the child spends in detention.

Where a child aged ten or 11 is to be kept in detention, he or she must be moved to local authority accommodation unless, for specified reasons (which must be recorded) 'it is impracticable to do so'.[38] The remand will be for a maximum of eight days. The court remanding the child or young person may impose any condition.[39] Where there is a remand to local authority accommodation the authority may ask the court for a Secure Accommodation Order.[40]

Moving a child over the age of 12 to local authority accommodation can be refused in circumstances where it is considered that such accommodation would not be adequate to protect the public from 'serious harm' from him or her.[41] In such cases a child between the ages of 12 and 17 may be sent to youth detention accommodation.[42] Before doing so, prosecutors are advised to consult the Youth Offending Team to explain the objections to bail and the reasons for seeking a remain to youth detention accommodation. An application for remand to youth detention accommodation should only be made after all the alternatives have been considered and found to be inadequate to protect the public.

Prosecution

In all cases, irrespective of age, there are two main factors which determine whether or not a person will be prosecuted and face trial. In England and Wales, the decision to prosecute lies with the Crown Prosecution Service, in Northern Ireland it lies with the Public Prosecution Service, and in Scotland with the Procurator Fiscal. The first factor is whether or not there is sufficient evidence against the accused person so that a prosecution has a reasonable prospect of succeeding. The second factor is whether or not prosecuting the accused is 'in the public interest'.

In relation to children there is a third principle that must be taken into account: the best interests of the child.[43] This applies to the decision whether to prosecute and to the decision to prosecute another person where a child is the victim of the alleged offence and/or will be called as a witness at any trial.

The Crown Prosecution Service (CPS) recognises that the younger the age of a child, the 'less likely it is that a prosecution is required'.[44] However, the CPS has to balance the interests of the child against the public interest in the prosecution proceeding. The seriousness of the offence, the suspect's past record if any, the harm caused, etc. must all be taken into consideration and the decision will involve balancing many factors in addition to the child's welfare and interests.

Children on trial

Article 6 of the European Convention on Human Rights (ECHR) states that:

> In the determination of his civil rights and obligations or of any criminal charge against him, everyone is entitled to a fair and public hearing within a reasonable time by an independent and impartial tribunal established by law.

Two cases brought before the European Court of Human Rights (ECtHR) alleging breaches of Article 6, the right to fair trial, have had a significant impact on improving the protection of children facing trial.

CASE FOCUS: *T AND V*[45]

In *T and V v United Kingdom* (1999), an application was made under the ECHR alleging that the proceedings in the Crown Court against two children accused of abducting and murdering a toddler, James Bulger, violated Article 6. The case attracted intense media and public interest. The ECtHR considered how the requirements of Article 6 should be adapted to reflect the needs of children and to promote their understanding and participation in the trial proceedings.

The fact that the children were represented by senior counsel was not sufficient: what was needed was a situation in which the child felt sufficiently comfortable that he or she could cooperate fully with his or her lawyers. The 'formality and ritual' of the Crown Court had an 'intimidating effect' on the child and the proceedings would have been difficult for him to understand. As a result of the children's inability to participate in the proceedings, there was a violation of Article 6.

Following this case a Practice Direction was issued stressing that measures had to be taken to enable a child to understand and participate in the proceedings and that the trial process had to be adapted to meet those needs.[46] In particular:

- the court should be arranged so that participants are on the same level;
- the child should sit with members of his or her family or others responsible for his or her care;

- the court is under a duty to explain the proceedings to the child;
- the trial must be conducted in a language that the child understands;
- robes, wigs, and uniforms should not be worn;
- frequent and regular breaks must be provided for.

CASE FOCUS: SC[47]

In *SC v United Kingdom* (2005), an 11-year-old child had been sentenced to two-and-a-half years detention for participating in an attempted robbery. He had complained that his rights under Article 6 had been breached, in that due to his age and low intelligence he was unable fully to understand and participate in the proceedings. The ECtHR accepted that it was not essential for a child to understand every detailed point of law or procedure. However, in order to participate in the proceedings, the child must be able to understand what is being said in court and to communicate effectively with his or her lawyers. The court ruled that SC's rights under Article 6 had been violated: his intellectual capacity was too low to enable him to understand the proceedings. What was needed was 'a specialist tribunal which is able to give full consideration to and make proper allowance for the handicaps under which he labours, and adapt its procedures accordingly'.[48]

Protecting children in court

The arrangement of the court

In the Youth Court the child, with his or her parent(s) or carer(s) will sit on the same level as the magistrates. A child under the age of 16 must have a parent or guardian with him or her in court, and those over 16 should be accompanied. Magistrates are encouraged to introduce themselves and explain the role of those present in court. The use of simple language is encouraged in order that the child can understand what is going on and participate in the proceedings and questions should be in plain language and legal jargon avoided.[49]

However, there are a number of problems with court hearings – whether in the Youth Court or Crown Court – as discussed by the *Review of the Youth Justice System in England and Wales* (the Taylor Review) 2016:

> Despite these adaptations and the best efforts of magistrates and judges, it is clear that the courts are simply not set up to ensure the full participation of children in criminal proceedings. Children are subject to what are essentially modified versions of the same process and procedures that apply to adult defendants. Too often children are alienated by the

frequent use of opaque legal argument and arcane terminology and not all magistrates do enough to explain what is happening in language that children can understand. The courts are often large spaces and the considerable distances between the different parties do not make for effective communication, not least because in order to be heard people have to raise their voices. Children are encouraged to address the Youth Court, but are asked to do so in an environment that is completely alien to any other situation in which they might find themselves asked to speak. On many occasions children leave the court confused by the outcome and need to have their sentence explained to them by a YOT worker. All these problems are exacerbated when cases are heard in the Crown Court or adult magistrates' courts where fewer adjustments can be made for children.[50]

The Review was also highly critical of the quality of representation for children before the Youth Courts, pointing out that the fee structure for representation results in barristers being paid three times as much for an adult hearing before the Crown Court than for a hearing before the Youth Court. The result is that children are often represented by junior barristers or solicitors and their representation is often poor.

For all these reasons, the Review calls for an end to court hearings for children and the introduction of children's panels which could deal with children's cases in a less formal, more individualised, manner (on the Scottish system of Children's Hearings, see below, page 216–218).

'Special measures'

Children who give evidence in court, whether as a defendant or a witness, have the right to special protection.[51] Either the prosecution or defence may apply to the court for 'special measures', and if no application has been made the court may decide to direct that such measures be taken to protect children. These measures can include:

- the use of screens to ensure that the witness does not see the defendant;
- the pre-recording of an interview with the witness to be produced at the trial;
- allowing evidence to be given from outside the court via a live television link;
- allowing cross-examination about the evidence to be recorded and then shown at the trial;
- clearing the court so that evidence is given in private;
- allowing a third party to help the witness communicate and allowing the use of communication aids;
- the lack of formal court dress of wigs and gowns.

Defendants are not allowed to personally cross-examine a child witness who is either the victim, or a witness to the commission of an offence in a case involving sexual offences, kidnapping or abduction, cruelty, or physical assault.

Reporting restrictions

Reporting restrictions and restrictions on publishing information that can identify alleged juvenile offenders and child victims of or witnesses to criminal offences apply from the time a criminal investigation into an alleged crime commences, and covers reporting anywhere in the UK, with the exception of proceedings in Scotland which has its own system of reporting restrictions.[52] Reporting restrictions on proceedings before the Youth Courts are automatic and prohibit the disclosure of the identity of victims, witnesses, and defendants under the age of 18.[53]

The powers of the Youth Courts

The Youth Court is a Magistrates' Court specialising in children's cases. Its special features include the absence of formality, the protection of the child's privacy through not allowing access by the public, and the prohibition on reporting the child's identity.

Consistent with the requirements of domestic law and the UN Convention on the Rights of the Child (CRC), when sentencing those under the age of 18, the court must consider two principal matters:

- the main aim of the youth justice system – the prevention of offending;[54] and
- the welfare of the child or young person.[55]

The Sentencing Council[56] states that:

> It is important to avoid 'criminalising' children and young people unnecessarily; the primary purpose of the youth justice system is to encourage children and young people to take responsibility for their own actions and promote re-integration into society rather than to punish. Restorative justice disposals may be of particular value for children and young people as they can encourage them to take responsibility for their actions and understand the impact their offence may have had on others.[57]

Sentencing

If the offence is relatively minor, the court may order a discharge: the offender is then free to go, with no further consequences. The court may also order a conditional discharge, subject to the single condition that the child does not commit any further offences within a specified time period. Only if the condition is breached will further action be taken.

Other than where there is a mandatory life sentence, or a statutory minimum custodial sentence, or orders under the Mental Health Act 1983, the court should adopt an approach to sentencing that is specific to the child and his or her needs. Consistent with domestic and international law, a custodial sentence is a last resort, to be imposed where the offence is so serious that no other sanction is appropriate.[58]

While the stated aim of sentencing is to encourage personal responsibility and promote reintegration into society (rather than punishment), the starting point in sentencing is nevertheless the seriousness of the offence and the sentence which an adult would have received (taking into account aggravating or mitigating factors and any credit due for pleading guilty). Having determined the adult sentence, the court then applies a reduction based on the offender's age. This is ordinarily between half to two-thirds for those aged 15 to 17, with the possibility of a further reduction for those aged under 15. In deciding what reduction should be applied, the court must consider the 'emotional and developmental age and maturity of the child or young person'.[59]

Referrals to the Youth Offending Panel[60]

Where a child is charged with an imprisonable offence[61] (i.e. an offence for which imprisonment is the punishment) for the first time, and pleads guilty, the Youth Court *must* make an order referring the child to the Youth Offender Panel. A Referral Order may also be made by the Crown Court when it is dealing with an appeal from the Youth Court.[62] The Referral Order is not available if the child pleads not guilty to the offence. A Referral Order cannot be made for an offence for which the sentence is fixed by law, for example where a child is convicted of murder and a mandatory sentence must be imposed.[63] The order is also not available if the court decides to make a hospital order or grant an absolute or conditional discharge.

A Referral Order requires the child to enter into a contract with a Youth Offender Panel (YOP).[64] The order lasts between three and 12 months, as determined by the court. It may be revoked or extended for three months, but last for no longer than 12 months. The court must explain to the child the referral process and what will happen if he or she does not comply with the terms of the contract which will be drawn up between the child and the Youth Offending Team and Panel.

The child will then be assessed by the Youth Offending Team (YOT) which then passes its assessment report to a Youth Offender Panel (YOP). The key elements of the contract are a form of reparation to the victim and/or wider community and a programme of activities designed to help the child move forwards without reoffending. Reparation may include a direct apology to the victim. There will be regular meetings with the child and his or her parent or carer to assess the progress being made. At the end of the contract, the criminal conviction which prompted the Referral Order will be 'spent'.[65] This means that although the conviction will remain on record (and it will only become relevant if the child reoffends), as noted above, it does not have to be disclosed to future employers or insurers. This is subject to defined exceptions which mainly relate to working with children, the sick or vulnerable, the administration of justice, and where matters of financial honesty are crucial.[66]

If the child refuses to agree a contract or then breaches its terms, the YOP can refer the child back to the court which can then revoke the RO and re-sentence the child for the original offence.

Youth Rehabilitation Orders

According to the Sentencing Council:

> Community orders can fulfil all of the purposes of sentencing. In particular, they can have the effect of restricting the offender's liberty while providing punishment in the community, rehabilitation for the offender and/ or ensuring that the offender engages in reparative activities.
>
> *General Principles*

Youth Rehabilitation Orders (a community order) may be imposed for an offence for which the punishment is imprisonment, and only where the offence is 'serious enough to warrant such a sentence'.[67] A Youth Rehabilitation Order (YRO) must be suitable for the individual offender, and should not conflict with his or her religious beliefs, or interfere with his or her education or training, and must take into account the ability of the offender to comply with its requirements. In addition to a YRO a fine may be imposed.

YROs consist of a range of requirements which will be adapted according to the seriousness of the offence for which the child or young person has been found guilty. These may include:

- unpaid work (16- and 17-year-olds), from 40 to 300 hours to be completed within 12 months;
- a specified number of days undertaking rehabilitation activities;
- prohibited activities;
- curfew requirements between two and 16 hours per 24 hours for a maximum term of 12 months;
- exclusion from a specified place/places for a maximum period of two years;
- residence requirement;
- education requirement;
- electronic monitoring requirement;
- foreign travel prohibition for a maximum of 12 months;
- mental health requirement;
- alcohol and drug dependency treatment;

- supervision requirements;
- a fostering requirement.

The supervision and fostering requirements are both intended to be a community alternative to custody. A YRO may be given with Intensive Supervision and Surveillance (ISS), on which see below. A court can only sentence a young person to a YRO with ISS when:

- the offence is punishable with imprisonment;
- the court is of the opinion that the offence is so serious that without ISS, a custodial sentence would be appropriate;
- for under 15s, only if they are a persistent offender;
- if the offence is non-imprisonable but the young offender is already in breach of a YRO, ISS is available only where the court considers that there has been wilful and persistent non-compliance.

Criminal Behaviour Orders[68]

Serious cases of antisocial behaviour will be dealt with by a Criminal Behaviour Order (CBO). These are available against both adults and children. A CBO can be issued by any criminal court against a person who has been convicted of an offence, on the application of the Crown Prosecution Service (on its own initiative or following a request by the police or local authority). The sort of conduct covered by a CBO may be drunkenness and aggression in a public place, threatening others, or being involved in burglary or street robbery. There is no necessary link between the offence for which the offender has been convicted and the basis for a CBO.

The test to be applied by the court is that the court is 'satisfied beyond reasonable doubt that the perpetrator has caused, or is likely to cause, harassment, alarm or distress to others' and that the CBO will help prevent any repetition of that conduct. For under 18s the local Youth Offending Team must be consulted. A CBO will state what an offender is not allowed to do and include positive requirements designed to address the underlying causes of the antisocial behaviour. These could include attendance at an anger management course; mentoring, substance misuse awareness training or a course designed to improve employment prospects. The CBO should not affect a person's education, training or employment.

For those under 18 the CBO will last for a minimum of one year and a maximum of three years, with an annual review to monitor progress. A person breaching a CBO commits a criminal offence carrying a maximum penalty of up to two years' detention and training for those under the age of 18.[69]

Unless the court has made an order prohibiting publication,[70] the police or local council may decide to publicise a CBO issued to a young person on the basis that this will reassure the local community that action is being taken and enable the public to report any further antisocial behaviour. Such publicity violates the young person's right to privacy,[71] and those considering whether to publicise the CBO must consider it a necessary and proportionate measure. The likely impact on the young person's behaviour must also be considered.

The Intensive Supervision and Surveillance Programme (ISSP)

Intensive Supervision and Surveillance (ISS) can only be imposed for an offence which carries a penalty of imprisonment. It is intended to be a community alternative to custody. Where the offender is under the age of 15, they must be considered to be a 'persistent offender'. ISS may be attached to a YRO or for those on bail or those on the community part of a Detention and Training Order, on which see below.

The ISSP was introduced in 2001 with the following three objectives:

- to reduce the reoffending in the garget group of offenders by five per cent, and to reduce the seriousness of reoffending;
- to tackle the underlying problems of the young people concerned, in an effective manner and with a particular emphasis on educational needs;
- to demonstrate that supervision and surveillance are being undertaken consistently and rigorously, and in ways that will reassure the community and sentencers of their credibility and likely success.[72]

The ISSP will last from six to 12 months and requires up to 25 hours of activities each week. Supervision is provided 365 days a year. All those on ISS are subject to an electronically monitored curfew, with any non-compliance being reported to the Youth Offending Service within 24 hours. A failure to comply with the requirements means they may be sent to custody.

Detention and Training Orders (DTOs)

The UN Convention on the Rights of the Child states, in part, that:

> Every child deprived of liberty shall be treated with humanity and respect for the inherent dignity of the human person, and in a manner which takes into account the needs of persons of his or her age.[73]
>
> *Article 37*

A Detention and Training Order is a prison sentence which may be imposed on 12 to 17 year-olds. A child below the age of 12 cannot receive a DTO and children aged between 12 and 14 may only receive a DTO if they are 'persistent offenders' (i.e. they have committed imprisonable offences on at least three occasions in the past 12 months).[74] The DTO will last for a specified period between four months and two years. The first half of the DTO will be served in custody;

the second half under the supervision of the Youth Offending Team. If the order is broken while under supervision, the child can be sent back into custody for up to three months. Before a DTO can be imposed the child must be legally represented, unless he or she has refused to apply for legal aid.

In 2015 there were 'around 1,000' children in custody for between two and five months as part of a DTO.[75] In the year ending March 2019 the average number of nights spent on a DTO was 90.[76] The 2016 Review of the Youth Justice System in England and Wales was highly critical of the custodial element of DTOs:

> These short custodial sentences often break vital links with family, education and support services and provide little opportunity for secure establishments to tackle the child's problems. Children fail to settle in secure provision and do not feel it is worth investing in the regime or building the relationships with staff members that would help their experience of temporary placements in foster care or children's homes.[77]

Moreover:

> The reoffending rages of children released from short custodial sentences are the highest of any cohort: 80 per cent for those serving under six-month sentences, and 73 per cent for those on six- to 12-month sentences.[78]

Ethnicity and detention

Children from Black, Asian, and Minority Ethnic backgrounds (BAME) make up a disproportionate percentage of children in custody.[79] Black people, who in 2015/16 made up around three per cent of the population, accounted for 12 per cent of adult prisoners and more than 20 per cent of children in custody. The BAME proportion of children offending for the first time rose from 11 per cent in the year ending March 2006 to 19 per cent in the year ending March 2016. The BAME proportion of child prisoners rose from 25 per cent to 41 per cent between 2006 and 2016.

Young Offender Institutions (YOIs)

The aim of a YOI is 'to help offenders to prepare for their return to the outside community'. This is to be achieved by a programme of activities, including education, training, and work. For those of compulsory school age, there must be 15 hours of education provided each week.

There are five Young Offender Institutions (YOIs) in England and Wales: Cookham Wood, Feltham A, Parc, Werrington, and the Keppel Unit at Wetherby. The Keppel Unit is a specialised high-dependency unit for boys aged between ten and 18. It enables the Youth Justice Board (which oversees the youth justice system) to provide a special level of care and support to vulnerable boys. In October 2019 there was a total of 606 boys aged 15 to 18 held in YOIs.

YOIs may be run by local authorities or by private companies.[80] On an inspection report on the children's prison inside Parc prison, Frances Crook, Chief Executive of the Howard League for Penal Reform, comments that G4S which runs Parc refused to allow the Howard League to visit: 'yet again', she writes, 'a private prison is being secretive …'.[81] She writes that the use of force by staff is high and that three-quarters of the boys said they had been physically restrained, in some cases with staff inflicting pain. There is also an apparent bias against BAME children with not one BAME child on the highest level of the incentives scheme. Boys were locked in their cells for 15 hours a day on average during the week and 18 hours at weekends, although the inspectors praised Parc for letting the boys out of their cells for longer than other prisons.

Secure Training Centres (STCs)

STCs accommodate boys and girls between the ages of 12 and 18. There are three STCs in England: Medway, Oakhill, and Rainsbrook. The Chief Inspector of Prisons Annual Report 2018–2019 expressed concerns over the conditions in all three. High levels of violence and the use of force continued to occur. Sixty-two per cent of children had been physically restrained since their arrival (compared with 49 per cent in YOIs).

CASE FOCUS: *GARETH*

In 2004 a 15-year-old boy who was three days into a 12-month sentence, Gareth Myatt, died as a consequence of physical restraint at Rainsbrook STC. He had refused to clean a sandwich toaster and was sent to his cell. Prison officers decided to separate him from others to enable him to calm down. When they started to remove his possessions from his room, including a piece of paper with his mother's phone number on it, Gareth became agitated and was reported to have punched an officer. He was then restrained by three officers. He complained that he could not breathe, to which an officer told him 'if you can talk, you can breathe'. Gareth slumped forward but the restraint continued. When it was stopped he was found to be unconscious and could not be resuscitated. The coroner gave a verdict of accidental death.

CASE FOCUS: *ADAM*

Also in 2004, at Hassockfield STC,[82] Adam Rickwood, aged 14, committed suicide by hanging. He had a history of self-harm and suicide attempts and had been placed a very long way from his home. He had earlier been restrained and a pain-inducing technique 'the nose distraction technique' had been applied. At a second inquest into his death it was concluded that the use of physical control at Hassockfield gave rise to an 'unlawful regime'; the use of force was ruled to be unlawful and contributed to Adam's death.[83]

Medway was inspected in 2018 by Ofsted.[84] The inspectors found that that most children had experienced the use of force or physical restraint; that there were high numbers of violent child-on-child incidents and that there was little being done to protect children from bullying. There were 330 incidents involving force in a six-month period, over 80 per cent of these involved the use of 'minimising and managing physical restraint' holds (MMPR). Restraint was found to have been used to control children's passive non-compliance, such as refusing to go to bed. On the infliction of pain, the inspection found that it had been used ten times over the previous six months, with the objective of making a child compliant. As the Report notes: 'deliberately inflicting pain significantly compromises children's safety and welfare'.[85] The Ofsted Report called for the use of force and restraint to be made compliant with STC Rules and for the end of pain-inducing techniques used on children.

The Medway STC was for years the subject of serious criticism for its treatment of children in its care and closed in 2020. It is intended to replace it with the first of a new type of secure accommodation: the Secure School (on which see below). Medway housed up to 67 girls and boys aged 12 to 18 years who were serving a custodial sentence or on remand.

Young Offender Institution rules[86]

The rules are complex, but the principal features from the point of view of the rights of detained children are as follows. A body search will be conducted on arrival. Within 24 hours of arriving at a YOI, written information about the rules governing the institution must be provided. Every YOI has a system of privileges which is linked to compliance with the rules. Privileges include earning money which may be spent within the YOI, and earning extra time outside the cell and meeting with others ('association'). Everyone is entitled to send and receive a letter on arrival at the YOI and thereafter one letter per week, and to receive a visit every fortnight unless the Secretary of State (in practice the governor of the institution) directs that he or she should only receive one visit every four weeks. There is a right to meet a legal adviser, out of the hearing of prison officers, and to correspond with a legal adviser and any court. However, if the governor 'has reasonable cause to believe' that the correspondence contains an 'illicit enclosure', or it might endanger the prison or others, or is of a criminal nature, the correspondence may be opened and stopped.

The governor has wide powers to ensure 'good order and discipline'. These include the power to remove an inmate from association with others, but for no longer than three days unless authorised by the Secretary of State or a member of the Board of Visitors.[87] Prison officers may use force if necessary, but that force must be no more than is necessary. Where an inmate is either difficult to control or violent he or she may be temporarily confined to a special cell until he or she stops being non-compliant or violent. To prevent an inmate from injuring him or herself or others, or to prevent damage to property to prevent a disturbance, the governor may order that an inmate is put under restraint. Restraint may not be used on those under the age of 17, other than placing him or her in handcuffs to prevent injury or damage. The rules set out the classes of disciplinary offences and the punishments that may be imposed when there is a finding of guilt. Punishments for offences against discipline include a caution, forfeiture of privileges, removal from activities other than education, training or work, imposing additional work requirements, stopping earnings, removal from his or her wing or living unit for up to 21 days. Where an inmate is found guilty of more than one charge, punishments may run consecutively.

Separation/solitary confinement of children

Under the Youth Offender Institution Rules, a child may be separated from others where 'it appears desirable, for the maintenance of good order or discipline or in his own interests'.[88] In its report, *Separation of Children in Young Offender Institutions*,[89] the Prison Inspectorate was highly critical of the conditions under which young offenders were kept in the five YOIs in England and Wales. In particular, the use of separation of a young person from his peers, often for many days at a time, is widespread. In the 2020 Report, between 54 per cent and 70 per cent of children reported having been kept locked up and stopped from mixing with others as a punishment. Most separated children spent long periods of time in their cells, with no human interaction. In the worst cases children had as little as 15 minutes out of their cells in a day: this amounts in many cases to solitary confinement which is defined as being 'the confinement of prisons for 22 hours or more a day without meaningful human contact'.[90]

The Report concludes that 'as a consequence of these failings most separated children experienced a regime that amounted to the widely accepted definition of solitary confinement'. And that, '…for some of these children, their solitary confinement was prolonged in nature'. Overall, the 2020 Report finds that the regime for children separated from others is generally poor and unsuitable for children. Segregation units varied, with conditions at one being described as 'dark, with small cells, often dirty and unventilated, walls and windows with graffiti and toilets dirty and stained'.

CASE FOCUS: *BOURGASS*[91]

In 2015, in a case concerning the legality of the solitary confinement of adult prisoners, the UK Supreme Court considered the evidence concerning the detrimental effects of segregation. A 2008 report, cited to the Court, for example, found that 'solitary confinement may cause serious psychological and sometimes physiological ill effects' and that 'between one third and as many as 90 per cent of prisoners experience adverse symptoms in solitary confinement'.[92] Equally a report of 2011 stated that solitary confinement can have extremely damaging effect on the 'mental, somatic and social health of those concerned' and that the risks increased with the longer the confinement lasted and 'the more indeterminate it is'.[93] If such risks may be experienced by adults they must surely also apply to children.

CASE FOCUS: *AB*[94]

In a legal challenge to the solitary confinement of a 15-year-old boy in Feltham the Court of Appeal ruled that his isolation had been unlawful on the basis that it breached the prison rules on the provision of education. The boy, AB, had been locked in his cell for over 22 hours a day for more than 15 days at a time. The Court referred to a statement made by the Committee on the Rights of the Child in 2007 on the use of discipline in institutions. This made clear that the use of corporal punishment, placement in a dark cell, closed or solitary confinement, or any other punishment that may compromise the physical or mental health or well-being of the child violated Article 37 of the CRC and 'must be strictly forbidden'. The Court ruled, however, that his isolation had not been a punitive measure, but imposed 'for his protection and for the protection of others'.

The Court also ruled that his detention did not amount to 'inhuman or degrading treatment' as prohibited by Article 3 of the European Convention on Human Rights. The opportunity to protect the rights of the child was lost.

The use of physical restraints against children

In its 2016 Report, the UN Committee on the Rights of the Child[95] expressed concern over:

> The use of physical restraint on children to maintain good order and discipline in Young Offenders' Institutions and the use of pain-inducing

techniques on children in institutional settings in England, Wales, and Scotland, and the lack of a comprehensive review of the use of restraint in institutional settings in Northern Ireland.

Staff in YOIs and STCs (but no other children's institutions) are permitted to use physical restraints for the purposes of 'discipline and good order'. While the number of children detained has fallen considerably over the past decade, those children who are detained are highly vulnerable and often have multiple problems which can result in disruptive, aggressive behaviour towards other children and/or staff. In the year ending March 2018, the Youth Justice Board reported that 'there were nearly 6,600 "use of force incidents" in YOIs and STCs on around 300 children, i.e. about one third of children experienced use of force almost twice a month on average'.[96] Some of these techniques deliberately inflict pain on the child for the purpose of making the child compliant. The evidence shows that the techniques are not being used as a last resort, but as a frequent occurrence. Moreover, they contravene international human rights standards; cause physical pain and psychological damage, create barriers to good relations between children and staff, and teach children that the use of force is an acceptable form of dispute resolution. The Joint Committee on Human Rights called in its 2019 Report for the use of force to be banned in YOIs and STCs, save for exceptional circumstances, and for the Ministry of Justice guidelines be revised accordingly.

In 2015 the Chief Inspector of Prisons wrote that:

> Some of what we describe in this report is deeply disturbing. Too many of our findings indicate little cultural change and, despite significant effort and some good practice, there is still much more to be done to ensure that the application [of restraint] locally is consistent with national policy guidance. Further progress is necessary both to ensure that past tragedies associated with the application of force by the state on children are not repeated – and to give staff the tools to better manage the behaviour of some of our most troubled and challenging children on a day-to-day basis.[97]

Among his recommendations were the following:

- that restraint should not be used for reasons relating to good order or security, and children should not be strip searched under restraint;
- pain-inducing techniques should not be used on children.

In 2019 the government issued new guidelines on restraint and restrictive intervention (RRI), although these do not apply to Secure Training Centres. The core values the guidance stresses are that the best interests of children and young people and their safety and welfare should underpin any use of restraint; that the risk of harm to children; young people and staff should be minimised; and that a decision to restrain a child or young person is taken to assure their safety and dignity and that of all concerned, including other children, young people, or adults present.[98] Recognising that restraint may be necessary to protect the child or others from serious harm or injury, the guidance states that restraint should only be used to prevent the risk of serious harm, that it should not be used to punish or with the intention of inflicting pain, suffering, or humiliation and that techniques used should be reasonable and proportionate to the circumstances.

Evaluating YOIs and STCs

The Annual Report 2016–2017 of the Chief Inspector of Prisons in England and Wales makes depressing reading in relation to the rights of children in custody.

> Perhaps the most concerning findings during the year emerged from our inspections of the custodial estate for children and young people.
>
> By February this year [2017] we had reached the conclusion that there was not a single establishment that we inspected in England and Wales in which it was safe to hold children and young people. The background to this dire situation is significant, and I make no apology for repeating here some of the relevant statistics. At that time there were around 609 children held in YOIs and 155 in STCs. The Youth Justice Board annual statistics for 2015–2016 showed self-harm rates running at 8.9 incidents per 100 children compared with 4.1 in 2011. Assault rates were 18.9 per 100 children, compared with 9.7 in 2011. Our own surveys showed that 46 per cent of boys had felt unsafe in their establishment. The number of those reporting being victimised by other boys had risen significantly and those who said they had been treated with respect by staff had fallen. Meanwhile, the proportion of boys engaged in a job (16 per cent), vocational training (11 per cent), and offending behaviour programmes (16 per cent) across the YOIs was lower in 2015–2016 than at any point since 2010–2011.[99]

As noted above, all detained children have a right to education, amounting to at least 15 hours a week. At Feltham A boys were receiving just half of the hours required.

In his Annual Report 2018–2019,[100] the Chief Inspector of Prisons noted that in YOIs and STCs:

- 49 per cent of children said they had been physically restrained;
- segregation units provided 'generally grim living conditions';
- 69 per cent of children were able to shower daily;
- healthcare provision was generally good;
- only two YOIs achieved the expected ten hours a day out of cell;
- between 44 per cent and 79 per cent of children had daily time in the open air;
- many children received less than the 15 hours' education they were entitled to;
- planning for release was undermined by there being a lack of suitable accommodation for children before their release.

The Annual Report of 2019–2020 recorded that few of the previous recommendations had been implemented. Living conditions and healthcare were 'mostly reasonable' and adequate and mental health services were of 'good quality'. Standards of care for children at risk of self-harm had improved in all YOIs, except Feltham where self-harm had risen 'dramatically'. On the other hand, the use of force had increased in all but one YOI and pain-inducing techniques continued to be used in all institutions despite earlier recommendations that these should not be used where there was no 'immediate threat of harm'. Separation practices continued to mean that many children experienced the equivalent of solitary confinement. The Chief Inspector called for 'an entirely new model of separation that enables managers to protect children from harm'.[101] In relation to Feltham A, an inspection in 2019 led to calls for the Justice Secretary to take 'decisive action' over the deficiencies. There were 'overwhelming problems' in safety including violence; self-harming levels were 14 times higher than in 2017; there were poor relations between staff and children; education provision and education was inadequate; there was too little time out of cells; insufficient contact between children and their families and many children released without 'stable accommodation, education, training or employment, or support from families'.

Secure Schools (SS)

As discussed above, in 2018 the Justice Secretary announced that Medway Secure Training Centre was to be replaced with a Secure School. Secure Schools are to be run by not-for-profit academy trusts and head teachers with expertise in working with children. The Covid pandemic delayed the planned replacement of Medway.

The plans for Secure Schools are the government's response to the Taylor Review on youth justice, discussed on page 200 above. The Ministry of Justice states that it intends to tackle violence against children and improve the outcomes of imprisonment for children by placing education and health at the heart of secure institutions.[102] The government hopes that they 'will be akin to a special residential school or Secure Children's Home and not simply prisons with education'. Secure Schools are to be inspected by Ofsted and the Care Quality Commission.

Secure Schools are to be privately run by specialist providers, with a specialised workforce. They will accommodate 60 to 70 young people who are currently sent to YOIs and STCs. The first two are to be located in the North West and South East of England (replacing Medway STC).[103]

Head teachers have the autonomy to develop the curriculum and timetable which must include English, maths, science, physical education, sports, and vocational training. The government hopes that children in secure units will make educational progress at the same level as children in other schools, and that on their release they will have education, employment, and/or training arranged.

Secure Children's Homes (SCH)

For the most troubled children who have been in the care of a local authority but have either absconded or committed offences and who are deemed to be at risk to themselves and/or others, accommodation within a secure unit may be considered necessary in order to provide the necessary support for the child. Secure Children's Home, run either by local authorities or the voluntary sector, give residential care, education facilities, and healthcare.

There are 15 Secure Children's Homes (SCH) in England and Wales. Each accommodates between one and 25 boys and girls between the ages of ten and 18. In Scotland there are five units, accommodating six to 24 children, with a total of 84 beds. In Northern Ireland there are four dedicated units. Seven of the 14 SCHs in England take welfare placements (those referred by local authorities) only; only two take placements from the youth justice system (i.e. those who have committed criminal offences). There is a lack of beds in the South of England, and no provision at all in the Midlands and East Anglia, with the likelihood that children will be accommodated far from home. The average length of stay is 4.5 months, although there is provision for 72-hour emergency placements. These may only take place once in a 28-day period, following which a secure order will need to be sought from the court.

A child or young person being cared for by a local authority may not be placed in an SCH unless certain legal criteria are met and the placement is authorised by a court. The criteria are that:

- he or she has a history of absconding and is likely to abscond from anything other than secure accommodation; and
- if he or she absconds he or she is likely to suffer significant harm; or
- if he or she is kept in any other accommodation, he or she is likely to injure him/herself or other persons.[104]

If these criteria are met, the court is under a duty to make the order.[105] The maximum period for which the child may be kept in secure accommodation must be stated by the court. The court may not make an order unless the child is legally represented, or having had the opportunity to apply for legal representation, has refused or failed to apply.[106]

In England the referral will be sent to the Secure Welfare Coordination Unit (SWCU) which coordinates all placements. If the child is under the age of 13, the consent of the Secretary of State (England) or Welsh Ministers is required.

SCHs are secure: the children are locked in their rooms at night. In all SCHs the children have access to the internet and there is provision for 27 hours of education. Judicial review is available to test both the legality of the detention and its continuation.

Child protection and youth justice in Scotland

The Children's Hearing System

The Children's Hearing System is a response to a review of youth justice published in 1964.[107] The Hearing System is a legal tribunal designed to deal with children in need of care and supervision and those in trouble with the law in an informal setting, thereby providing a unique care and justice system for children.[108] There are no Youth Courts in Scotland, and children will not be dealt with by the courts unless there is a serious charge such as murder or rape.

Children who have committed offences and those who are victims of offences are dealt with in the same forum. A child may be brought before a hearing on a number of grounds. These include a crime having been committed against the child or the child is at risk of being abused or harmed. Having committed an offence is a ground for referring to the Hearing System, as is the misuse of alcohol or drugs and behaviour which is likely to have a serious adverse effect on the child or another child, or that the child is beyond control.[109]

The first point of contact with the system is a referral to the Children's Reporter who will take the decision whether the child should attend a hearing or whether the problem can be dealt with without a formal hearing. The Hearing System involves the child, his or her parents or carers, professionals, and Children's Panel Members who work together to identify the best way to ensure that a child offender does not reoffend and that all vulnerable children in need, including offenders, are supported in the best way possible. In relation to children who have committed criminal offences, by exploring the reasons for offending behaviour and uncovering the root cause of it, it is hoped that the hearing can reach an outcome to support the child and his or her welfare.

At the heart of the system is the children's panel, a force of some 2,500 volunteers. Children's Hearings Scotland (CHS) is a national body set up to support the Hearings System and headed by the National Convener. There is a Principal Reporter with responsibility for arranging all Children's Hearings. The National Convener is responsible for ensuring that the children's panel is sufficiently staffed from people from the local community.[110]

Guiding principles

The paramount consideration for those dealing with children whether at the Children's Hearing, or a pre-hearing panel or in court (see below), is the need to safeguard and promote the child's welfare throughout childhood. The views of the child are placed centre-stage. There is a presumption that a child aged 12 or more is capable to forming a view, and hearing should take into account the views of those under the age of 12 where the panel considers that he or she has sufficient understanding to form a view. A third guiding principle is the 'no order' principle. This requires that a hearing (or court) should only make orders/arrangements where to do so is better for the child than making no order/arrangements. Every Children's Hearing is under a duty to consider whether a Safeguarder should be appointed to look after the interests of the child involved in the hearing.

The Children's Panel

In 2019 to 2020, there were 30,363 Children's Hearings involved in supporting 13,316 children. Panel members are drawn from the local community and must live or work in the local authority area in which they sit on Children's Hearings, and receive both pre-service and in-service training. Members are appointed for a renewable, three-year term. Three panel members will sit at a hearing.

The hearing

The hearing is a legal meeting with wide-ranging powers. It is held in private, with the child and his or her parents or carers, the Panel members, and a social worker. There are no prosecutors or police present. Helping the child – rather than punishing him or her – is at the heart of the system. With effect from 2020 a specialist advocacy service for children and young people has been introduced with a view to strengthening children's rights within the hearings system.

Child Assessment Orders and Child Protection Orders (CPO)

If a local authority is concerned that a child is at risk it may apply to the sheriff for a Child Assessment Order, lasting three days, in which the child's health and well-being will be assessed. The consent of the child to a medical assessment is needed if he or she is, in the opinion of a medical practitioner, capable of understanding the 'nature and possible consequences' of the procedure.[111] If the sheriff considers that a child is in immediate risk of harm, he or she may make a CPO instead of a Child Assessment Order.

If a child is believed to be at immediate risk of significant harm any person may apply to the sheriff for a Child Protection Order.[112] If granted, the order may provide for a child to be taken to a place of safety, or if in such a place, not to be removed from it. Conditions may be applied. An attempt must be made to implement the order within 24 hours and it will lapse if not implemented within six days. Once the order is implemented there will be a hearing to review the order.

Exclusion Orders

Where the risk of harm is attributable to a 'named person', the local authority can apply to the sheriff for an Exclusion Order which requires the person to leave the child's home.[113] The sheriff can also attach conditions and can issue the police with a power of arrest without warrant if the Exclusion Order is breached.

Compulsory Supervision Orders (CSO)

The Hearing Panel (or sheriff) may impose a Compulsory Supervision Order. A CSO lays down specific requirements with which a child must comply and imposes duties on local authorities to provide for the child's needs. The CSO may stipulate where a child is to live, with whom he or she may (or may not) have contact, activities which are restricted, and any arrangements which must be made regarding the child's health or treatment.[114] There is power to authorise a child to be placed and kept in secure accommodation within a specified residential establishment.

Summary

The Youth Justice System in England, Wales, and Northern Ireland, in spite of its stated aim of preventing offending and/or reoffending by children and young people remains heavily reflective of the adult justice system with its emphasis on guilt and innocence and punishment. The age of criminal responsibility in England, Wales, and Northern Ireland, set at ten, is too low, and when compared with most continental countries, draconian, drawing children in need of care and support into a system not geared to cater for their well-being.

While there are mechanisms for diverting children out of the criminal justice system – cautions, community orders, and injunctions – these operate within the mainstream court system, rather than in community-based child-centred agencies focusing on guidance and support. When children are subject to custodial orders, as has been reported by those reviewing the system, the institutions to which they are sent and the treatment they receive while there are not conducive to guiding a child towards a fulfilling trouble-free adult life. Children's rights, if they exist, lie in the formal procedural rather than substantive realm. The welfare of the child may be a dominant principle in decision-making relating to children, but it has a hollow ring when considered against the reality of English juvenile justice.

The Scottish system, by contrast, puts the child and his or her problems and needs at the heart of the system. The rights of the child, and his or her welfare, have a resonance which is lacking in the youth justice system in the rest of the United Kingdom.

Notes

1 Member States shall seek, in conformity with their respective general interests, to further the well-being of the juvenile and her or his family. UN Standard Minimum Rules for the Administration of Juvenile Justice: the 'Beijing rules', rule 1.1 Crime and Disorder Act 1998, section 37.
2 Family Law Reform Act 1969, section 1 lowering the age of majority from 21. The Children Act 1989, section 105, defines a child as a person under the age of 18.
3 Crime and Disorder Act 1998, section 117.

4 Youth Offending Teams were introduced under the Crime and Disorder Act 1998.
5 Under the Human Rights Act 1998. Note that the Conservative government in 2020 stated that the Human Rights Act is to be reviewed by a constitutional commission.
6 Children and Young Persons Act 1963, section 16.
7 Criminal Procedure (Scotland) Act 1995.
8 Inserted by the Age of Criminal Responsibility Act (Scotland) 2018.
9 General Comment No 10: Children's Rights in Juvenile Justice: CRC/C/GC/10, 25 April 2007.
10 In 2020 MPs called for a formal review.
11 [1986] AC 112.
12 Crime and Disorder Act 1998, section 11.
13 Under the Children Act 1989, section 31.
14 Crime and Disorder Act 1998, section 11. Child Safety Orders replace Anti-Social Behaviour Orders (ASBOs).
15 Crime and Disorder Act 1998, section 13.
16 Crime and Disorder Act 1998, sections 8 and 9.
17 Legal Aid, Sentencing and Punishment of Offenders Act 2012 (LASPO): inserts sections 66ZA and ZB into Crime and Disorder Act 1998.
18 Crime and Disorder Act 1998 as amended by section 41 of the Criminal Justice and Courts Act 2015.
19 Antisocial Behaviour, Crime and Policing Act 2014.
20 There are also Community Protection Notices where there is persistent antisocial behaviour in an area which is harming the community. These are available against young people over the age of 16, have no fixed duration, and if breached may result in a fine between £100 and £2,500.
21 In relation to (b), this applies only where the injunction is applied for by a housing provider, local authority or chief officer of police.
22 Antisocial Behaviour, Crime and Policing Act 2014, Part 1.
23 ibid. Schedule 2, Part 2.
24 The police may alternatively apply to the court for a warrant.
25 Antisocial Behaviour, Crime and Policing act 2014, section 9.
26 Antisocial Behaviour, Crime and Policing Act 2014, Schedule 2, Part 2.
27 Ministry of Justice, 30 January 2020.
28 Excluding figures from the Lancashire police force.
29 *Kenlin v Gardner* [1967] 2 QB 510.
30 Contrary to section 51(1) Police Act 1964.
31 UNCRC Article 3 and Article 37(c).
32 *R (HC) (a child) v Secretary of State for the Home Department* [2013] EWHC 982 (admin).
33 Bail Act 1976.
34 Police and Criminal Evidence Act 1984, section 38.
35 *R (B) v Brent Youth Court* [2010] EWHC 1893 (Admin).
36 *R (B) v Brent Youth Court* [2010] EWHC 1893 (Admin).
37 Legal Aid and Sentencing of Offenders Act 2012, section 91.
38 Bail Act 1976, section 3(6).
39 Under section 25 Children Act 1989.
40 Legal Aid and Sentencing of Offenders Act, sections 98 and 99.
41 Meaning accommodation provided for the purpose of restricting liberty: ibid. (6A).
42 As required by the UN Convention on the Rights of the Child, Article 3.
43 CPS Guidance: cps.gov.uk-guidance/safeguarding-children-victims-and-witnesses.
44 (1999) 30 EHRR 121.
45 [2000] All ER 285.
46 (2005) 40 EHRR 10.
47 ibid., paragraphs 34–35.
48 Judicial College, *Youth Court Bench Book,* 2017.

49 Review, paragraph 91.
50 Youth Justice and Criminal Evidence Act 1999, Part II.
51 ibid.
52 Children and Young Persons Act 1933, section 49.
53 This requirement does not apply where a life sentence must be imposed or when making some orders under the Mental Health Act 1983.
54 Children and Young Persons act 1933, section 44(1); article 3.1 UN CRC.
55 The Sentencing Council is an independent non-departmental public body with responsibility for developing guidelines and monitoring their use Established in 2010, the Sentencing Council replaced the Sentencing Guidelines Council and Sentencing Advisory Panel.
56 Sentencing Children and Young People, Definitive Guideline, 2017.
57 ibid., *paragraph 1.4.*
58 Youth Sentencing Guidelines, paragraph 6,46.
59 Sections 16–28 Powers of the Criminal Courts (Sentencing) Act 2000.
60 An imprisonable offence is defined as 'an offence punishable in the case of an adult with imprisonment': LASPO Act 2012, Schedule 11.
61 Senior Courts Act 1981, section 48(4).
62 Powers of Criminal Courts (Sentencing) Act 2000, section 90.
63 Youth Justice and Criminal Evidence Act 1999, section 6.
64 Rehabilitation of Offenders Act 1974.
65 See the Rehabilitation of Offenders Exceptions Order 1975.
66 Criminal Justice Act 2003, section 148(1).
67 Antisocial Behaviour, Crime and Policing Act 2014, sections 22–33.
68 Antisocial Behaviour, Crime and Policing Act 2014, section 22.
69 Children and Young Persons Act 1933, section 39.
70 Protected under the European Convention on Human Rights, Article 8.
71 Youth Justice Board, ISSP: the Final Report, 2005.
72 Article 37.
73 Sentencing Guidelines Council, Overarching Principles, paragraph 6.5.
74 Review of the Youth Justice System in England and Wales, Cm 9298, 2016.
75 Ministry of Justice, Youth Justice Statistics, England and Wales, April 2018 to March 2019.
76 Cm 9298, paragraph 97.
77 ibid. From Ministry of Justice Proven Reoffending Statistics Quarterly, July 2013 to June 2014, Table C2b..
78 The Lammy Review into the treatment of, and outcomes for, Black, Asian and Minority Ethnic Individuals in the Criminal Justice System, September 2017.
79 Criminal Justice Act 1991, section 84.
80 howardleague.org/blog/parc-prison-and-its-unit-for-children/
81 Hassockfield was closed in 2015.
82 HM Inspectorate of Prisons, *Behaviour management and restraint of children in custody,* November 2015.
83 The Office for Standards in Education.
84 Ofsted, Inspection Report on Medway Secure Training Centre, 2018, paragraph 32.
85 The Young Offender Institution Rules 2000, SI No 3371.
86 The Board of Visitors must visit the YOI regularly, and is tasked with overseeing the state of the premises, the administration of the institution and the treatment of inmates.
87 Rule 49, Young Offender Institution Rules 2000, SI No 3371.
88 HM Inspectorate of Prison, January 2020.
89 UN Standard Minimum rules for the treatment of Prisoners (the Nelson Mandela Rules), Rule 44.

90 *R (Bourgass) v Secretary of State for Justice* [2015] UKSC 54. The Supreme Court ruled that the solitary confinement for seven months was unauthorised and therefore unlawful.
91 Instanbul Statement on the Use and Effects of Solitary Confinement, 2008.
92 European Committee for the Prevention of Torture and Inhuman or Degrading Treatment or Punishment, 21st General Report of 2011.
93 *R (AB) v Secretary of State for Justice* [2019] EWCA Civ 9.
94 Concluding observations on the fifth periodic report of the UK of Great Britain and Northern Ireland, paragraph 38.
95 Joint Committee on Human Rights, *Youth Detention: solitary confinement and restraint,* 19th Report, HC 994, HL Paper 343, April 2019.
96 HM Inspectorate of Prisons, *Behaviour management and restraint of children in custody,* November 2015, page 7.
97 HM Government: *Reducing the Need for Restraint and Restrictive Intervention,* June 2019.
98 Chief Inspector Of Prisons for England and Wales, *Annual Report 206 - 17,* Page 9.
99 HC 2469 2019.
100 See: https://www.justiceinspectorates.gov.uk/hmiprisons/wp-content/uploads/sites/4/2020/01/Separation-of-children-thematic-Web-2019.pdf
101 *The Government Response to Charlie Taylor's Review of the Youth Justice System, Cm 9382, 2016;* Ministry of Justice, *Our Secure Schools Vision,* July 2019.
102 The Medway Secure School is to be run by Oasis Charitable Trust which operates academies in the UK's most deprived areas.
103 Children Act 1989, section 25; Social Services and Well-being (Wales) Act 2014.
104 *Re M: (secure Accommodation Order)* (1995) 1 FLR 418.
105 Children Act 1989, section 25(6).
106 Lord Kilbrandon: *The Kilbrandon Report: Children and Young Persons, Scotland.* 3rd edn., London: TSO 1995.
107 The system is administered by two non-departmental government bodies, the Scottish Children's Reporter Administration (Local Government (Scotland) Act 1994) and Children's Hearing Scotland (Children's Hearings (Scotland) Act 2011.
108 Children's Hearing (Scotland) Act 2011, section 67.
109 Children's Hearings (Scotland) Act 2011, section 1.
110 Age of Legal Capacity (Scotland) Act 1991, section 2.
111 Children's Hearings (Scotland) Act 2011, section 37.
112 Children (Scotland) Act 1995, section 75(1).
113 Children's Hearings (Scotland) Act 2011, section 83.

8

CHILDREN: CONTRACT AND EMPLOYMENT

Introduction

This final brief chapter brings together two aspects of children's rights: the right to enter into contracts and employment rights. Each of these matters is a complex area of law and it must be stressed that what follows is a brief introduction.

Contract

Introduction

Children's contracts are regulated by common law (decisions of the courts) and statute, principally the Minors Contract Act 1987. In England, Wales, and Northern Ireland the age of majority for the purposes of entering into valid contracts is 18; in Scotland the age is 16.[1] This is an area of law where the rights of children are well-protected, the law recognising the vulnerability of children. It is for this reason that, for the most part (but see below on exceptions) contracts entered into below the age of majority will not be upheld by the courts.

Categories of contract

Contracts – irrespective of the age of the parties – may be *illegal*, *void*, or *voidable*.

A contract may be *illegal* under common law or statute (Act of Parliament). Under common law, judges regard contracts to commit crimes or to regulate sexual relations as illegal and has no legal effect: it is void and unenforceable. An illegal contract is 'any contract which involves (in its formation, purpose, or performance) a legal wrong ... or conduct contrary to public policy'.[2] The courts have held that contracts which are 'contrary to good morals' or which undermine family life are illegal on grounds of public policy. On the other hand, not

DOI: 10.4324/9780429452710-8

all contracts affected by illegality will be unenforceable. It is also possible that the illegal aspect of a contract can be severed from the rest of the contract which can then be enforced. A contract may be illegal from its inception (e.g. a contract to commit a crime), or it may be illegal in the manner in which it is performed. Here a valid and enforceable contract may become unenforceable because of the way it has been executed/performed. As a general rule the courts will not allow a wrongdoer to profit from his or her wrongdoing. However, adopting a rigid formal rule denying any remedy could cause injustice. What is needed is a more flexible approach, taking into account all the circumstances, including the seriousness of the conduct and the respective culpability of the parties to the agreement.[3]

CASE FOCUS: *PATEL V MIRZA*[4]

In this case Mr Patel gave Mr Mirza £620,000 to place bets on a bank's share prices with the benefit of insider information. There was expected to be a government announcement about the bank but this did not happen and the bet was not placed. Mr Patel sought the return of his money, which Mr Mirza refused on the basis that the agreement with Mr Patel involved illegality. Could Mr Patel recover his money?

The Supreme Court ruled that he could. Mr Patel should not be debarred from claiming his money only because the money was paid for an illegal purpose. Restoring the money to Mr Patel was doing no more than returning both parties to the agreement to the position they would have been in had the agreement not been made: he was therefore not 'profiting from his own wrong' in the classic sense.

A *void contract* is one which has no legal effect: it is treated as if it was never made and there are no legal consequences arising from the agreement. Examples of cases where a contract may be void include a fundamental mistake over the existence of goods, or where both parties think that they are dealing with X when in fact they are dealing with Y. A contract may also be void where both parties mistakenly think that it is capable of being performed, but in fact it is not. It may be physically impossible to perform the contract (the goods do not exist, or the contract fixes a price on a crop based on a fundamental error over whether the land can yield the amount of the crop contracted for), or it may be legally impossible (a fundamental mistake over the ownership of property which is the subject of the contract), or commercially impossible to perform the contract (for example the event for which the contract has been formed is cancelled).

A *voidable contract*, on the other hand, is one which is valid until one party avoids, repudiates, or otherwise sets it aside. In the case of children's contracts, all contracts which are not void are voidable. The child may repudiate the contract up until the age of majority. On the other hand, if there is no repudiation of the contract it becomes fully valid and enforceable once he or she has reached the age of majority.

Capacity to contract

There is a legal presumption that a child under the age of seven lacks the capacity to enter into a binding contract. Between the ages of seven and 18 (16 in Scotland), a child (or minor, in the language of contract law) may enter into a contract. The general rule is that a contract between and minor and an adult will be binding on the adult but not on the minor. There are exceptions to this rule: necessities, contracts which benefit the child (beneficial contracts), contracts for the acquisition of property with duties attached (e.g. a leasehold property which requires the payment of ground rent). If a minor enters into a contract it is voidable (the minor can 'avoid' or cancel it) before reaching the age of 18 or within a reasonable time after that without giving any reasons. The other party to the contract, however, remains bound by it: there is an in-built inequality between the parties to the contract. If the contract endures until the age of 18, without being repudiated by the minor, it becomes binding.

Contracts for necessities and contracts of employment, apprenticeship, or education

Contracts for necessities, of employment or apprenticeships or education are areas which mark the exception to the general rule that children's contracts are invalid and unenforceable. In relation to necessities, a contract entered into by a child will be valid and binding if it is for 'necessities'. The Sale of Goods Act 1979 states that:

> … where necessaries are sold and delivered to a minor…he must pay a reasonable price for them. 'Necessaries' means goods suitable to the condition in life of the minor…and to his actual requirements at the time of the sale and delivery.

The problem with the Sales of Goods Act statement lies in its vagueness and the need for an interpretation which inevitably requires value judgments to be made, and in the case of a dispute this task will fall on the courts. Food, clothing, and medicines are obvious examples of necessities, although in relation to each there are grey areas. Food will include dietary staples such as bread, but beyond the essentials what is 'necessary' may be determined by a child's standard of living. A warm coat will be necessary, but would that cover a designer coat? To decide this the courts need to look to 'the condition in life of the minor', and this entails an assessment of the child's circumstances. For example:

CASE FOCUS: *INMAN*

Inman was a minor studying at the University of Cambridge. Nash sold him some cloth, on credit, valued at approximately £145 for 11 waistcoats. Inman refused to pay. The judge ruled that Inman had sufficient clothing and that therefore the contract with Nash was not one for 'necessities'. Nash was therefore unable to recover the money.

Contracts of apprenticeship, employment, instruction, or service are also treated as contracts for necessaries, provided that the terms of the contract overall have the effect of benefitting the minor.[5] In other words, they are binding on minors unless by the terms of the contract they are more burdensome than beneficial. The legal position is explained in *Chitty on Contracts*:[6]

> The principle that contracts beneficial to a minor are binding on him is not confined to contracts for necessities and contracts of employment, apprenticeship or education in a strict sense. It extends also to other contracts which in a broad sense may be treated as analogous to contracts of service, apprenticeship or education. So, for instance, a contract by a minor (who was a professional boxer) with the British Boxing Board of Control whereby he agreed to adhere to the rules of the Board was held binding on him because he could not have earned his living as a boxer without entering into the agreement.

CASE FOCUS: *DF*[7]

A 14-year-old girl entered into a contract as an apprentice dancer. The contract was to last for seven years. It prohibited the girl from marrying or from accepting any work with other employers without the owner's consent. The contract did not guarantee that the girl would be given any work and entitled the owner to cancel the contract at any time. The Court of Appeal ruled that the contract was unenforceable: it conferred no obligations on the owner and overall was not beneficial to the girl.

The *Wayne Rooney* case[8] also illustrates the rule. The question here was whether a contract entered into by Rooney at the age of 17 and a sports management company was binding on him. If it was binding, then a third party who later contracted with Rooney could be liable for causing Rooney to breach his contract with the first company.

Under the Football Association Rules, no one could be contracted as a player before the age of 17. At the age of 15 Wayne Rooney became a trainee player with Everton Football Club. He entered into a contract with Proform Sports who would act as his agent. Another company, Proactive Sports sought a contract with Rooney and was subsequently accused of unlawful interference with and/or procuring a breach of contract with Proform. Central to the question whether Proactive had caused a breach of contract was the question whether the contract with Proform was binding on Rooney. The judge ruled that it was not binding. The agreement between Rooney and Everton FC clearly fell within the definition of a beneficial contract, i.e. a contract for necessaries, contracts of employment, apprenticeship, or education. He was already engaged with Everton and would enter into a contract with them when he was 17 (although it would be voidable and Rooney could set it aside before the age of 18 if was not 'genuinely for his benefit'). The same could not, the judge ruled, be said of the contract with Proform: given his relationship with Everton for whom he intended to play once he turned 17, Wayne Rooney did not need their services. As a result, the Proform contract was not binding on Wayne Rooney and Proactive Sports was not therefore liable for causing a breach of contract.

However, where the minor reaps a benefit from the contract, which is not otherwise void, the courts may rule that the minor is bound by the contract and its terms.

CASE FOCUS: C[9]

The publisher had agreed to publish the autobiography of the son of Charlie Chaplin while the son was still a minor. The autobiography was to be written by others from material received from the minor and his adult wife. He approved the final proofs and had received advanced royalties from the publisher. Before publication, however, the son sought an injunction to stop publication on the basis that the book contained inaccuracies.

The court refused the injunction and the son was bound by the contract: the contract had enabled the son to become an author and he had received royalties. Overall the contract was to his benefit and he was bound.

CASE FOCUS: *DOYLE*[10]

A minor entered into a contract with the British Boxing Board of Control, under which he received a licence. He agreed to abide by the Board's rules.

Under the contract, if he was disqualified in a fight he would lose the sum of money which he would have otherwise been paid, whereas the normal rule was that a boxer was paid where he lost the fight. There was therefore a detriment to the boxer. However, the court ruled that he was bound by the contract: it enabled him to fight and earn a living.

Another type of contract binding on a minor is the right to hold a lease on property and this is an important right within the context of a child's right to a home and security. Although a child is unable to own a freehold interest in property, this prohibition does not apply to leasehold property. Where a child holds an interest in property, he or she is bound to pay rent or other liabilities according to the terms of the contract (unless these are so onerous as to be unlawful and unenforceable).

CASE FOCUS: *MARIE*[11]

The tenant of a property owned by the local authority died. Living with him at the time of his death were his daughter Wendy and her daughter, Marie, then aged 13. Under the Housing Act 1985, Wendy was not eligible to succeed to the tenancy, but Marie, having lived there for about three years, was. The local authority was granted a possession order, later set aside to decide the question of whether Marie could succeed to the tenancy. The judge ruled that she could, and the local authority appealed.

The Court of Appeal dismissed the local authority's appeal. It was accepted that no minor could hold a legal estate in land.[12] However, there was no law stopping the authority entering into a contract with a minor to grant him or her a lease, and it was clear that a minor could succeed to a tenancy held by a deceased secure tenant. The local authority argued that the word 'person' in the Housing Act referred only to adults. That was swiftly dealt with by Justice Hale who said caustically that 'it might be suggested that Parliament simply forgot that children are people too' but that there was 'ample evidence to conclude that minor children are not "non persons" in the law of landlord and tenant let alone the law of property generally'. Marie succeeded to the tenancy.

The Minors Contract Act 1987

The Minors Contract Act was passed to avoid some of the uncertainties in the law and to prevent injustice arising out of the minor's protected status in relation to contract.

Where a minor's contract is unenforceable due to age at the time the contract was entered into, a court may, 'if it is just and equitable to do so', require the minor to transfer to the other party any property acquired under the contract, or any property representing it.[13] This rule applies also where a contract is voidable and the minor has cancelled/repudiated it. This is the principle of restitution and it softens the harshness of a seller's position vis-à-vis the minor by enabling him or her to recover the property acquired by the minor (as in *Nash v Inman* above). However, the Act does not define 'property' and it is unclear whether it includes money. The court will not order the return of property where the minor has disposed of it and received nothing in return.

Employment

Introduction

The employment of children is subject to detailed regulations to protect children, prevent their exploitation, and ensure that school-age children are in full-time education. The matter is devolved to the nations of the UK which provide both equivalent rights and restrictions on employing children. Within the nations, the detailed regulation of employment is controlled by local authorities who should be consulted if employment is being considered.

Both the European Convention on Human Rights (ECHR) and the UN Convention on the Rights of the Child (CRC) also provide for child protection from exploitation. The CRC, for example, provides that:

> State Parties recognise the right of the child to be protected from economic exploitation and from performing any work that is likely to be hazardous or to interfere with the child's education, or to be harmful to the child's health or physical, mental, spiritual, moral or social development.
>
> *UN Convention on the Rights of the Child, Article 32*

In addition to Article 32 above, the CRC requires that States provide for minimum age or ages for entering employment, the regulation of hours of work and conditions of employment, and the availability of penalties or sanctions to ensure enforcement of the rules. Article 4 of the European Convention on Human Rights prohibits slavery, servitude, and forced or compulsory labour (on modern slavery and trafficking see Chapter 5).

The employment of children in the UK has a very long history, much of it characterised by abuse, cruelty, and neglect. The regulation of that employment stems only from the nineteenth century. Apprenticeships date back to the Middle Ages:

> Indentures (written contracts) were drawn up, binding servant to master and vice versa; in which the master personally taught the apprentice;

took responsibility for the latter's moral welfare; and gave him board and lodgings.[14]

Orphans and children abandoned by their families came under the care of the Poor Law, and from there through apprenticeships into the care of their masters. Early official concerns over the plight of working children focused on those employed from an early age as chimney sweeps: 'climbing boys'. An Act of 1788 imposed a minimum age of eight years. In 1834 a Chimney Sweeps Act was passed prohibiting apprenticeships for boys under the age of ten, and providing that no child under 14 years of age could be employed as a chimney sweep, the age raised to 16 under the 1840 Chimney Sweeps Act. The Parish Apprentices Act 1802 restricted the hours which Poor Law apprentices were allowed to work in factories and in cotton mills for no more than 12 hours a day. The problem with this and other legislation was that there were no enforcement mechanisms and widespread flouting of the law.[15]

By the 1830s, the plight of children working in mills and factories had attracted political attention. The 'Ten-Hour Movement' led by Anthony Ashley-Cooper MP (later Lord Shaftesbury) campaigned to reduce the number of hours worked by children under the age of 16 and a Factory Act of 1831 limited working hours for those under the age of 18 to 12 hours in the cotton mills. The Factory Act 1833 extended the scope of control, prohibiting children under the age of nine from working in factories; for those aged between nine and 13, eight hours a day and for those aged between 13 and 18 to 12 hours a day. The 1833 Act also established an enforcement mechanism: a four-person inspectorate of factories (for over 4,000 mills).

In 1844 Parliament passed a Factory Act addressing the safety of working conditions.[16] It became a criminal offence to fail to securely fence off dangerous machinery and prohibited children from cleaning machinery while it was in operation. The 1844 Act further restricted the working hours of children, limiting them to six and-a-half hours with three hours' education. For children aged 13 to 18 there was a maximum 12-hour day.

In 1878 the Factories and Workshop Act consolidated earlier legislation and regulated the hours of work and education requirements of children under the age of 14. But legal reform was not universally welcome. Professor Stephen Cretney writes of these restrictions that:

> Later generations may find difficulty in understanding how there could be any opposition to legislation which would prevent children of four or five years of age being dragged from bed at four in the morning and made to toil in the dark for perhaps 18 hours a day, sometimes chained to trucks which they had to drag on all-fours through mine shafts. But at the time there were many people who thought it better for children to be employed in a cotton mill or factory than to be running uncontrolled in the streets of the large industrial cities, and certainly there was a general

concern (mingled no doubt with a measure of fear) about 'the hordes of neglected and destitute children who frequented the streets begging and thieving, without homes or teaching or indeed anyone apparently to care for them'.[17]

The 1891 Factory Act raised the minimum age for employment in factories to 11.

The condition of women and children working in coal mines also attracted official attention. Children aged eight, or younger, were employed. In 1842 the Mines and Collieries Act was passed, prohibiting all underground work for women and girls and for boys under the age of ten. The minimum age for boys was raised to 12 in 1860.[18]

The decline of child labour coincided with, or was caused by, the growth in compulsory education. The Education Act 1880 made schooling compulsory until the age of ten, later raised to 12. By 1900 all children were required to be in school up to the age of 12. Note that the school/education leaving age is England is 18; in Scotland and Wales it is 16, and in Northern Ireland the school leaving age is dependent upon the child's date of birth. Children turning 16 between 1 September and 1 July may leave school after 30 June whereas those turning 16 between 2 July and 31 August must remain in school until the end of the following June. On education see Chapter 3.

Permitted working hours[19]

In the UK children under the age of 13 are generally prohibited from employment. Exceptions exists in relation to sport, advertising, modelling, films and theatre for which a local authority licence will be required. Local authorities have the power to make byelaws regulating the types of work and hours of work for children between the age of 13 and 16, and these may vary across the country. For details of a particular area, the relevant local authority should be consulted.

In general, children are not allowed to work:

- in factories or on industrial sites;
- during school hours;
- before 7 am and after 7 pm;
- for more than one hour before school;
- for more than 12 hours in any week in which he or she is required to attend school;
- for more than four hours without taking a break of at least one hour;
- in any work that may be harmful to their health, well-being, or education;
- without having a two-week break from any work during the school holiday in each calendar year;
- without an employment permit issued by the education department of the local council, if this is required by local byelaws.

In term time, children can only work a maximum of 12 hours a week. This includes:

- a maximum of two hours on school days and Sundays;
- a maximum of five hours on Saturdays for 13 to 14 year-olds, or eight hours for 15 to 16 year-olds.

During school holidays 13 to 14 year-olds are only allowed to work a maximum of 25 hours a week. This includes:

- a maximum of five hours on weekdays and Saturdays;
- a maximum of two hours on Sunday.

During school holidays 15 to 16 year-olds can only work a maximum of 35 hours a week. This includes:

- a maximum of eight hours on weekdays and Saturdays;
- a maximum of two hours on Sundays.

If a child is employed in contravention of byelaws or regulations, the employer commits an offence and is liable to a fine of £50, or for second or subsequent offences, £100.[20]

An employment permit for children under the school leaving age will be required according to local byelaws. If it is required, it must be applied for before any work begins and be registered with the local authority.

The effectiveness of the regulation of child employment and the local authority system of registration in England has been subjected to criticism for failing adequately to protect children's rights. Commissioned by the Department for Education before the 2010 general election, the research examined the current system of regulation and registration and considered options for reform.[21] In summary, the current registration system is failing because of a 'substantial number' of employers who do not report employing children of school age, and only a minority of working children obtain permits. Moreover, where permits are obtained there are few checks on whether any conditions laid down in the permit are being complied with.

The principal explanations for the failing of the current system include the following:

- the multiplicity of legislation relating to child employment;
- variations between local authorities in byelaws;
- a limited awareness of issues surrounding the employment of children, including health and safety requirements and the need to protect children's schooling;
- councils which have no policy on child employment;

- employers' ignorance over the legal requirements;
- limited local authority resources;
- the need for more effective monitoring and enforcement of the system.

Of the options for reform the research findings favoured the introduction of a national regulatory framework for child employment. This would introduce consistency, clarity, fairness across local authorities, the introduction of national standards, and a possible simplification of the rules which act as a deterrent to employer compliance.

Health and safety requirements

All employers must, as far as reasonably practicable, ensure the health and safety of all employees, regardless of age. In relation to children, however, there are additional considerations and requirements designed to protect their rights. Employers must ensure that children are protected from any risks to their health or safety which might arise:

- because of their lack of experience;
- lack of awareness of existing or potential risks; or
- from the fact that they are not yet fully mature.[22]

In assessing risks to child employees, the Health and Safety at Work Regulations require that an employer considers:

- the layout of the workplace;
- the physical, biological, and chemical agents they will be exposed to;
- how they will handle work equipment;
- how the work and processes are organised;
- the extent of health and safety training needed;
- risks from particular agents, processes, and work.

Children should not be employed for work:

- which is beyond his or her physical or psychological capacity;
- which involves harmful exposure to toxic or carcinogenic substances, or cause heritable genetic damage or harm to an unborn child, or which in any other way chronically affects human health;
- which involves harmful exposure to radiation;
- which involves the risk of accidents which may be reasonable assumed cannot be recognised or avoided by young persons owing to their insufficient attention to safety or lack of experience or training; or
- in which there is a risk to health from extreme cold or heat, noise, or vibration.[23]

Children must never carry out work involving the above risks. Exceptions to the above restrictions apply to young people, defined as over compulsory school age but under 18, where the work is necessary for his or her training and he or she will be supervised by a competent person and where any risk will be reduced to the lowest level that is reasonably practicable.

Live performances: theatres, etc.

Children under school leaving age participating in live performances require a licence from the local authority.[24] Licences are granted where the local authority is satisfied about a child's fitness and about provisions made for his or her health, treatment, and education. Regulations impose strict limits on participation:

- children from nought to four may be at the place of performance or rehearsal for a maximum of five hours; those aged five to eight a maximum of eight hours and those nine and over a maximum of 9.5 hours';
- depending on age, regulations provide for the earliest and latest times permitted at the place of performance or rehearsal;
- depending on age, there is a maximum period of continuous performance or rehearsal;
- depending on age, the maximum total hours of performance or rehearsal;
- minimum intervals for meals and rest;
- education requirements;
- minimum breaks between performances;
- maximum days to take part in performances.

Employment in the armed forces

The UN Convention on the Rights of the Child (CRC) Optional Protocol on Involvement of Children in Armed Conflict, requires that States will not recruit or conscript children under the age of 18 to send them into the battlefield. It is contrary to international law to recruit children as soldiers under the age of 15.

In the UK, children can be recruited into the armed forces from the age of 16 and can apply from the age of 15 years and nine months. They should not engage in military conflict until the age of 18, but there is evidence that children served in both Iraq and Afghanistan between 2003 and 2010. The UK recruitment age is out of line with all EU Member States, in which the earliest age children can be recruited is 17. Worldwide, 134 countries have prohibited the recruitment of children, and 37 recruit from the age of 17. The UK is one of only 20 countries in the world to recruit 16 year-olds. The UK has been criticised by the Committee on the Rights of the Child (the CRC monitoring body) which has called on the government to end the recruitment of children. It is not the only body to do so: the Joint Committee on Human rights called in 2009 for the government to raise the minimum age.

When children have been in the forces of six months and have not left, they are committed to remaining until the age of 22, a total of six years – two years longer than an adult would serve.[25] Up until six months, children under the age of 18 are entitled to a discharge as of right by giving 28 days' notice (for adult recruits only 14 days' notice is required). Thereafter any release from service before the age of 22 is at the discretion of the commanding officer: it is not a right. The lack of clarity over terms of service contained in the Enlistment Paper signed by recruits on joining has been criticised as difficult to understand, a problem compounded by research finding that 50 per cent of recruits joining the army at non-officer level have a reading age at or below that of an average 11 year-old.[26]

Summary

The law of contract provides good protection for the rights of children. In relation to employment, the vulnerability of children through age and the need to ensure that they are in full-time education is also well recognised and protected through detailed rules. However, although the law provides for equivalent restrictions on the employment of children throughout the UK, what is permissible depends partly on the nation's school leaving age and also on the type of employment permitted under local authority bye laws. It is essential, therefore, to consult the local authority if there is doubt as to whether a particular form of child employment is permitted.

Notes

1 The Family Law Reform Act 1969, Age of Majority (Northern Ireland) Act 1969, Age of Legal Capacity (Scotland) Act 1991.
2 Law Commission, *Illegal Transactions: the Effect of Illegality on Contracts and Trusts*, LCCP N 154, 1999.
3 *Patel v Mirza* [2016] UKSC 42.
4 ibid.
5 Per Hodge, J, *Proform Sports Management Ltd v Proactive Sports Management Ltd* [2006] EWHC 2903 (Ch).
6 *Chitty on Contracts*, 29th edn., 2004, paragraph 8–028.
7 *De Francesco v Barnum* (1889) 45 Ch D 430.
8 *Proform Sports Management Ltd v Proactive Sports Management Ltd* [2006] EWHC 2903, Ch.
9 *Chaplin v Leslie Frewin (Publishers) Ltd* [1996] Ch 71.
10 *Doyle v White City Stadium* [1935] 1 KB 110.
11 *RB of Kingston Upon Thames v Wendy Price, Marie Emma Prince* [1998] EWCA Civ 1891.
12 Law of Property Act 1925, section 19(1); Settled Land Act 1925, section 27(1).
13 Minor's Contract Act 1987, section 3.
14 C. More, *Skills and the English Working Class* Croom Helm, 1980, p. 4.
15 Graphically described by Karl Marx in *Das Kapital: A Critique of Political Economy*, 1867. Volume 4.
16 Following the *Report of the Royal Commission on the Employment of Children and Very Young People in Mines and Factories*, 1842.

17 S.M. Cretney, *Family Law in the Twentieth Century: A History,* Oxford UP, 2003, page 629, citing *Home Office Note to the Machinery of Government Committee on Home Office Functions in relation to Child Welfare,* December 1944, PRO MH102/1379, paragraph 1.

18 The Coal Mines regulation Act 1860.

19 UK Government, *Child employment: Restrictions on child employment.* Children and Young Persons Act 1933, section 18(1).

20 See Children (Protection at Work) Regulations 1998, SI No. 276; Children (Protection at Work) Regulations 2000, SI No 1333 and Children (Protection at Work) (N0 2) Regulations, 2000 SI No 2548.

21 Department for Education: *Research Report DFE-RR 124, The Regulation of Child Employment and options for reform,* University of West Scotland, 2011.

22 Management of Health and Safety at Work regulations 1999, SI 1999/3242.

23 ibid., Regulation 19.

24 Children and Young Persons Act 1963, sections 37–43 and Regulations.

25 Terms of Service Regulations.

26 MOD evidence to House of Commons Defence Select Committee in 2004–2005, cited by ForcesWatch, *The Recruitment of under 18s into the UK Armed Forces.* www .forceswatch.net

CHILDREN APPENDIX

Introduction

The age of majority is 18. However, as seen throughout this book, the law lays down different ages at which children are entitled to do certain things. In this Appendix, these different ages are brought together for ease of reference, dealing with the individual issues in alphabetical order. Where relevant, the chapter number in which the issue is discussed is also given. The data below refers to the position in England, although there is general equivalence across the nations of the UK.

A

Accommodation: local authorities are under a statutory duty to provide accommodation for homeless 16 to 17 year-olds, and to care leavers between the ages of 18 and 21. Both categories are defined as having priority needs.

Adoption: a child can be adopted up to the age of 18. **See Chapter 6.**

Age of criminal responsibility: ten in England, Wales, and Northern Ireland and 12 in Scotland. **See Chapter 7.**

Air rifles and shotguns: it is an offence for a child under the age of 18 to buy or hire an air weapon, or ammunition, or for someone to make them a gift of an air weapon or ammunition. A child under the age of 14 cannot own or hire an air weapon or ammunition at any time. They may shoot an air weapon on private premises, provided it is with consent and under the supervision of a person over the age of 21. From the age of 14 to 17, a child may borrow an air gun from a person over 18 and use it on private premises without supervision.

Shotguns require a firearm certificate which may not be granted to a child under the age of 14. From the age of 15 a child may have an assembled shotgun but only when under the supervision of a person over the age of 21, or where the gun is securely covered, and cannot be used.

Alcohol: sales of alcohol are prohibited to those below the age of 18 and under-18s may not buy or be served with alcohol in licensed premises. It is an offence to purchase alcohol for an under-18 year old.

Armed forces: a 16 year-old may join the army, navy, or air force but not be engaged in active duty until the age of 18.

B

Bank accounts: the minimum age for opening a current account is 11; some accounts are restricted to age 16. Overdrafts are not permitted. The minimum age for opening a savings account is seven.

Being left alone at home: parents are under a legal duty to ensure the safety of their children up to the age of 16. There is no age laid down in law at which a child can be left alone. If being left alone would lead to neglect or physical or psychological harm, a person over the age of 16 who has responsibility for the child is guilty of a criminal offence. The NSPCC advises that children under the age of 12 should not be left alone 'for long'; under-16s should not be left alone overnight or for long periods of time and that no child should be left alone if it puts him or her at risk.

Buying a pet: from age 12.

C

Cigarettes: see **Tobacco**

Contract: a child below the age of seven may not enter into a contract. Over the age of seven, a contract for necessities, contracts for employment, apprenticeships, or education will be binding on the child (but not the adult). **See Chapter 8.**

D

Driving: subject to testing, a child may drive a moped at 16. Cars and motorcycles can be driven from the age of 17 (larger motorbikes have an age restriction of 21 or 24). All require testing which comprises Basic Compulsory Basic Training, a theory test, and a practical test. A provisional licence can be applied for from the age of 15 years and nine months. Special rules apply to tractors, heavy goods vehicles, horseboxes, etc.

E

Education: in England a child must be in full-time education from the age of five to 16, and in education or training from the age of 16 to 18. In Scotland, Wales, and Northern Ireland a child must be in full-time education until the age of 16 (the school leaving date depending upon the child's date of birth). **See Chapter 4.**

Employment: a 13 year-old may work part-time, with some exceptions to the type of work and restrictions on hours worked. From the age of 16 a child may work up to a maximum of 40 hours a week. Note, however, that detailed regulations are the responsibility of local authorities who should be consulted where the employment of under-18s is being considered. **See Chapter 8.**

F

Films and videos: British Board of Film Classification, 12A cinema release suitable for 12 years and over; other classifications, 15 and 18, are suitable for 15 and 18 year-olds.

Fireworks: sales of fireworks to those under the age of 18 are prohibited.

Flying: the minimum age for a Private Pilot Licence is 16; for a Commercial Pilot Licence or Airline Transport Pilot Licence, 18. A child of 14 can fly a glider solo; to get a Glider Private Pilot Licence the minimum age is 16. A written knowledge test and practical test must be passed.

G

Gambling: the minimum age is 18 for all adult gaming centres, betting shops, bingo halls, casinos, race tracks, and online gambling. See also **Lottery** below.

H

Horse riding: at any age (subject to the relevant adult's liability for failure to care for the child); without a safety helmet from the age of 14.

J

Jury service: a child cannot be called for jury service below the age of 18.

L

Leaving home: the law in relation to leaving home is very unclear, creating and sustaining uncertainty over the rights of both children and parents and other carers.

Every year thousands of children leave home for various reasons (**See Chapter 6** on missing children). The vast majority of these will be found and return home. Where a child becomes homeless, they are defined as 'children in need' and local authorities have a duty to provide accommodation. **See Chapter 6** on the duties of local authorities towards children in need.

Under the Children Act 1989 a court cannot make an order under section 8 (relating to where a child is to live) for a child over the age of 16, unless there are 'exceptional circumstances'. Should a dispute arise over where a child is to live, the decision of the court will be determined by the principle of the best interests of the child (the welfare principle). Central to this will be the age and maturity of the child, his or her financial resources, and the circumstances in which he or she is living. A court may not make a Care or Supervision Order in relation to a child who has reached the age of 17 (or 16, if the child is married) (**See Chapter 5** on local authority duties and powers).

Surviving outside the family home is difficult for a child, particularly for those in full-time education who cannot also be in employment. The right to State benefits (see Welfare benefits below) begins at 18, subject to limited exceptions.

The Child Abduction Act 1984, makes it a criminal offence to 'take or detain' a child under the age of 16 if this keeps him or her 'out of the lawful control' of the person (usually a parent) who has the right to the lawful control of the child. 'Detaining a child' includes inducing a child to remain.

Lottery: the minimum age is 16, but is under review.

M

Marriage: at the age of 16 a child may marry with the consent of a parent or a court of law. Without parental consent a valid marriage may be entered into at the age of 18.

Medical treatment: at the age of 16 a child may consent to medical treatment. Below that age, the right to consent will be determined by the concept of the 'mature minor', the test being whether a child has sufficient maturity and understanding to make the decision which in turn involves a number of considerations and whether the treatment is in the best interests of the child (the welfare principle). The right to refuse medical treatment will also be determined by the mature minor test and the welfare principle. **See Chapter 3**.

Military service: applications to join the armed forces may be made from the age of 15 years and nine months. The minimum age for recruitment is 16. The minimum age for active service is 18 years. **See Chapter 8**.

P

Parliament, stand for: at age 18.

Passports: at 16 a child may apply for a passport in his or her own right. Before that age, parents must apply on behalf of the child.

Property: a child under the age of 18 may not own a legal estate in land. Under the age of 18 a child may contract for a lease and be responsible for the rent, etc., on the property.

S

School governor: minimum age is 18.

Sexual intercourse: a child under the age of 16 may not lawfully consent to sexual intercourse.

T

Tattoos: a child under the age of 18 cannot lawfully get a tattoo.

Taxation: from the age of 16 a child may be taxed on earned income. In 2020/2021, tax is payable on income of over £12,500 and on interest of over £100 paid on money from parents.

Tobacco: a child under the age of 18 cannot lawfully purchase tobacco.

V

Videos: British Board of Film Classification: video release classified as 12 is suitable for 12 years and over; others classified as suitable for 15 and 18 year-olds.
Voting: in England, Wales, and Northern Ireland, the right to vote is from the age of 18. In Scotland the right to vote arises at age 16.

W

Welfare benefits: A child under the age of 16 may apply for a Disability Living Allowance (DLA) if he or she needs extra help or has difficulty with mobility: the DLA is not means-tested.

Eligibility for Universal Credit starts at 18 years. There are exceptions for 16- and 17-year-olds. These include being in full-time education and entitled to a Personal Independence Plan or Disability Living Allowance; having medical evidence and awaiting a Work Capability Assessment; having responsibility for a child or caring for a severely disabled person; being pregnant with less than 11 weeks before the date of childbirth; having had a child within the previous 15 weeks.

A 16 or 17 year-old may also be eligible if he or she does not have parental support through being estranged from his or her parents and not being in the care of the local authority.

Wills: a child below the age of 18 cannot make a valid will.

INDEX

abduction 12–15
abortion 61
abuse 118–156
accommodation 161–163
adoption 49, 167–170
age of criminal responsibility 190–191
alternative provision 106–107
Anti-Slavery Commissioner 140–141
arrest 195–198
asylum 176, 179–183

bail 197–198
Blackstone, William (Sir) 2

CAFCASS 25
care and supervision orders 165–166
care plans 161
Child and Adolescent Mental Health
    Service 76–77
Child Assessment Orders 163
childhood 4–5
child refugees 176, 178–183
Children Act 1989 17, 160
children in need 159–160
Child Safety Orders 191
circumcision 79–81
civil injunctions 193–194
Cleveland Inquiry 121–122
confidentiality 64
contract 222–227; capacity 224;
    necessities 224–227
corporal punishment 123–124
County Lines 137–137
Court structure 26–27

Cretney, Stephen 229–230
Criminal Behaviour Orders 193, 205
Crown Prosecution Service 198–199

Declaration of Incompatibility 16
Detention and Training Orders 206
disability 72–75
discrimination 20–21; protected
    characteristics 20

education 86–114
Education, Health and Care Plans
    100–101
Education Supervision Order 88, 167
Emergency Protection Order 163–165
employment 228–234; armed forces 233;
    live performances 233; working
    hours 230
equality 41–43
Equality Act 2010 20–21
European Convention on Human Rights
    8–16, 92
exploitation 136
extremism 146

Female Genital Mutilation 80, 129–134;
    Female Genital Mutilation Protection
    Orders Statistics on 131–132
forced marriage 125; Forced Marriage
    Protection Orders 127–129

gender 49–54
GIDS: Gender Identity Development
    Service 53

Gillick 53, 62–65, 190
guardianship 168–170

Hague Convention on
    Abduction 12–15
Heywood, Colin 4
humanitarian protection 180–181
Human Rights Act 1998 15–16

identity rights 42–48
immunisation 70
Independent Inquiry into Child Sexual
    Abuse 143
independent schools 108–109
inherent jurisdiction 21–23
Intensive Supervision and Surveillance
    Programme 206
internet abuse 144, 146

Jehovah's Witnesses 77
Judicial review 23–24

legal aid and advice 25–26, 197
local authorities: duties of 171–184;
    liability of 171–174
Locke, John 2

Magistrates' Court 192, 202
medical treatment 53, 83; consent to 61;
    financial resources and 81–82; refusing
    consent to 64; withdrawing 66;
    withholding 66
mental health 60, 75
missing children 171

National Referral Mechanism (NRM)
    139–140

Official Solicitor 25
off-rolling 107
Ofsted 90

parentage 43
parental responsibility 31–33
Parenting Orders 191–192
police protection 164–165
prevent strategy 146–151
prosecution 198

refugees 174–184
religious education 93–94
remand 197–198
reporting restrictions 20

safeguarding 40–41
schools: admissions 91; bullying 95–96;
    class sizes 91; discipline 94–95;
    exclusion 103–106; governance 90;
    independent 108; liability of 111–112;
    managed moves 107; off rolling 107;
    Ofsted 90; religious education 93;
    standards 90; truancy 96; uniform 92;
    unregistered 110
Scottish Hearing System 216–218
Secure Children's Homes 215
Secure Schools 214
Secure Training Centres 208–209
SEND 97–99
sentencing 202–207
sexual exploitation 141–144
slavery 138–139
solitary confinement 210, 214
Special Educational Needs 73, 97–98
Special Guardianship Orders 168–169
special measures 201–202
standard of living 59
Supervision Orders 166
surrogacy 48

trafficking 137–141
truancy 96

UN Convention on the Rights of the
    Child 7–8

wardship 21–23
welfare 34–36
working hours 230–231

Young Offender Institutions 207–216
youth cautions 192
Youth Courts 190, 200, 202
youth crime statistics 194–195
Youth Offending Panels 189, 203
Youth Offending Teams 189, 192, 198,
    203, 205
Youth Rehabilitation Orders 204

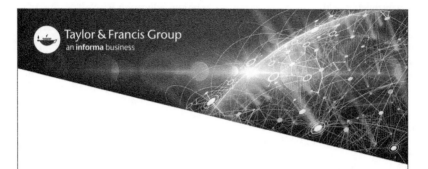